When Christians Disagree
Series Editor: Oliver R. Barclay

The Church and its Unity
Editor: Alan F. Gibson

Also in this series

The Role of Women
Editor: Shirley Lees

Politics and the Parties
Editor: Jonathan Chaplin

The Church and its Unity

Editor: Alan F. Gibson

Michael Cole
Eryl Davies
Graham Harrison
David Holloway
Gordon W. Kuhrt
David Matthew
Derek Prime
Harry Uprichard

When Christians Disagree
Inter-Varsity Press

INTER-VARSITY PRESS
38 De Montfort Street, Leicester LE1 7GP, England

First published 1992

British Library Cataloguing in Publication Data
A catalogue record for this book is available from the British
Library.

ISBN 0-85110-959-4

Set in Linotron Melior

Photoset in Great Britain by Parker Typesetting Service,
Leicester
Printed in Great Britain by
Cox & Wyman Ltd, Reading, Berkshire

*Inter-Varsity Press is the book-publishing division of the
Universities and Colleges Christian Fellowship (formerly the
Inter-Varsity Fellowship), a student movement linking Christian
Unions in universities and colleges throughout the United
Kingdom and the Republic of Ireland, and a member movement
of the International Fellowship of Evangelical Students. For
information about local and national activities write to UCCF,
38 De Montfort Street, Leicester LE1 7GP.*

Contents

Part 4 The issue of charismatic experience

Part 5 Conclusion: Where does this leave us?

When Christians Disagree

Introducing the series

There are many subjects on which the teaching of the Bible is quite clear. There is a substantial core of Christian theology and ethics that we can confidently proclaim as 'biblical teaching', and those rejecting as well as those accepting the authority of that teaching will agree that such a core exists.

As we try to work out the application of biblical teaching in detail, however, we find areas in which there is no such clear consensus. Christians who are trying equally to be obedient to the teaching of Christ and his carefully instructed apostles come to different conclusions about such subjects as baptism and church government. Some of their differences have been resolved after debate. In Protestant circles, for instance, few would now wish, as some once did, to excommunicate people for advocating birth control. Further discussion has brought substantial agreement. Some questions, however, are not so easily resolved at present; and there is a need for healthy discussion among Christians so that we may arrive, if possible, at an agreed view. If that is not possible, then all of us need to re-examine our view in the light of Scripture and to exchange views, so that we may ensure that our position is not the product of wishful thinking, but is really faithful to the Bible. All of us are influenced in our thinking by our traditions, our education and the general climate of thought of our age. These forces tend to mould our ideas more than we realize, and to make us conform to the fashion of our time, or the traditions in which we were brought up, rather than to revealed truth.

This series of books under the title of *When Christians Disagree* attempts to tackle some of these current debates. Each book has the same fundamental structures. A series of starting 'theses', or a statement of a position (usually excluding the more extreme views on either side), has been sent to the writers. They have been asked to agree or disagree with the 'theses' and to set out a Christian position as they see it. They then have the opportunity to respond to one or more of the other articles written from a different point of view from their own. A short closing summary attempts to clarify the main issues in debate.

All the contributors seek to be ruled by Scripture. Since they do not agree between themselves, the crucial issue is whether one view or another is more consistent with the teaching of the Bible. Some of the problems arise out of the impact upon us of new cultural patterns. These new patterns may or may not be healthy, and that has to be judged by the application of biblical truth which is always health-giving – the good and acceptable and perfect will of God. We are not arguing whether it is easier to believe or do one thing or another in today's world. We are not even asking whether a Christian position seems stupid to the cultured person of today. We are asking whether there are revealed principles that give us at least some guidelines, and perhaps even a clear answer to our problems.

The Bible is authoritative in more than one way: in some areas explicit teaching is given; in other areas the question is left open in such a way that we know there is no universal 'right' answer. Worship provides an example. There are some broad principles; but the Bible seems authoritatively to allow, and perhaps implicitly to encourage, variety in the details of the style and ordering of worship. In such cases we will solve the problem in our own age and culture in obedience to the more basic explicit teachings that we have.

In the areas that this series explores there are some things laid down clearly in Scripture and some that are not. There is, for instance, no biblical instruction as to whether husband or wife should dig the garden; there are no explicit limits drawn to the coercive powers of the state, nor any delineation of the nature of the world before the fall – except that it was very good.

The arguments, therefore, concern first of all whether the Bible does or does not settle certain questions and secondly how far we can go in confident application of those biblical truths that we are given. The demarcation line between these here is important. If we can agree what is clearly taught then all else is in a secondary category, where we know that human opinion is fallible. Some of our discussion is above the line and is therefore most important. Some falls below it and cannot be as vital, even if in practical terms we have to adopt a policy.

Oliver R. Barclay

Introduction:
Why bother with all this?

Ours is a highly individualist generation. Democracy and the right to personal freedom are taken for granted, even among Christians. The corporate concept of the church is not so highly regarded today. Charged with bureaucracy, with irrelevance, or with quenching the Spirit, the view from the pew is that the church needs to get its act together if it is to regain the support it claims.

No Bible-believing Christian can, however, deny the importance of the church in God's saving purpose. The Saviour committed himself to its structure by saying, 'I will build my church.' The New Testament traces its first rapid, if faltering, stages of growth. In subsequent centuries the church has had an enormous influence on the destiny of nations, whatever the secular historians may say. At a personal level, generations of lonely and discouraged believers have had reason to thank God for the mutual encouragement provided by the body of Christ.

Of which church, however, are we speaking? There are so many to choose from. Anyone who has moved to study or work away from home has experienced the problem. Gone are the days of only one church or chapel in the village. The ecclesiastical supermarket offers a bewildering complexity of options. Whilst not all may be represented in every town, a MARC Europe survey has located fifty-three denominational groupings, each with more than fifty congregations in Britain. And as for the United States, well, that really is something else, as they say over there.

We are not surprised that some rationalizing of resources is under way. The cynical might suggest that the pressure for unity is coming from the churches' finance officers. (Small may be beautiful but it is hardly economic!) In fact, the modern ecumenical movement had its origins in the missionary concern of the early twentieth century. Its support today can seem to owe more to a popular reductionist theology, a theology which finds the perpetuation of traditional denominational differences simply unnecessary.

In 1990 Britain's ecumenical map was re-drawn. The five-year Inter-Church Process, given direction by the 1987 Swanwick Declaration, led to the disbanding of the former British Council of Churches and the founding of new relationship structures. In these new structures, the four separate bodies in England, Wales, Scotland and Ireland are now being co-ordinated by the Council of Churches for Britain and Ireland (CCBI). Several new features were introduced. Strenuous efforts have been made to establish horizontal consultation procedures at every level from the bottom up, encouraging all church members, whatever their particular interests, to own the ecumenical dimension of their ministry. With some unease over past failures, the black-led churches have been incorporated into the scheme. The Roman Catholic Church, although not a member of the international body, the World Council of Churches, has committed itself to the CCBI with enthusiasm.

Some, but by no means all, evangelicals have gone along with these changes. In fact, they represent an historic departure from the post-Reformation position. However it is viewed, 1990 marked a significant milestone in the ecumenical pilgrimage.

If only briefly, some mention must be made of the concept of para-church ecumenism. Recent decades have seen a proliferation of trans-denominational evangelical bodies ranging from the world-famous Keswick Convention to the specialist agencies for the support of AIDS sufferers. Whilst most of these societies see themselves as providing a service to local churches, their contribution to ecumenism has been mixed. The undoubted strength of their co-operation has been in introducing evangelicals to other Bible-believing Christians from backgrounds different from their own. The stimulus of bodies like the

Universities and Colleges Christian Fellowship has been of immeasurable blessing as student co-operation has been fostered around an agreed Basis of Faith. Many have profited from having their own practice and theology exposed to the challenge of another's equally sincere assumptions. The range of friendships forged in student days with Christians from other denominations have frequently become prayer partnerships of life-long significance.

Such para-church bodies have reflected the undoubted reality of the universal church in which denominational labels are subsumed under the banner of 'All one in Christ Jesus'. So rich has been their contribution to evangelism, publishing, Bible teaching and social concern that it may seem invidious to say anything negative about them. Perhaps a doubt could best be expressed in the form of a question. Is it not possible that para-church bodies can become a substitute for the church itself? Has the very success of this evangelical networking diverted attention from the role and significance of local churches and their need to relate to each other?

This book is concerned with the church and its unity. When all the fine work of para-church bodies has been recognized, and God thanked for their contribution, we are still left with the institution of the church itself. That is our immediate interest, for reasons which will become apparent. Not the least of these reasons is the prominence given in the Bible to the gathering of saints Christ is graciously pleased to identify as his body.

It is the shared life in the family of God which lends a unique character to the discussions of this book. The distinctive badge of Christian discipleship is love. Love for the brothers and sisters from whom we differ will temper our language and our attitudes to each other. We shall look for the strongest and best expression of our opponent's position to counter. It does not take love to knock down a straw man. Christian controversy has not always been marked by courtesy and mutual respect, especially where a church has been rent by schism. It is never easy to speak warmly of those who have left our fellowship to shelter in another flock. Nor is that made easier if we suspect that the other under-shepherd has encouraged the move!

The task before us, however, is not optional. The New Testament exhorts us to make every effort to express the unity Christ died to achieve. We are to consider one another, to encourage one another, to submit to one another and to provoke one another (but only to love and good works!). If we are concerned to be Bible Christians what we cannot do is to ignore the church unity question and hope that it will go away.

Our basic agreements and issues for discussion

This book is an exercise in respectful confrontation. Before embarking on a discussion of their differences, all the contributors assured each other of their evangelical credentials. Their common ground is summarized in the following eight propositions, grouped under two headings.

The authority of Scripture

1. Christ rules his church by Scripture, God's written word, which is her final authority in all matters of faith and practice. The teaching of Scripture is therefore sufficient to determine all that is essential to the life, order and discipline of the church.

2. The teaching of Scripture is clear on a massive core of doctrine and ethics, including much about the nature, purpose and ministry of the church. We rejoice in the unity of faith of all who have been renewed by the Holy Spirit and who accept the authority of Scripture for their own obedience to Christ.

3. Whatever is not found in Scripture, whether deduced by human reason, dignified by tradition or received from

any contemporary insight, cannot be held to possess the same authority as Scripture itself without impugning its finality and sufficiency.

4. All Christians in every generation need the illumination of the Holy Spirit to understand Scripture rightly. Our limited response to its teaching is neither a reflection on the clarity of God's word, nor on the adequacy of his help, but rather on our weakness.

These four principles are what the authors understand to be the evangelical view of Scripture. Whilst genuinely born-again individuals, unreservedly regarded as members of the church universal, may yet retain some confusion over Scripture, the unity of the church catholic is related in the Bible to her acceptance of this common foundation.

The evangelical use of Scripture

Widely different conclusions about the doctrine of the church are drawn from Scripture by evangelicals equally committed to its authority. Whilst this may disappoint us, it should not surprise us, given the following four propositions.

5. Scripture is not exhaustive; it does not deal explicitly with every question which might be asked. We cannot settle with absolute certainty from Scripture a number of issues relevant to the church today. Some problems had not yet arisen in the first century, such as those posed by the establishment of the church by civil authority. That concept was not an option in New Testament times.

6. All Christians recognize a link between the Old Testament people of God and the New Testament body of Christ. Some significant differences in church practice arise from divergent understandings of this continuity/discontinuity balance.

7. Whilst sharing a common faith, the churches of the New Testament period were not identical and some features called for particular counsel from the apostolic writers. Subsequently Christians have drawn differing

conclusions about which aspects of New Testament church practice and teaching were specific to the original readers and which remain normative for the whole church throughout this age.

8. Individual Christians and churches today are called upon to make decisions in many areas for which no explicit biblical guidance is to be expected. They will seek to make deductions from principles found in Scripture. Whereas in some matters a church will make a corporate decision and its members will accept that, there are other matters which the church will be content to leave to the conscience of the individual.

Where the lines diverge

The end-products of ecclesiastical diversity are all too evident in the twentieth century. Furthermore, various national, denominational and independent models of the church are espoused by evangelicals. The debate which follows will show, however, that in practice the role they give to Scripture is not identical. Some seek to be controlled by Scripture alone but differ in their interpretations of particular texts, showing a greater or lesser degree of toleration of those holding other positions. Others start not from Scripture itself but from their prior commitment to the institutional church. They point to the mixed character of all churches in an imperfect world and fear that an appeal to Scripture alone is simplistic. Yet others regard the appeal to normative Scripture as inadequate without the exercise of contemporary gifts to apply Christ's rule over his church.

Let us now sharpen up the issues about the church and its unity which we propose to discuss.

The issue of membership

Is the biblical pattern that of a national church or of a

gathered church? Who should be accepted as members of a local church? Professing believers only? Baptized believers only? Believers and their baptized children also? How do we regard regular adherents who remain uncommitted and unbaptized? How are the spiritual qualifications for a profession of faith to be discerned? Is 'folk-religion' a superstition to be refuted or an opportunity to be grasped?

The issue of denominations

Does the Bible validate a structured connectionalism or the autonomy of independency? Is any kind of disciplined structure needed to enable churches to fulfil their positive mission in the world? Does such co-operation restrict or enhance the local church in its relationship to Christ as its head? If denominational labels do exist, should they be ignored in favour of para-church co-operation?

The issue of doctrinal purity

Should churches be doctrinally comprehensive or entirely separated from error? How far can a gathered church, seeking to maintain a realistically pure membership, enjoy fellowship with another local church which seems to accept a more mixed membership? Does it make any essential difference if that other local church itself maintains a vigorous evangelical testimony within a denomination in which other churches do not? Is the lack of clarity in a mixed body too high a price to pay?

The issue of charismatic experience

Are charismatic experiences to be expressed by the renewal of traditional denominations, or by establishing new fellowships in which God's gifts are being restored? Is it the gospel alone which constitutes the ground of unity within and among local churches, or do different experiences of spirituality and the exercise of gifts of oversight call for new structures of church order today?

Part 1

The issue of membership

David Holloway and Derek Prime

- *Is the biblical pattern that of a national church or of a gathered church?*
- *Who should be accepted as members of a local church – professing believers only, baptized believers only, believers and also their baptized children?*
- *How do we regard regular attenders who remain uncommitted and unbaptized?*
- *How are the spiritual qualifications for a profession of faith to be discerned?*
- *Is 'folk-religion' a superstition to be refuted or an opportunity to be grasped?*

The national church

David Holloway

Presenting problems ● Distinctions ● Church
and sect ● Church and state ● Infant baptism ●
Conclusion

Presenting problems

There is a paradox: the church as it is, and the church as it is
meant to be. Archbishop William Temple once wrote:

> Those who know anything about the Church of
> the ninth and tenth centuries, before the Hil-
> debrandine Reformation, or about the Church of
> the fifteenth century just before the Lutheran,
> Calvinist, and Ignatian Reformations, find con-
> spicuous difficulty in applying to it the glowing
> phrases of St Peter and St Paul.[1]

And it was the Anglican Dean Inge who refused to

> suppose that the forms which Christianity has
> so far assumed – Jewish-Christian Messianism,
> the paganized Christianity of Western Catholic-
> ism, the fossilized Christianity of the East, the
> disrupted and fissiparous Christianity of the
> North – are any better than caricatures of what
> Christ meant his Church to be.[2]

Nobody, however, who honestly studies the New Testament can argue that history reveals the church in a *complete* slide from the high ground of the New Testament church. Look at the epistles to Corinth! You do not even have to read between the lines to see that here was a church with serious moral and theological problems. The letters to the churches in the book of Revelation (chs. 2 – 3) show further serious faults in the early apostolic church.

There are some who agree with all this. They say, however, that a real and new problem started in the fourth century with Constantine when he proclaimed 'the peace of the church'. Soon afterwards matters became even worse when Theodosius gave the Christian church official status in 381 and outlawed paganism. The church then began its move from being a simple federation of *gathered* churches to being a set of established regional or national churches. The ultimate disgrace, it is claimed, was at the Reformation with the principle of '*cuius regio, eius religio*' – 'your region (or nation) determines your religion' (but these critics sometimes forget that this also meant your religion will determine your region's religion). Here, however, was the 'modern' national church inevitably full, they say, of nominal believers who were in fact unbelievers.

So what we now have to do, the critics continue, is to get rid of established and national churches. We are not going to criticize the Reformers, they concede, for they knew no better. Indeed, some of the anabaptists these Reformers were opposing were so extreme that we can understand why they wanted to hold on to the 'establishment'. But the situation in the twentieth century is completely different. Let us now disestablish. True, we shall not end up with an absolutely pure church – we shall only enjoy that in heaven. The whole Christian community, however, will be improved by the demise of national churches. At the very least we will tighten up on the issue of membership.

Put like that, the argument for disestablishment looks persuasive. Unfortunately, things are not so simple. That there are still questions over the nature of the church, and who should be in it, is not surprising. These are questions that have been on the Christian agenda since Luther nailed his ninety-five theses to the door of the castle church at Wittenberg on that eventful day of 31 October 1517.

The Reformation in the sixteenth century focused on two issues: how to relate in true worship to a loving heavenly Father, and where to find the true church. The first issue was better solved than the second. Agreement over the doctrine of justification by grace through faith came relatively easily among those eager for reform. Agreement over the doctrine of the church has yet to be reached. Those who are the product of the European Reformation are still arguing – witness this book!

Some, of course, have a good grasp of the theological and sociological problems that lie behind the issue of the national church over against a gathered church. Many, however, see the issue simply pragmatically. Nowhere do they believe they see it more clearly than in what are called 'the occasional offices' – baptisms, weddings and funerals. They see the national churches baptizing, marrying and burying all and sundry, and do not like the spectacle.

Of these three, baptism (especially infant baptism) presents the chief problem as far as membership is concerned. We shall deal with this issue later.

Distinctions

Discussions over national churches can be very confused, for national churches are all so different. By a 'national' church many people mean an 'established' church. But what is an established church?

Establishment occurs when the state or nation legally recognizes one church and not another. As the Chadwick 'Report on *Church and State*' made clear in 1970:

> The words 'by law established' were originally used to denote the statutory process by which the allegiance of the Church of England to the Sovereign (and not the Pope) and the forms of worship and doctrines of that church were imposed by law. The phrase distinguished the

legality of the national church from other
churches which were then unlawful and whose
worship and doctrines were then proscribed.[3]

Today, however, this distinction has disappeared. All
the churches in the United Kingdom have a basis in law.
Their constitutions, property and even some forms of
worship are secured by law. The Church of England, the
national English church, is distinguished by being bound by
more of the law and more of the national constitution than are
other churches and, in return, by having more privileges.

In the former Soviet Union, however, the national
church, the Russian Orthodox Church was, by law,
deprived of its privileges in 1918. It, however, continued to
be *de facto* the national church.

In Germany there are two national churches! The 'basic
law' operates a separation of church and state – a 'free
church in a free state' – but this does not stop significant
co-operation especially between the state and the two
largest churches, the 'Evangelical' Church in Germany and
the Roman Catholic Church. The state, for example,
enables the churches to use the machinery of taxation to
acquire funds (except from those who choose to opt out).

Some can be forgiven if they, therefore, conclude that a
national church is simply one that has been on the ground a
long time, or is sufficiently large in terms of membership,
and so can influence the national culture. For this reason
the Southern Baptist Church in the United States is felt to
be akin to a national church – at least in the areas where it is
strong. Such a view gains all the more credence when it is
remembered that Billy Graham, the most distinguished of
Southern Baptist ordained clergy, is asked to pray at the
inauguration of Presidents.

So what are we *really* talking about when we distinguish
two sorts of churches – a national church and a gathered
church? That there are these two sorts of church does seem
self-evident for all our difficulties of definition. The two
seem to result from two factors: firstly, the factor of church-
state relations and, secondly, the factor of two structures
for mission.

The Bible in a very real sense introduces us to the 'national church' in the Old Testament. The New Testament makes it quite clear that the church is the continuation and fulfilment of the historic people of God, called first in the covenant with Abraham. The story of the Old Testament is, however, of how God's people, after being a pilgrim, 'gathered' people, eventually became settled with their own land and laws. The 'church' and nation, if you like, then became one: here was the first national church!

Following the disobedience of his people, however, God's purposes were narrowed down and fulfilled in Jesus Christ – the one obedient, suffering servant. There then began the 'new' covenant church of the apostolic age. It was again a pilgrim, gathered church of loosely connected Jewish-Gentile Christian synagogues at first unsettled and scattered around the Mediterranean world. The church then grew and became more settled; and, as we have seen, in the fourth century it was on its way to becoming a national – indeed international – church.

Becoming a national church, however, did not, and does not, depend so much on its character as on the wider society and culture. When the state authorities were persecuting the early church, it was the church of the catacombs and 'gathered'. When, however, the state authorities ceased persecuting and accepted the Christian way, the church, almost inevitably, became the church of the Roman Empire. Similarly, ceasing to be a national church will usually depend on state initiative, as the Russians learned under Lenin.

We can view the church, however, not only from the perspective of national versus gathered churches and state approval or disapproval. We can also view it from the perspective of two structures for mission. The early church, like its Jewish counterpart, was not just made up of settled Jewish-Gentile Christian synagogues. There were also 'missionary bands'.

The Jews of the Diaspora had two ways of functioning. They not only had their own Jewish settled synagogues, but also people who, Jesus said, 'travel over land and sea to win a single convert' (Mt. 23:15). These Jewish proselytizers would have travelled around the Mediterranean.

Similarly, it seems that the early Christians had travelling missionaries alongside the increasingly settled Christian synagogues. Paul himself had created such missionary bands. He worked with colleagues who travelled together as the church of Christ. In no way did he think of himself as 'para-church'. The church, the body of Christ, was big enough to include not only groups of people in given localities, but also people like Paul, who though 'not physically present', was 'with you in spirit' (1 Cor. 5:3) – indeed he might even be in prison!

Sadly, today, we too readily identify the church with groups of people defined by *structures*, using *buildings* and having specific *routines*. The early church defined itself more in terms of people whom Christ had called (Jn. 15:16) and who had responded in faith and obedience. Structures, buildings and routines were, even then, no doubt, necessary but quite secondary.

We have too rigid a model of the church – often a box (or association of boxes) with a parish, or specific territorial area. The early church, the post-apostolic church and the medieval church, however, had no problem in viewing itself more flexibly, for at least it had these *two* structures – local congregations and travelling missionaries – making up the church.

In time the loose groupings of Christian synagogues became connectional churches in dioceses with bishops. In time, too, the Pauline missionary bands were succeeded by monastic missionary bands working out of monastic houses under abbots or abbesses. Indeed, the story of the conversion of northern Europe and the United Kingdom in particular is the story of monastic missionary bands. Columba, Aidan and Cuthbert were missionary monks working in the north of the United Kingdom, and Augustine was a missionary monk working in the south. These missionary bands in turn established settled churches.

True there was a rivalry at times between these two structures. But Ralph Winter has argued that

the great achievement of the mediaeval period is

the ultimate synthesis, delicately achieved, whereby Catholic orders were able to function along with Catholic parishes and dioceses, without the two structures conflicting with each other to the point of a setback to the movement.[4]

One of the tragedies of the Reformation was that there was a renewal of settled churches, but no renewal of missionary bands. There was, instead, a dissolution of monasteries. This has meant that, in time, in the western Protestant tradition, there has had to be independent pressure for 'renewing structures' of committed men and women. This has resulted in missionary societies for world evangelization, and gathered churches for local evangelization – witness John Wesley and the Methodist churches. To this day when it is felt that an established church is not meeting the spiritual needs of people in a given area, some may set up a house church or some new community church as a response.

Church and sect

The issues are complex. Part of the problem is that in discussing the church we are discussing, as the Anglican divine Richard Hooker reminded us, both a 'society and a society supernatural'. We cannot view the church only from its ideal and God-intended position as the society that is the supernatural 'bride of Christ'. Hooker argued that we must distinguish 'first between the Church of God mystical and visible, then between the visible sound and corrupted'. The church 'militant here on earth' is a sociological reality. It is a *human* society. Grace perfects nature; it does not destroy it. And Christian groups do not cease, by virtue of being Christian, to be subject to the normal patterns of healthy human interaction, behaviour and development. The theological and historical analysis of the church needs (critically) to be supplemented by sociological analysis.

The analysis of Ernest Troeltsch in *The Social Teaching*

of the Christian Churches is undoubtedly inadequate and defective in part, but it cannot be ignored. His contrast between the sect-type of Christian organization and the church-type is instructive for our discussion.

Troeltsch saw the church-type as an organization that was essentially conservative, accepting the secular social order and concerned to influence the masses.

> It desires to cover the whole of life. The sects, on the other hand, are comparatively small groups; they aspire after personal inward perfection, and aim at a direct personal fellowship between the members of each group. From the very beginning, therefore, they are forced to organize themselves in small groups, and to renounce the idea of dominating the world. Their attitude towards the world, the State, and Society may be indifferent, tolerant, or hostile, since they have no desire to control and incorporate these forms of social life ... The fully developed Church, however, utilizes the State and the ruling classes, and weaves these elements into her own life; she then becomes an integral part of the existing social order; from this standpoint, then, the Church both stabilizes and determines the social order.[5]

The church-type, Troeltsch argued, works 'downwards from above' – being associated with the upper classes. The sect-type works 'upwards from below' being 'connected with the lower classes, or at least with those elements in Society which are opposed to the State and to Society'.[6]

Troeltsch saw the value in both the church-type and the sect-type. He saw the church-type as following in Paul's footsteps.

> Paulinism, in spite of its strongly individualistic and 'enthusiastic' features, had already led the way along this line: it desired to conquer the world for Christ; it came to terms with the order

of the State by interpreting it as an institution ordained and permitted by God; it accepted the existing order with its professions and its habits and customs.[7]

He saw the value of the sect-type, however, in keeping alive elements of the Christian faith that can get obscured, as 'the mainstream of Christian development ... flows along the channel prepared by the church-type'. The sects

> always appeal to the Gospel and to Primitive Christianity, and accuse the Church of having fallen away from its ideal ... the sects, with their greater independence of the world, and their continual emphasis upon the original ideals of Christianity, often represent in a very direct and characteristic way the essential fundamental ideas of Christianity.[8]

Troeltsch also noted that the sect 'is a voluntary community whose members join it of their own free will'. Infant baptism, which they see in the church-type, 'is almost always a stumbling-block'.[9] A sect objects to the concept of being born into a church.

Both church-type and sect-type, he argued, are there in embryo in New Testament times.

> If then in reality both types claim, and rightly claim, a relationship with the Primitive Church, it is clear that the final cause for this dualistic development must lie within primitive Christianity itself.[10]

We have already seen how there are contrasts between the social ordering and style of the 'settled' people of God in the Old Testament and that of the first scattered early Christian synagogues. We have also seen how there were at least two different New Testament structures for mission, one of which was more church-type, the other more sect-type.

If, therefore, both types are valid as Christian responses to the work of God in his world, and both can claim scriptural authority, there does not seem to be a blueprint in the Bible for the relationship of the church and state that would favour either model. In the wise words of Sir Timothy Hoare:

> Each generation of Christians must accept, discern and adapt what they receive . . . Perhaps the problem of finding the ideal relationship between any church and any state, 'will never be solved until the coming of the Son of Man, when there shall be no King but Christ and all nations, people and languages shall bow down before Him' (Browne).[11]

For that reason there is no universal answer to the question: Is it right to be a church-type or a sect-type? It depends on the history and the growth of your church. It seems, however, almost inevitable that as a church grows and is concerned for the Lordship of Christ in the whole of life and society, it will move from being a sect-type to becoming a church-type.

The key is social influence. That is why the old categories of 'national church' versus 'gathered church' are not always reliable. In the changed situation today in northern Europe and the United States some of the old national churches contain within them sect-types, while some of the independent gathered churches operate as church-types.

The United States has moved in its short history from having a formal religious establishment to disestablishing churches and then insisting on a separation of church and state. But with 40% of the population weekly in church, many churches will be and, indeed, are functioning as church-types. Indeed, the 'moral majority' movement of the Reagan era was evidence of a number of conservative sect-type churches adopting a church-type posture. Some of the huge American churches, with congregations of thousands, are clearly church-types.

In England, by contrast, some elements of the national church, the Church of England, are now having to function as sect-types. This is inevitable where individual churches are so weak and so thin on the ground. Ironically, those parishes that are operating most as church-types in terms of social influence are often growing, Anglican evangelical churches. It is ironic, for these churches in the past have often been criticized by liberal hierarchies for operating within the Church of England as gathered churches and sects!

Church and state

The issue of membership is less of a concern for a national or church-type church. This is not because there is no concern for commitment or truth, but because the truth of Jesus' words in Matthew 13:24–43 becomes so apparent. The field, the world, does contain both wheat and weeds and these are so close together it is hard to distinguish between them. There are also wise and foolish virgins (Mt. 25:1–13). The early church showed, right from the start, that the visible church of Christ would contain nominal believers (Acts 5:1–11).

If people join the church, they do so on a profession of faith. The church cannot read the hearts of men and women. They have to be taken on trust. There is, however, less *angst* in a church-type church over mistakes. For the church is not seen just in relation to itself, and thus its purity. It is also seen in its responsibility to the world. It does not, therefore, believe in putting up unnecessary barriers between itself and the world. Inevitably this will mean that proportionally more will jump over those barriers than jump over the greater barriers that a sect-type church erects. The church-type church, however, does not have to be unconcerned when this happens. Indeed, there can and should be a proper biblical discipline in such a church, and certainly relating to leadership.

The perspective in the church-type church is the wider community. The state is seen as God-ordained (Rom. 13).

This is, however, no more than biblical orthodox Christian theology. Yes, the state can become demonic (Rev. 13), but until it becomes so, it is seen as God's instrument.

Augustine saw the God-given function of the state as restraining evil. Luther saw the state as God's left hand, and the church, or the kingdom of grace, as his right hand. He also stressed not only the negative function of the state in restraining evil but the positive function of the state in promoting peace and order.

Calvin saw the state as being separate from the church, but he argued that a state composed of Christian citizens has the duty of aiding the church. It ought 'to cherish and support the external worship of God, to preserve the pure doctrine of religion, to defend the constitution of the Church'.[12] Calvin did not have in mind a theocracy so much as a situation where the state and the church were complementary and in a dialectical relationship.

In various measure these approaches have informed the Christian, or the church's, response to the state over the centuries. The church cannot ever turn its back on the state. It cannot, that is, if it and its members are to be obedient to Jesus' command to, 'Give to Caesar what is Caesar's' (Mt. 22:21), let alone his command to 'go and make disciples of all nations' (Mt. 28:18).

Alec Vidler put the duty of the church well in his book *The Orb and the Cross*:

> A Church to be worthy of the name, however small a minority it may be in any given society, is charged with the responsibility of bearing testimony to God's sovereignty and God's will before kings and rulers and the whole people. It must declare man's civic duties as well as ecclesiastical duties. It must teach the law of God, as well as preach the Gospel of God. It must denounce injustice and sin wherever they are to be found, and call upon all men to repent and return unto the Lord their God by obeying His Law in their common life.[13]

A national or church-type church finds it easier to do that. When, of course, a national church fails in this duty, it incurs the judgment of God.

In our present environment, however, we must not be trapped into old stereotypes or old ways of thinking. There is a growing awareness that our corporate life in society is not just a matter of individuals and states. Nor is it just a matter of some churches, national or church-type churches, working alongside the 'powers that be', while gathered or sect-type churches concern themselves with individual needs and problems.

A recent analysis of modern western life is that in addition to the private and public worlds of the individual and the state there is an intermediate area. This is serviced by 'mediating structures' that function as bridges between the private and the public worlds. This area and these structures are crucial to human well-being. Fundamental to this area are the mediating structures of the family, the school and the church (of all types). These are the 'value carriers' in modern society. The health of the state (social and spiritual) and the health of the individual (personal and spiritual) depends to a great degree on the health of these mediating structures.

All this means that the Christian in the last decade of the twentieth century must be concerned for individual conversions to Christ, for influencing the wider social order, but also for church renewal, church growth and church revitalization. Praise God for some sect-type churches that are better than some church-type churches at church renewal. Praise God for some church-type churches that are better at church growth and evangelism, and influencing the wider social order. The total church is one body but 'members do not all have the same function'. So Paul says, 'We have different gifts according to the grace given us', and exhorts us to use them (Rom. 12:4, 6).

There is still, however, the issue of baptism and in particular, infant baptism. For all the theorizing and the value seen in a national church-type church, if something is wrong and contrary to apostolic teaching and practice, then it is wrong!

Infant baptism

So as a postscript we must now answer the objections many feel about baptism in national churches. There are usually two main objections.

The first objection is, as we have suggested, that national churches practise infant or paedo-baptism alongside adult baptism. True, some gathered churches are also paedo-baptist: and a quasi-national church like the Southern Baptist Church in the United States is obviously adult-baptist. Be that as it may. Many critics of national churches argue that a policy of exclusive adult baptism produces, and would produce for them, a more healthy membership.

The second objection is that national churches not only practise infant baptism but they also baptize infants indiscriminately. An easy way to eliminate indiscriminate infant baptism, it is then argued, is to eliminate infant baptism itself.

Baptism, of course, is central to the question of church membership. In New Testament times you became one of the 'saints', or you were identified with the church, by being identified with Christ. On the human side this initiation was marked by receiving the apostolic word and being baptized (Acts 2:41).

So baptism was a sign of having started rather than of having arrived. The New Testament suggests that the qualifications for baptism were fairly minimal. Of course, there were tighter qualifications for officers in the church, as we can see from the pastoral epistles. The basic baptismal confession, however, was probably in line with Romans 10:9, 'if you confess with your mouth "Jesus is Lord," and believe in your heart that God raised him from the dead, you will be saved.'

As for the meaning of baptism, we need to go back to the day of Pentecost. On that occasion Peter said (addressing adults), 'Repent and be baptised every one of you in the name of Jesus Christ for the forgiveness of your sins. And you will receive the gift of the Holy Spirit' (Acts 2:38).

This suggests there are three strands in Christian initiation – one is ours (repentance), one is the church's (baptism), and one is God's (the gift of the Holy Spirit). Baptism (the church's rite) is therefore associated with something that we do *and* something that God does. So, baptism is not just a symbol of our penitent response. It is also a symbol of God's gracious action in bringing us to new life and power by his Holy Spirit. That is important.

Fundamental to the Christian experience are a 'new heart' and a 'new spirit'. This was the promise in Ezekiel 36:26. Jesus' own baptism was especially linked with the reception of the Spirit (Jn. 1:32). So we must see at the heart of the symbolism of baptism God's initiative as he works in our lives by his Holy Spirit, and not just a human response as we repent and confess Christ. Those who see baptism in terms only of a person's response rather than divine grace will clearly have problems over infant baptism.

Infant baptism only becomes a practical issue when believing parents have children, or when adults who already have children become believers. The majority of people in the history of the church have judged that baptizing these children is appropriate. God's initiative of grace is working in the lives of children while they are receiving Christian nurture at the hands of their parents and the local fellowship. Parents, on the basis of their own faith, may, it is argued, symbolize this in the baptism of children. Are they right to do so? What guidance can we get from the Bible?

Part of the background to Christian baptism is Old Testament circumcision – it is interesting to note that on one occasion Paul uses circumcision as a metaphor for Christian initiation (Col. 2:11–12). Circumcision was a sign of God's covenant with Abraham (Gn. 17:10). It was not an automatic guarantee of blessing (both Jacob and Esau were circumcised but the line of blessing was through Jacob alone). Along with adult males, however, male infants were also circumcised; such was the concept of family solidarity. So here was a religious rite that marked God's initiative and Jewish faith at the same time, but it also involved infant children.

Another part of the background to Christian baptism is

John the Baptist. We come across baptism in New Testament times first with John. Indeed, he was challenging some of the assumptions behind the Jewish circumcision philosophy. But what did John's baptism mean?

The Jews had water-rites for proselytes, Gentile converts who wanted to be admitted to the Jewish community. There were also water-rites associated with the Qumran community. So what was remarkable about John the Baptist? It was obviously not the water-rite as such. Rather, it was the fact that he called the *Jews* to baptism. It was a statement that not just Gentile proselytes but Jewish people as well needed to repent and get right with God.

It follows that, unless we have evidence to the contrary, we must assume that John's water-rite in its administration was not radically different from other Jewish water-rites. As there is evidence that children were baptized along with their parents in proselyte baptism, we may infer that they were also baptized along with their parents in John's baptism. And as Christian baptism evolved from John's baptism, it is to be assumed that, in the early church, when households were baptized along with the main convert (Acts 16:15, 33), children of the believing convert were also baptized.

This seems to be confirmed by Paul in 1 Corinthians 7:14 where he argues that 'the unbelieving husband has been sanctified through his wife, and the unbelieving wife has been sanctified through her believing husband. Otherwise your children would be unclean, but as it is, *they are holy*'. Paul was arguing from the known to the unknown. Everyone of these Christian wives or husbands knew that their children were holy; the trouble was with their unbelieving partners. But how did they know their children were 'holy' except for their having been baptized? A 'holy one' or 'saint' is the common New Testament term for a church member. As the New Testament does not seem to know of any unbaptized church members, it is hard to see how these children could not have been baptized. At any rate, this passage clearly implies that family solidarity was still strong as a concept in the early church. It was not confined to pre-Christian Judaism.

It is hard to argue that the New Testament is against infant baptism where there are believing parents. Certainly the consensus of Christians down the centuries has not been against it. The post-apostolic church practised infant baptism; such early dissenters as we know of seem more concerned to put baptism off, not until adulthood, but death! The 'baptist' position simply emerged as one minority position at the time of the Reformation.

A final consideration is that there are pastoral reasons for infant baptism. If you do not baptize the children of Christian parents, how are those parents to bring up their children? As non-Christians to be converted? But when those children pray to Jesus (albeit in a child-like way), are they exercising faith? Luther said such children exercised *infans fides* – infant faith. They do not have mature faith; but they confess Jesus as Lord in their own terms. Sometimes, sadly, some seem to fall away, but so do people baptized as adults.

There is an ambiguity here. A number of national churches and other church-type churches that practise infant baptism get over the ambiguity by, in effect, extending the ritual of initiation. It begins with the water-rite and concludes with the profession of faith some years later at confirmation. This happens in the Church of England.

The objection that national churches practise infant baptism is a weak one. More serious is the objection that national churches baptize infants indiscriminately. Clearly, indiscriminate baptism is wrong. Such a practice, however, often arises because of the indiscipline of the minister in not making clear to the parents what the church requires before infant baptism can properly take place, rather than the principles of the church itself.

As an example, the Church of England is committed to discrimination in baptism, even though some accuse it of being indiscriminate. Its new Prayer Book, the Alternative Service Book, begins the service of 'The Baptism of Children' by asking the parents and Godparents if they are willing by prayer, *example* and teaching to help and encourage the child, not only in trusting God, but also in public worship and private prayer. The service does not continue until an assurance has been given. The parents and Godparents then have to make a profession of faith *themselves*. For Anglicans it is, therefore, obviously inappropriate to baptize the children of parents who will never engage in public worship. Otherwise there will not be the 'example' required. That this sometimes happens is an 'abuse'. But as Augustine said: *abusum non tollit usum* – the abuse does not deny the true use.

Conclusion

Most Christians agree that the New Testament is not clear on many matters of church order. In such cases the national and church-type churches tend to take seriously, if not follow, another maxim of Augustine, 'In matters where the Scripture has not spoken clearly, the custom of the people of God or the institutions of our predecessors, are to be held as law.'[14]

The gathered or sect-type churches probably have less of a regard for history and tradition. As someone who has a commitment to a national church, the Church of England, I feel that such disregard is not always wise. True, it has an attraction in the modern world because of the legacy of the European Enlightenment which saw history and tradition as a burden to be rejected. Immanuel Kant, after all, defined 'enlightenment' as, 'man's emergence from self-incurred immaturity. Immaturity is the inability to use one's own understanding *without the guidance of another*.'[15]

Too many in the modern world, however, are wanting to be 'open' to everything and to 're-invent the wheel'.

It would seem best if the church of Christ avoided following this now nearly dead fashion, and learnt lessons from the past.

Response to David Holloway

Derek Prime

A more urgent issue

David Holloway seems to assume that the establishment or disestablishment of the national church is a principal issue under debate when we consider church membership. I wonder if this is an Anglican preoccupation? While I should not wish to dismiss it as unimportant, the far more urgent question is: How does one become a member of the church of Jesus Christ – irrespective of its local manifestation or name? Unless we relate ourselves to this question, discussions about the nature of the church become woolly and pragmatic rather than scriptural.

David suggests that there are still questions about the nature of the church and who should be in it. Among evangelical believers that is rarely the case. The church is made up of those who know in experience the reality of 'justification by grace through faith' – a doctrine David rightly says we are all agreed upon. That truth has immediate relevance to the issue of membership. To be members of the church of Jesus Christ men and women must have faith in him – they must be believers.

This truth, in turn, influences how we view young children before they are old enough to respond to the gospel's call. The New Testament nowhere instructs us to admit infants to church membership, and such action is never assumed. Whatever may have happened in proselyte baptism certainly has no authority for Christian practice. Furthermore, there is no evidence of John the Baptist baptizing infants, and the baptism our Lord himself instituted was clearly in harmony with John's.

Circumcision and baptism

The placing of circumcision alongside baptism, and the suggestion that the background to Christian baptism is Old Testament circumcision, is nowhere explicitly taught in the New Testament. It has to be argued for – and that in itself makes it suspect. We must not forget that the Jews themselves all too easily fell into the snare of trusting in the outward physical act of circumcision to the neglect of the spiritual relationship it was intended to signify. Paul makes the point that visible membership of the people of God under the old covenant was not enough (Rom. 2:28–29) – he knew that from personal experience.

I should not want to dismiss as unimportant 'tradition' and 'consensus' – the words used in reference to infant baptism – but all traditions and convictions must be tested by the Scriptures themselves.

The children of Christian parents

The pastoral reasons suggested for the baptism of children of Christian parents, besides being without biblical warrant, do not stand up to close scrutiny. We should bring up children as those who need to be converted. To give the impression that they are secure because of their parents' faith is neither biblical nor true. All the time they are not of an age to believe for themselves, it seems right to regard them as being in a special relationship to God because of their identity with their Christian parents. This is a truth more than hinted at in 1 Corinthians 7:14

40

although not expanded upon in a way that would lead us to presumption or indifference to our children's need of personal faith and salvation. (There seems to be no justification for the suggestion that the grounds for an infant being described as 'holy' in 1 Corinthians 7:14 was the fact of its baptism. If an unbelieving husband did not need to be baptized in order to be sanctified through his wife, why should children need to be baptized?)

Our children should indeed be taught and encouraged to pray. While God makes special promises to believers about prayer, he hears the prayers of all who call upon him in truth. Our responsibility is to teach and encourage our children to exercise personal faith in God through Jesus Christ so that they may enter into the glorious relationship with God he has made possible by his atonement.

The vital question

To use the fact that some who are baptized as adults fall away afterwards as an argument for baptizing infants, who may later make no confession of faith, carries little weight. Just in the practical terms of the numbers involved, the former are few in comparison with the latter. The vital question, however, is not, 'Do people stand after baptism?' but 'Who are the proper subjects for baptism?' In the New Testament it is a sign of incorporation into Christ, and an expression of God-given repentance and faith which are more than just a human beginning or a sign of having started the Christian life.

I feel, however, that we should not allow ourselves to be side-tracked by arguments concerning baptism. We must be influenced in our church practice and conduct by the more important question: How do we become members of the body of Christ? – irrespective of the mode of baptism, or the age at which it may be administered. The answer the New Testament plainly gives – as distinct from other positions which have to be argued for – is that the church is made up of believers, those who are 'in Christ'. Whether a company of believers is a 'church-type' or a 'sect-type' –

a way of putting things that sounds rather derogatory with regard to the latter – the key question is: Is this a company of true believers? The parables of the weeds (Mt. 13:24–43), and of the wise and foolish virgins (Mt. 25:1–13), which David referred to, give no grounds for not questioning and testing the reality of people's Christian profession.

Influencing society for good

I wonder if the claim that the national and established churches are seen as stabilizing and determining the social order in a way other churches do not stands up to examination. To suggest that it is only the 'church-type' churches who take their responsibility to society seriously is manifestly wrong. What effect, honestly, do the pronouncements of 'church leaders' have upon the affairs of a nation compared with the influence of ordinary Christians – irrespective of their church affiliation – who genuinely function as salt and light, whether in the Civil Service, the government, the Health Service, teaching, business, commerce or in family life? I do not wish to make an issue of this since it is not really our subject, but nonconformists – the so-called 'sect-type' churches – have been prominent in social reform and missionary endeavour, and it is significant that the phrase 'the nonconformist conscience', has entered the English vocabulary. Christians – whether of the 'church-type' or 'sect-type' – are salt and light. They cannot be faithful disciples without functioning as such. The best influence for good the church can give to society is that of changed lives – lives committed to righteousness (1 Pet. 2:24).

The gathered church

Derek Prime

Personal experience ● What is 'the church'? ●
The local church in the New Testament ●
Where do these conclusions lead us? ● Procedures for admittance into church membership ● The position of young children in the
church ● How important is baptism as a qualifi-
cation for church membership? ● The benefits
of the gathered church concept

We cannot help but approach the issue of church membership in the light of our own experience and background. We are often influenced as much by
circumstances over which we have had no control as by
our convictions – a truth we may sometimes be reluctant
to admit. This is certainly the case when we consider who
are the appropriate persons to admit to the church's visible membership.

Personal experience

My own background is not untypical of many in our
unchurched society. My parents were not professing

Christians but, having been baptized and married in an Anglican church, they regarded themselves as members of the Church of England. Born prematurely, there were fears that I might not live, and so I was hurriedly baptized. I have wondered if this was because of the churchmanship of a doctor or nurse present at the time. A little while later my parents decided I should be baptized 'properly', with an aunt, who made no Christian profession, as my God-parent. My own church connection thereafter was with two local Anglican churches through membership of their Cubs and Scouts.

In my early teens I was introduced, by school friends, to an independent evangelical church. After about a year I came under conviction of sin and realized my need of salvation. I professed faith in Christ and found myself immediately at home in that church fellowship. Soon afterwards I faced up to the matter of baptism. The church, through whose witness I had been converted, practised only believer's baptism, although it was not a condition of church membership. The explanation for this was that although baptism was regarded as important, living faith in Christ was regarded as more important, and the intention was not to refuse church fellowship to any whom Christ had received.

As I read the New Testament for the first time I became aware that baptism invariably followed faith rather than preceding it. My parents were horrified at my contem-plating baptism. Was I not a Christian already? Had I not been baptized as a child? Had I not, in fact, been baptized twice? Their questions were understandable from the standpoint of their nominal membership of the Anglican Church, but they only served to strengthen my conviction that I must obey the New Testament instruction to confess my faith in Christ by baptism and to link it with member-ship of the local church.

Now I readily admit that my parents' understanding was not what all Anglicans would encourage, and that perhaps some Anglican ministers would have declined my parents' request to baptize me, or would have been concerned about my Godparents' inability to instruct me.

Whatever may be the criticisms of that situation, however, the truth is that my parents – and I too through them – had the mistaken idea that we were members of the church of Christ on account of infant baptism and our loose attachment to Anglicanism, and these mistaken convictions actually constituted a hindrance to understanding the real truth of the gospel.

It may be suggested that my adopting what is known as the 'gathered church' position is the consequence of my background and experience – and there must be some truth in that. At university I studied first history and then theology, convinced that God was calling me into the ministry. At that time I had to determine to which denominational group I should apply, both for training and eventual ordination. Because of the influence of many of my friends who were going into the Anglican ministry, I seriously considered doing the same. It was, however, the issue of church membership, and especially the baptism of infants – with the implications of baptismal regeneration on the part of some at least in Anglicanism – that convinced me that it was not the right way forward for me.

The words in the Prayer Book, said after the baptism of a child, contradicted what I knew from the Scriptures and from my own experience: 'Seeing now, dearly beloved brethren, that this child is by Baptism regenerate and grafted into the body of Christ's Church, let us give thanks unto Almighty God for these benefits.' I found myself similarly unhappy with the answer to the second question of the Catechism when a confirmation candidate says, 'My baptism wherein I was made a member of Christ, a child of God, and an inheritor of the Kingdom of Heaven.' Although the Prayer Book Service is not used now as frequently as it was, the Alternative Service Book of 1980 still has the priest praying, 'We thank you that by your Holy Spirit these children have been born again into new life, adopted for your own, and received into the fellowship of your Church.'

What is 'the church'?

Our convictions concerning church membership stem from our view of the church universal and especially of the local church. I understand the church universal to be composed of all who are 'in Christ', those 'who have been chosen according to the foreknowledge of God the Father, through the sanctifying work of the Spirit, for obedience to Jesus Christ and sprinkling by his blood' (1 Pet. 1:2) – in other words, born-again believers. Those who are 'in Christ' are the church, whichever part of the visible body of Christ they belong to, or even if they are not part of the visible body of Christ, as may be the case for some. The identity of those who are 'in Christ' is known for certainty by God alone, although there are clear evidences of being 'in Christ' which we are encouraged to look for. Paul sums up the situation in 2 Timothy 2:19:

> God's solid foundation stands firm, sealed with this inscription: 'The Lord knows those who are his,' and, 'Everyone who confesses the name of the Lord must turn away from wickedness.'

It is not inappropriate to speak of the invisible church, particularly when we refer to the church universal (and in a limited way of the local church also), in the sense that all its members are not visible to us, as they are to God. 1 John 2:19 gives some warrant for the common distinction between the visible and invisible church. The local church's *professed* membership is, however, visible to us. We are therefore bound to ask the question: What relation should the local church's membership bear to the invisible and universal church, made up as it is of all who are 'in Christ'? The answer must be that the local church should match as nearly as possible the make-up of the invisible church in that all its members should be 'in Christ' and give evidence of saving faith. The identity of the two will never be perfect, but our aim must be to make their boundaries coincide as nearly as possible. It was for this reason that Paul urged professing Christians at Corinth to examine themselves to ensure they were in the faith (2 Cor. 13:5).

The local church in the New Testament

Basic to right action with regard to church membership is the truth that the local church is a fellowship of believers. It is obviously important that we should now consider the grounds for this assertion, and we do so by looking at four fundamental conclusions to which New Testament teaching and practice point us.

1 The early church was a fellowship of believers

The whole emphasis of the apostolic preaching was upon the necessity of a personal and individual response to the message of the gospel as it was preached. When the crowds in Jerusalem on the day of Pentecost asked, 'What shall we do?' they were told:

> Repent and be baptised, every one of you, in the name of Jesus Christ for the forgiveness of your sins. And you will receive the gift of the Holy Spirit. The promise is for you and your children and for all who are far off – for all whom the Lord our God will call (Acts 2:38–39).

The mention of children is not a reference to their immediate inclusion in the church as members but a promise that the gospel will save them as they believe it even as it will save others who have not yet heard it. Men and women were urged to repent and to turn to God (Acts 3:19) and receive the forgiveness of their sins through Christ (Acts 16:31). The early church was synonymous with those who 'believed and turned to the Lord' (Acts 11:21), in whom there was 'the evidence of the grace of God' (Acts 11:23).

47

The terms used to describe Christians in the Acts of the Apostles all point to and demand a personal response to the gospel: believers (the verb 'believe' is used thirty-nine times), 'disciples' (thirty-one times), and followers of 'the Way' (Acts 19:9; 22:4; 24:22). If we accept the usual Protestant interpretation of Matthew 16:16–18, then we believe we are built upon the rock of Jesus' Messiahship and Sonship as we personally confess him as the Son of God.

2 The early church was a fellowship of believers who professed their faith through baptism

In the early church baptism always followed faith; it never preceded it. On the day of Pentecost, after listening to Peter's proclamation of the gospel, 'those who accepted his message were baptised' (Acts 2:41). When the Ethiopian put his faith in Jesus as the Messiah and Saviour he had been looking for, the first question he asked on seeing water was, 'Look, here is water. Why shouldn't I be baptised?' (Acts 8:37). Paul's immediate action after his conversion, upon receiving his sight back, was to be baptized (Acts 9:18). He plainly knew this to be Christian practice, and it may have been part of the instructions given to him by the Lord Jesus, either directly or through Ananias. The same was true for Cornelius. It is significant that it was when Peter saw the evidences of new birth both in Cornelius and the members of his household that he concluded that baptism should take place (Acts 10:47–48). Even though it was in the early hours of the morning, the Philippian jailer and his family professed their faith by means of baptism (Acts 16:33). Everything in Acts points to this as the established pattern.

More important, however, than even the Acts narratives is the Lord Jesus Christ's plain command to his disciples to 'make disciples of all nations, baptising them in the name of the Father and of the Son and of the Holy Spirit' (Mt. 28:19), and his words recorded in Mark 16:16, 'Whoever believes and is baptised will be saved, but whoever does not believe will be condemned.' Here baptism clearly follows faith, and is seen as the badge of discipleship. Whatever views we take of Mark's longer ending, it relates our Lord Jesus Christ's instruction which regulated early church practice.

3 Believer's baptism and church membership were synonymous in the early church and New Testament period

The apostles and first disciples formed the embryonic church. On the day of Pentecost those who were baptized on repentance and profession of faith in Christ 'were added to their number that day' (Acts 2:41), and 'They devoted themselves to the apostles' teaching and to the fellowship, to the breaking of bread and to prayer' (Acts 2:42). The stress was upon 'believers' being together (Acts 2:44), and as people entered into salvation so they were added to the church (Acts 2:47).

It has only been because of so much confusion over baptism – its meaning and to whom it should be administered – that baptism and church membership have tended to be separated. To be a Christian is to be 'in Christ' and baptism has at its heart the truth of our union with him (Rom. 6:1–5). Baptism does not itself create that union but it expresses it. A wedding ring expresses the union of two people; it does not create that union, and it may be worn without such a union existing. Where a union is contracted, however, the ring's symbolism is meaningful to both parties, and expresses to the world at large both belonging and commitment. So it is with baptism. Baptism also symbolizes admittance into the visible body of Christ, but it does not achieve that admittance – such is through faith in our Lord Jesus Christ alone, and the merits of his atoning sacrifice.

When the early believers confessed their faith in Christ by baptism they were automatically regarded and received as part of the visible community of believers where they lived. Baptism is an ordinance of belonging. There are two places in Acts where baptism 'into the name of the Lord Jesus' reflects an expression used in a commercial context of the legal transfer of property (Acts 8:16; 19:5). Writing to the Romans, Paul addresses the church members as 'those who are called to belong to Jesus Christ' (Rom. 1:6).

4 The New Testament descriptions of members of a local church demand and take for granted the existence and profession of personal faith in Christ

Paul describes the Corinthians as being part of the church because they 'call on the name of our Lord Jesus Christ' (1 Cor. 1:2); the Ephesians as 'the faithful in Christ Jesus' (Eph. 1:1) or 'believers who are in Christ Jesus'; the Philippians as those in whom God has begun his good work of regeneration (Phil. 1:6); the Colossians as 'the holy and faithful brothers in Christ' (Col. 1:2); and the Thessalonians as those who 'turned to God from idols to serve the living and true God, and to wait for his Son from heaven' (1 Thes. 1:9–10). Peter writes of church members as having come to Christ 'the living Stone' to become themselves living stones in God's building or temple, the church (1 Pet. 2:4–5).

Since the New Testament descriptions of a Christian and of church members require the existence of faith, and its confession *before* baptism, church membership should be restricted to those who make this profession of faith, and ideally to those who confirm it by believer's baptism. There is a complete absence of any command to baptize infants in the New Testament.

Some would suggest that the three 'household' baptisms recorded in the Acts of the Apostles – those of Cornelius (Acts 10), Lydia, and the Philippian jailer (Acts 16) – argue for infant baptism and therefore the membership of infants in the church. We must consider this possibility. It is important to remember that no important doctrine of the faith rests upon implications drawn from narrative, but that all that Christians are found to believe and practise is clearly commanded. Having established

50

that important truth, the Acts narratives themselves by no means point in the direction of infant baptism, or the admission of infants into the membership of the church.

I am unconvinced by the arguments of those who put forward infant baptism in Christian households for a number of reasons. Firstly, in not one of the household baptisms in Acts are infants mentioned. Anything so important as the practice of infant baptism must surely be based upon New Testament instruction and not upon the doubtful implications of narrative, and especially its silences.

Secondly, if we look at the three cases themselves, the emphasis in two is upon the complete households sharing faith, so that they all rejoiced in salvation. Children who are old enough to understand the gospel are old enough to respond to it by faith and baptism. It is sometimes said that the three households were bound to have had very young children within them. As we consider the little we know of their circumstances, the opposite case can be legitimately argued. Cornelius was a centurion and therefore no young army recruit. Lydia was a business-woman and probably a widow (in that there is no mention of her husband) and so more likely than not any family she had was grown up. Jailers in a Roman colony such as Philippi were usually retired Roman soldiers, and so the jailer too probably had a grown-up family. Whatever the details of these families, however, in the cases of Cornelius and the jailer, the narratives specifically refer to all the household personally believing (Acts 10:44; 16:32, 34).

Thirdly, the rest of the New Testament makes no reference at all to the baptism of children, either before the age of understanding or after. I recognize that many argue for infant baptism through their convictions concerning covenant theology, but it is significant that the case has to be argued, whereas believer's baptism is plainly the New Testament practice without the necessity for argument.

Fourthly, there is no doubt that Christian baptism is in complete continuity with the preparatory work of John the Baptist in baptizing, and also our Lord's own practice of baptism during his ministry – the latter being often overlooked. John the Baptist – who no doubt knew his Old Testament covenant theology as well as any – is nowhere said to have baptized children. His emphasis was upon a personal response of repentance on the part of all who submitted to his baptism. Likewise, our Lord, while receiving children and blessing them, did not baptize them, which we may assume he would have done if it had been his purpose for his church. Rather, he baptized 'disciples' (Jn. 4:1–2), although leaving the actual baptizing to others rather than doing it himself, presumably so that people would appreciate that the value of baptism is not in the one who baptizes but in its significance.

Where do these conclusions lead us?

They lead us to define a church as a group of believers who, knowing themselves to be 'in Christ', and to be born again of his Spirit, also know themselves to be joined together as members of his body, and brothers and sisters in God's family. The real church is an association of believing people, of committed and practising Christians. The key requirement for church membership is that an individual is 'in Christ'. We must exercise great care, therefore, in our admission of people to membership. While a totally pure membership is impossible, that is no reason for low standards of admission to church membership which may contradict the gospel. It is our duty, therefore, to examine carefully and charitably those who ask for membership of the local church.

We should not first ask someone if he or she has been baptized – at whatever age or by whatever form – but we should enquire as to their faith and their understanding of the person and work of our Lord Jesus Christ. We should not receive them into membership simply because they have been in church membership elsewhere: far more important than that is their personal faith in Christ, their relationship to him, and their determination to 'live a new life' (Rom. 6:4).

In the two churches to which I have belonged we have

never automatically received people into membership on the grounds that they have already been church members elsewhere. A membership interview by the elders to discover and test their Christian profession was considered as necessary for such people as for anyone else. If, as occasionally happened, there seemed any surprise or even resentment at this procedure, it simply underlined the importance of the interview to point out the priority of a living relationship with God through our Lord Jesus Christ, and there were cases when the surprise and resentment sprang from a nominal rather than a living faith. Difficult as such situations were, they delivered the church from receiving into membership those who were only nominal believers, and it helped to save nominal believers from a false assurance and sense of spiritual security to which they had no real claim. In all the cases I can recall, such interviews led to people being brought to personal faith. These situations obviously needed great care in their handling, but good alone resulted as people were made to realize our complete dependence upon Christ alone for salvation.

Procedures for admittance into church membership

If the key requirement for church membership is that a person is 'in Christ', what are the procedures for church membership? What do we expect as proof of a person's union with Christ? The three evidences of a genuine Christian profession, which John gives in his first epistle, are what we must look for: a confession of faith in Jesus as the Messiah and Son of God (1 Jn. 5:1), righteousness of life (1 Jn. 2:29) and love for other Christians (1 Jn. 3:14). These cannot be observed in a moment or in a brief interview with a person, and so there is wisdom and benefit in someone applying for church membership only when he or she has been fellowshipping, for a while at least, with a church. There has to be some membership procedure, therefore, which provides the opportunity to discern these evidences.

It would probably be best if I related the procedures with which I am familiar in two churches, and the following is an amalgam of the two.

We discouraged people from applying for membership until they had attended the church for a few months, so that we had a chance to get to know them, and they us. If they happened to be transferring membership from a church in the locality, we took no action for at least three months, and more usually six, and then only after consultation with the church fellowship concerned.

We also produced an application form for prospective members. It asked the following questions:

- Have you received the Lord Jesus Christ as your Saviour? (Jn. 1:12; Acts 13:38–39; Rev. 3:20).
- When and where (or about what period) did you thus receive the Lord Jesus Christ?
- Have you confessed the Lord Jesus Christ to others? (Lk. 9:26; Rom. 10:9–10).
- Have you been baptized as a believer? If you have, when and where?
- If you have not been baptized, are you prepared to make this public confession of Christ? (Mt. 28:19–20; Acts 2:38–41; Rom. 6:4).
- Are you now in membership with a church? If so, please say which, and why you wish to leave.
- If you are not now in membership with another church, have you ever been, and, if so, why did you leave?
- Why do you wish to join this church fellowship?
- As a Christian, do you see the necessity of paying close attention to how you live (Rom. 12:17; Eph. 5:15), so as to lead a self-controlled and godly life (Tit. 2:12) and to be an example of a Christian believer in your speech, conduct, love, faith, purity (1 Tim. 4:12) and separation from all that is dishonouring to God (2 Cor. 6:14–18)?
- Are you engaged in any Christian work? Give particulars.

- Are you prepared to render active help in the work of the church fellowship if called upon? (Rom. 12:11).
- Do you pledge yourself conscientiously to contribute, according to your means, towards the financial requirements of the Lord's work in the church?

At the conclusion of the form there was the doctrinal statement of the church, parallel with that of the UCCF, with additional clauses relating to baptism and the nature of the church. The concluding questions were: Do you pledge yourself, by the grace of God, to live at all times a life that befits a true Christian and a member of this church? Do you promise to take a conscientious part in the life and support of the church, regularly attending its various services when possible, and exhibiting willingness to help in whatever way you can in its service and witness for our Lord Jesus Christ? The final question related first to the doctrinal statement and then to all the previous answers the individual had provided: Do your beliefs and intentions fully agree with the above?

It can happen that a young or weak Christian applies for church membership who, while clear concerning the fundamentals of the gospel, has areas of uncertainty on other points of doctrine or conduct. He or she should be accepted without first attempting to settle these doubtful points (Rom. 14:1).

The benefit of such an application form was that it indicated at least what was looked for in those applying for church membership, and something of the expectations the church had of the life and conduct of church members. It also gave the elders some understanding of a person's background, convictions and spiritual standing, so that they could ask appropriate questions at the next stage in the membership procedure – an interview with three of the elders. This interview took place after the application had been brought before the elders at their monthly meeting. It was likely that some of the elders already knew the applicant, and their observations were important, especially if they had doubts about the person's spiritual standing, or if they knew of matters relating to the person's character or conduct which ought to be discussed in order to help the prospective church member.

If it was obvious that the application was straight-forward, and the person already well-known and estab-lished as a Christian, the interviewing elders did not need to bring the application back to the elders' meeting. If, however, they had any doubts following the interview, they then told the applicant. 'We have been glad to meet you, and we will share our conversation with the elders at their next meeting, and we will be in touch with you.' I remember, for instance, the interviewing elders meeting with an older man who had started to come to church with great regularity, and who fairly soon afterwards asked for membership. It was plain that, although gen-uinely seeking, and in earnest, the evidences of new birth were not apparent. The elders felt they could not accept him, and I was delegated to talk with him and to explain their hesitancy at his readiness for church membership, and to suggest that he should join the discipleship classes. This he did, and as a result he came to clear assurance of faith in Christ, and later to baptism and church member-ship. In similar situations, one of the three interviewing elders might offer to do a weekly Bible study with such a person, and we had women church members who could do the same with women on a one-to-one basis.

Each interview would be different in so far as the infor-mation upon the application form sparked off appropriate questions. But there were basic questions I would invariably ask, such as, 'Would you share with us, please, the circumstances of your conversion?' 'If someone asked you, "How do you know that you are a Christian?" how would you answer?' 'Why do you want to be a church member, and what makes you believe that this local church is the one you should join?' 'Do you find God speaking to you through his word here as you hear it taught and preached?' 'Are you aware of spiritual gifts and abilities God has given you, and are there particular forms of service in which you feel you would like to offer your help?' 'Why do you feel church membership is important?' 'Do you find you have many opportunities for witness to

Christ where God has placed you?' Answers to questions like these revealed much of a person's faith and convictions, and prompted helpful discussion and conversation. Once a person was approved for church membership, he or she was received into membership at the next occasion the church met around the Lord's Table, and was then placed under the care of one of the elders, and joined his pastoral group.

The position of young children in the church

If church membership is solely for those who are 'in Christ', what is the position of children, and in particular the children of Christian parents? Children are 'in Christ' only as adults are 'in Christ', through personal faith in our Lord Jesus and the experience of new birth. However, children of Christian parents are – until they are old enough to understand and to be responsible for their actions – in some way 'sanctified' and 'holy' (1 Cor. 7:14), and are to be viewed as a part of the church family. The conversion of such children is frequently gradual and almost imperceptible, until they arrive at their teens when what has been hidden is so often publicly declared. Our Lord's invitation, 'Let the little children come to me, and do not hinder them, for the kingdom of God belongs to such as these' (Lk. 18:16) clearly implies that children are the objects of God's love and grace, and, while young, children may be regarded as benefiting from our Lord's saving work until they are old enough to understand the gospel. It is interesting to note that our Lord's familiar words of welcome to children are closely followed by his speaking of 'these ones' *believing* in him (Mt. 18:6; Mk. 9:42) – a fact often overlooked in the discussion of his words.

The task of parents and of the local church is to teach children the Scriptures and the gospel so that hopefully when they are no longer children – and thus become responsible for their own faith and actions – they may profess personal faith and be baptized as members of the body of Christ. If children die before reaching the age of understanding, we may be confident that the saving grace of Christ covers them. While young, they should be considered part of the church family, although not included in its ordinances until they personally confess faith. If, however, they reach the age of understanding and reject the gospel, they are in exactly the same position as other unbelievers (Mk. 16:16).

Although I am not at all convinced by covenant theology, being unsure of its validity, I can appreciate the sincerity of those who argue it in relation to the children of Christian parents. It is vitally important, however, that children of such parents should not be given a false sense of security about their position before God, as may so easily happen. The inwardness of faith, and the priority of personal experience of Christ, must constantly be implied and taught to our children. As some may rest today in a false assurance on account of their covenant theology, so may Jews. Paul, the Jew, wrote:

> A man is not a Jew if he is only one outwardly, nor is circumcision merely outward and physical. No, a man is a Jew if he is one inwardly; and circumcision is circumcision of the heart, by the Spirit, not by the written code. Such a man's praise is not from men, but from God (Rom. 2:28–29).

In the context of the churches to which I have belonged, parents are encouraged to bring their children as babies to church, when the whole church family is present, for a brief service of thanksgiving, for the dedication of themselves to God in the exercise of their parenthood, and, as far as it is possible, to dedicate their children to God. The stress, however, is upon the parents' dedication rather than the child's. The promises parents make relate to their thankfulness to God, their conduct as parents and their discipline and instruction of their children in God's word and the gospel of Christ. The whole church then rises to its feet as a symbol of its commitment to join with the parents in their prayers and endeavours for the spiritual well-being of the child, and unites in prayer for the child's conversion in the years of understanding.

I believe in child conversion, and our Lord's words about little ones believing in him are the strongest possible encouragement to do so. Any sample survey of church members will probably reveal that the majority were converted as children. Since most who are baptized as believers are in their late teens and older, it is seldom that children – influenced by the example of those they see – ask for baptism before they are in their teens. I believe it is unwise to set an ideal or a minimum age as each case must be looked at individually. There have been occasions when those barely in their teens have asked for baptism, and I have always felt it important to take time to speak to them carefully. My approach has been to suggest they first join the discipleship class – something we usually require of all who request baptism. I then also raise the question of their age, saying something along these lines, 'Some will feel that you are too young to make such a public profession, and that perhaps we as a church or your parents are putting wrongful pressure on you. Now we know that isn't the case, but others don't. Let's pray together now, that we will know the right time for you to make this profession of faith, and once you have completed the course of discipleship classes, let's meet together again to talk about it.' This has never failed to be workable and helpful. The important thing is to maintain a pastoral relationship with such young people so as to encourage them and to avoid them being made to stumble in any way.

There are no biblical grounds for separating baptism from church membership, and really the two should be synonymous. For this reason alone care must be taken as to the time at which children and young people are baptized. It is not without significance that those who practise infant baptism find themselves needing to have confirmation or some other public admission into adult membership of the church. It is obviously far better if that public act of identity with the body of Christ can be the biblical one of believer's baptism. A further obvious advantage – no doubt intended by God – is that it stresses the importance and priority of faith in Jesus Christ rather than dependence upon the church relationship or a Christian family background.

How important is baptism as a qualification for church membership?

Basic to our answer is the truth that baptism is an ordinance rather than a sacrament. To call it a sacrament may imply that grace is mediated by it – a suggestion the New Testament does not substantiate. Acting upon the principle established in Romans 2:28–29 already referred to, baptism is not as important as the possession and profession of living faith in Jesus Christ (*cf.* Rom. 10:6–13). We should not first ask prospective church members, 'Are you baptized?', but 'Do you have living faith in Jesus Christ as your Saviour and Lord, and are there evidences of it in your life?' Baptism is not essential to salvation; it is, however, more important for discipleship, since it is a command of Christ for his disciples (Mt. 28:19).

Because there is so often confusion in people's minds about baptism, and because of the varying backgrounds from which they come, it is imperative that baptism and how it is administered (including the amount of water used) should not be an obstacle to church membership. After all, the basic purpose of church membership must be to receive all whom Christ has received (Rom. 15:7). An illustration may help here. How ludicrous it is that we might ask someone to preach the word of God in our church fellowships (because like us he is 'in Christ' and is faithful to the gospel) but if he came to live in our neighbourhood we might refuse him church membership because his baptism was different in some way from our own. Baptism should unite Christians, not divide them.

Since differing views of baptism may divide Christians, I would prefer a local church to have an 'open' membership, with the membership procedures already described, so as to be able to receive all applicants who are genuinely 'in Christ'. Otherwise Christians who have not been baptized as believers may be regarded as merely adherents. Every church inevitably has its adherents, many of whom may be uncommitted to Christ. It is often difficult to know at what stage such people are spiritually, and the prayers and actions of God's people should be focused upon their conversion, and their being added to the church of Christ.

Many adherents will be genuine seekers, and as the seed of God's word is sown in their hearts, a harvest will follow. Pastoral contact is important to ensure they do not fall into the snare of depending upon church attendance for acceptance with God. I favour the practice of inviting to the Lord's Table all who love the Lord Jesus Christ in sincerity. As soon as a previously uncommitted adherent participates we should seize an early opportunity to enquire graciously what has prompted this step, so that pastoral care and instruction can be given. But it would be sad if other adherents, who are undoubted believers and whose right to participate in the Lord's Supper cannot be questioned, were denied church membership because their church background means that they have not been baptized as believers. Such people are often in a quandary since they do not wish to be baptized again simply as a means of gaining church membership; if they are to be baptized, they want it to be on the grounds of honest conviction.

My experience, in one church which was open in its membership and another which offered full membership only to those baptized as believers, is that as many, if not more, such adherents faced up to the issue of baptism, were baptized and entered into church membership in the former as in the latter. One undoubted reason was that they were able to think believer's baptism through on its own, without the complication of wondering if their motives were mixed in with their desire to come into church membership.

The benefits of the gathered church concept

Neglect of this understanding of the gathered church – the understanding I believe the New Testament gives – has led to woolly thinking among God's people and even superstition among those who are not yet his people. I recognize that many will feel that a drawback of the gathered church position is that there is not the same pool of unconverted people in the local congregation in which to 'fish', but this view of a congregation is not in harmony with the New Testament conception of the church. I recognize too that evangelicals in national churches, whether Anglican or Presbyterian, will strive after purity of membership. But they have to fight many battles which I believe we are not intended to fight.

The gathered church avoids many of the perils to which my nominal Anglicanism exposed me as a child. Firstly, it demonstrates that church membership has nothing to do with a merely nominal relationship with a church. Secondly, baptism is kept until it can be the proper mark of faith in Christ and membership of his body. Thirdly, neither baptism nor church membership are viewed as synonymous with the experience of salvation. Fourthly, children are delivered from a false assurance and, at the same time, become the particular object of the church's prayers and endeavours to win them to Christ.

Response to Derek Prime

David Holloway

Questions and comments

Is Derek Prime's position really more biblical than mine? He talks of 'neglect of this understanding of the gathered church – understanding I believe the New Testament gives'. But is it the New Testament position? I believe he is too confident. Surely the New Testament does not give a blueprint for church order. There are principles, but much is 'grey' and not 'black and white'. Indeed, on much the New Testament is quite silent. For that reason it is no good Derek simply saying that 'there is a complete absence of any command to baptize infants in the New Testament'. There is also an absence of any prohibition *against* baptizing them. The argument from silence works both ways. We have to argue about what was likely. Of course, the norm was, and is, adult baptism. But as Derek says, children of Christian parents should be viewed as part of the church family, particularly as the conversion of such children is frequently gradual. Does the New Testament forbid beginning their baptismal initiation in infancy? What about the children addressed in Colossians 3:20? Were they or were they not baptized? (*Cf.* Col. 2:12.)

In these 'grey areas', where all is not clear, I believe we

need to work with the '60% rule'. That is to say, if you are convinced of your position by only 60%, it is no good someone pointing out the 40% that is against you. Until you are convinced by 51% that you are wrong, you should not shift your ground. With regard to baptism I am not totally convinced of my position; but I find Derek's position less convincing.

In fact, his position is not nearly as 'biblical' as he seems to be suggesting. Towards the end of his paper he argues, 'There are no biblical grounds for separating baptism from church membership, and really the two should be synonymous' (p. 59). Earlier, however, he had argued, 'It has only been because of so much confusion over baptism ... that baptism and church membership have tended to be separated' (p. 49). So something is tolerated in the gathered churches where the New Testament would suggest something different. Also Derek's understanding of membership is linked to a profession of faith rather than baptism – 'church membership should be restricted to those who make this profession of faith, and ideally to those who confirm it by believer's baptism.' So believer's baptism, he argues, is the 'ideal', while profession of faith is the essential. But that is not what was taught on the day of Pentecost, 'Repent, and be baptised every one of you, in the name of Jesus Christ for the forgiveness of your sins. And you will receive the gift of the Holy Spirit' (Acts 2:38).

In this portrait of the gathered church, membership seems to be an honour you earn. It is what you receive when you 'graduate' in the school of discipleship. Similarly baptism seems to be the sign of 'having arrived' or being a mature Christian. That may be pastorally helpful, but surely you cannot argue for it as New Testament practice. Derek rightly says, 'those who are "in Christ" are the church'. But you can be 'in Christ' and still be pretty immature – witness the Corinthians. Yet they were all members at Corinth. Paul says so in 1 Corinthians 12:12–13.

Derek says, 'we must exercise great care, therefore, in our admission of people to membership'. So he advocates a 'maximalist' approach. The approach to the new member is to test his or her maturity. This can be seen from the 'application form for prospective members'. But the New Testament seems more 'minimalist' than that. On the day of Pentecost Peter only asked for repentance (Acts 2:38). The crux for the Philippian jailer was 'believe in the Lord Jesus' (Acts 16:31). Paul and Silas had less than sixty minutes to give pre-baptismal instruction and to test the credentials of the jailer and his household, but 'immediately he and all his family were baptised' (Acts 16:33).

That leads on to the matter of 'proof'. Derek rightly says that the key requirement for church membership is that a person is 'in Christ'. He then says that there are 'three evidences of a genuine profession' – a confession of faith, righteousness of life and love for other Christians. But how can you be sure about these evidences? Is intention or achievement what should be looked for? Derek obviously saw his elders as being very thorough in their interviewing. But what happens when you get someone who says they believe the creed; they are willing to say publicly (as they are required to do in the Anglican ASB baptismal service), 'I turn to Christ', 'I repent of my sin' and 'I renounce evil'; and they are serious in what they are saying? Is the leadership entitled to refuse membership or baptism because they are not yet convinced of the candidate's 'righteousness of life' or 'love for other Christians'? If there is flagrant sin, that is one thing. But how 'righteous' and how 'loving' do you have to be before being admitted to baptism? Is baptism the beginning of a process or the end? I am not arguing that the answer is simple – there was a 'catechumenate' in the post-apostolic church that would support Derek's proposals, and it was found to be pastorally helpful. But let us not say this is the New Testament model.

I should have liked to comment at length on other matters. For example, Derek criticizes the Book of Common Prayer wording, 'this child *is* by Baptism regenerate', but he doesn't point out that the child '*is* regenerate' only to the same extent as he or she has made the promises. The child has not *directly* made those promises yet, they have been made 'in the name of the child' by Godparents. To put it crudely, the 'is' becomes more real as the child grows into what was promised 'until [as the service says] he come of age to take it upon himself'. Also I should have liked to have discussed more whether baptism is fundamentally a symbol of human response or God's grace. Then I should have liked to have discussed the matter of how the language of ritual works. Often 'the part' can stand for 'the whole'. Baptism 'saves you' says Peter (1 Pet. 3:21). He was referring, however, to more than the water-rite – 'not the removal of dirt from the body but the pledge of a good conscience towards God. It saves you by the resurrection of Jesus Christ.' So 'baptism' can stand for all that is involved in Christian initiation *and* the application of water by itself – that is one of the issues lurking in the background of this discussion. Space, however, forbids fuller discussion.

Part 2

The issue of denominations

Eryl Davies and Harry Uprichard

- *Does the Bible validate a structured connectionalism or the autonomy of independency?*
- *Is any kind of disciplined structure needed to enable churches to fulfil their positive mission in the world?*
- *Does such co-operation restrict or enhance the local church in its relationship to Christ as its head?*
- *If denominational labels do exist, should they be ignored in favour of para-church co-operation?*

Independency

Eryl Davies

Observations ● The issue ● Local churches are
independent ● Local churches are interrelated
● Local churches are interdependent

What do the terms 'connectionalism' and 'independency'
convey to you? Take, for example, connectionalism. No, it
has nothing to do with a T.V. quiz programme, or with a
train timetable. The word comes from a basic verb meaning to tie or fasten together. In a church context, the word
denotes the establishing of a relationship or association
between a group of churches. There are certain doctrines
and practices which link churches together within a
structured group such as Presbyterian, Methodist or Episcopal. Another word used to describe the linking together
of churches in this way is 'denomination'.

What about the term independency? Americans could
be forgiven for thinking it has something to do with their
national holiday on 4 July – Independence Day! In
ecclesiology, however, the term denotes the idea that each
local church is autonomous; no other church or group of
churches or church dignitary, like a bishop or pope, exer-
cises control over it.

Observations

Before examining these terms in more detail, here are some preliminary observations by way of introduction to this important but difficult subject.

Firstly, there is an important sense in which independency supports and practises connectionalism. Are you surprised? Well, remember that independent churches where the Bible is preached are connected dynamically by virtue of their union with the exalted Christ, their submission to Christ as the church's head, and their obedience to the word of God. The connection between them, therefore, is spiritual and is expressed in mutual, spontaneous fellowship with, and concern for, other local churches. While there is this spiritual connection between Christians and churches, independency insists that each local church is self-governing.

Secondly, we need to recognize the different expressions of connectionalism. One such expression is episcopacy. This claims that by the end of the second century AD, the office of 'bishop' had emerged, carrying with it authority over a plurality of churches within a geographical area. Episcopalians attempt to link this elevated office of bishop with the New Testament word *episkopos* which is translated in the AV as 'bishop' but more helpfully as 'overseer' in modern translations. However, the New Testament uses the terms *episkopos* and *presbyteros* interchangeably to describe the elders/overseers within a local church (*cf.*, for example, Acts 20 where the same officers are called 'elders' in v. 17 and 'overseers' in v. 28).[1] Equally unconvincing in support of what is known as the 'monarchical episcopate' is the appeal to the position of James in the Jerusalem church council (Acts 15). Certainly James was respected in the church for his godly life and his relationship to the Lord Jesus. James may have acted as chairman in the council but what he suggested there was discussed then agreed by the leaders of the Jerusalem and Antioch churches. There was no imposition of authority here on the part of a 'bishop'. Historically, however, the Orthodox, Roman Catholic, Anglican and a few other denominations have used this kind of episcopacy for church government.

Another expression of connectionalism is presbyterianism which insists, unlike episcopacy, that the words *episkopos* and *presbyteros* are used interchangeably in the New Testament to describe the office and work of elders in local churches. This also argues for the plurality and parity of elders; their task is to rule (1 Tim. 3:5–6; Heb. 13:7), govern (1 Cor. 12:28, 'administration') and feed the church (Acts 20:28; 1 Pet. 5:2). As an independent I accept this view of eldership but do not accept that elders can meet together in Presbyteries and Assemblies to govern large numbers of local churches. On the basis of the Jerusalem council (Acts 15:6–29), presbyterians assume that the decisions made at church courts are binding for local churches. I shall discuss the significance of this council later but independents insist it was only advisory with no legislative power over the churches.

Thirdly, there are different connotations of the term 'independency'. For some, independency is equivalent to isolationism; in other words, a local church can function as if no other churches existed. I am not defending this attitude nor is it representative of genuine independency. Traditionally, independency has more often been identified with a congregationalist form of church government. Congregationalists believe that all members of a local church are equally responsible to Christ for deciding all matters relating to their church. The church members' meeting, therefore, determines all church business and polity. R. W. Dale (1829–1895), for example, has a useful defence and exposition of this position.[2]

Nevertheless, in 1966 changes occurred within British congregationalism when many of its churches covenanted to form a more centralized Congregational church. The latter then merged with the Presbyterian Church of England to form the United Reformed Church. In order to maintain traditional congregational church government, some churches formed the Congregational Federation while others associated together in an Evangelical Fellowship of Congregational Churches.

The term 'independency' is also used in a sense wider than congregationalism. During the past twenty years, many independent churches have been established in Britain. Some of these churches seceded from various denominations for doctrinal reasons but others are new churches. Amongst these independent churches, the overall pattern is one of strong leadership by local elders coupled both with the full agreement of members and the desire to safeguard the church's autonomy. This type of independency is certainly not a new, modern phenomenon. In Wales, for example, some independent causes last century were called presbyterian because of the strong leadership role exercised by local church elders, yet each church remained self-governing. My personal sympathies lie with this third type of independency for it retains the most biblical elements within both congregationalism and presbyterianism.

The issue

By now, you may have appreciated the point at issue between independency and connectionalism, namely, how is the relationship between local churches to be described and expressed? Is the relationship one of spontaneous fellowship alone between self-governing local churches or should there be denominational structures which, in varying degrees, direct local church life? Furthermore, are there advantages within denominational structures which enable local churches to fulfil their mission more effectively in the world? These are the questions which need to be answered, but first a brief word about procedure.

I am proceeding on the assumption that churches must be governed in ways clearly authorized by New Testament principles and practice, but this has wide-ranging implications. One of these implications in relation to episcopacy is underlined by a presbyterian: 'the development whereby diocesan episcopacy has gained currency in the government of the church is without any warrant from

Scripture and, therefore, can plead no sanction from the head of the church'.[3] Positions like archbishop, cardinal, and pope, *etc.* are also unauthorized by the New Testament.

At a local level, presbyterianism is more scriptural with its emphasis on eldership. 'It is in the local congregation', writes John Murray, 'that the presbyterian principle must first be exemplified'.[4] Provided this leadership by elders is exercised biblically and with the concurrence of church members, an increasing number of independents today would be happy. Nevertheless, independents challenge the legitimacy of an area Presbytery or Assembly of elders as a means of governing local churches. While there are some differences of emphasis and interpretation (e.g. over Acts 15) between independents and presbyterians yet there are also significant statements by presbyterians implying that biblical support for their position is weak. Consider the acknowledgment, for example, by Louis Berkhof:

> Scripture does not contain an explicit command to the effect that the local churches of a district must form an organic union. ... In fact, it represents the local churches as individual entities without any external bond of union.[5]

Independents agree! Why then impose a denominational structure on local churches?

John Murray makes a similar acknowledgment to that of Berkhof: '[it] should be recognized that there is much in the form of the organization and procedure adopted in the Presbyterian churches that cannot plead the authority of the New Testament'.[6]

Murray then finds justification for aspects of presbyterian polity in the 'light of nature and Christian prudence'. Whether we favour connectionalism or independency, our submission to Scripture and to the headship of Christ demands that we re-assess the validity of our forms of church government in the light of the word of God. There are weaknesses, too, in independency especially when there is dissension within the local church. All our cherished traditions and practices need to be radically re-appraised at the bar of Scripture.

I now intend to discuss the issue of independency and connectionalism in the context of three propositions relating to the church:

– Local churches are independent
– Local churches are interrelated
– Local churches are interdependent

Local churches are independent

In the New Testament, the important Greek word translated 'church' is *ekklēsia* and its dominant meaning is the assembly or gathering of people together (see e.g. Acts 19:32, 39, 41 where the word is used in a secular context only). The Old Testament background to *ekklēsia* is important and confirmatory. Passages like Deuteronomy 9:10; 10:4 and 18:16 are significant as they refer to God's people meeting formally together before the Lord on 'the day of the assembly' (*qāhāl*) to worship. Interestingly, the first Greek translation of the Hebrew Old Testament, the Septuagint, consistently used the word *ekklēsia* to translate the Hebrew *qāhāl*.

The important question concerns the way *ekklēsia* is used in the New Testament. Both independents and connectionalists agree that *ekklēsia* refers to the local church in many instances but there is disagreement whether it is used in only one or at least two further ways. At this point I shall underline the local church reference of *ekklēsia*.

Matthew 18:17 is the first occasion where the word is used in this restricted local sense but it is used many times later in Acts and the epistles to describe a specific church in a locality whether at Jerusalem, Antioch, Ephesus, Cenchrea, Corinth, Laodicea or Thessalonica, and the like.[7] Naturally, the word *ekklēsia* is also used in the plural to describe a number of local churches, for example, 'all the churches of the Gentiles' (Rom. 16:4); 'all the churches of Christ' (Rom. 16:16); 'the churches of God'

(1 Cor. 11:16; 2 Thes. 1:4) and 'all the congregations of the saints' (1 Cor. 14:33).

This restricted use of *ekklēsia* to refer to the local church has four implications:

1 The local *ekklēsia* is a genuine church

By this I mean that the New Testament regards the local church as a church in its own right; nowhere is it regarded as being only a partial church. Admittedly, the local church is an expression of the universal church yet it is never described or looked upon as an incomplete church. The local church at Corinth, for example, was immature and full of problems yet the apostle did not hesitate to call it 'the church of God' (1 Cor. 1:2). Later, he tells the same church, 'you are the body of Christ' (1 Cor. 12:27). The local *ekklēsia* then is a microcosm and expression of the universal church; it is a church in its own right for it is a spiritual organism,[8] receiving leadership and ministry from Christ its head through elders (Acts 20:17–28; Tit. 1:5, 7, etc.). Such a local church is not subject to the decisions of a larger group of churches or their leaders. This individual entity of the local church is a creation of the gospel, indwelt by the Holy Spirit, governed and equipped by the Lord Jesus Christ. The local church, therefore, governs its own affairs according to the revealed will of God.

2 The local *ekklēsia* is a gathered church

By means of the preaching of the gospel and the regenerating work of the Holy Spirit, men and women are brought as sinners to trust and obey the Lord Jesus Christ; it is such people who meet together and constitute the church within a locality. On the day of Pentecost, for example, 3,000 people were converted through the preaching of the apostle Peter. They were converted within the context of the church and immediately integrated into the life and witness of the church at Jerusalem (Acts 2:41–46); this was the consistent pattern throughout the New Testament period. As God blessed the preaching of the apostle Paul in different cities and countries, local churches were established (e.g. Acts 14:23) and these were gathered churches of believers. It is into the bosom of the church, wrote John Calvin, that 'God is pleased to collect his children'[9] for the purpose of nourishing and perfecting them in the faith.

The principle of the gathered church of believers challenges the traditional distinction between the 'invisible' and 'visible' church. This distinction was used by the Reformers and remains popular with some connectionalists today. As mixed, denominational churches often include significant and even large numbers of unregenerate members, the distinction can be useful to connectionalists. For example, the mixed membership is sometimes referred to as the 'visible' church whereas the term 'invisible' church is used to refer only to true Christians who are difficult to distinguish in many denominational churches. While no church on earth is perfect, the New Testament underlines the fact that only believers should belong to the local church. For example, 'the church of God at Corinth' did not have a mixed membership of believers and unbelievers for Paul goes on to describe all the members as those who were 'sanctified in Christ Jesus and called to be holy' (1 Cor. 1:2). In other words, the Corinth church was a gathered, visible church of believers. Yes, there are invisible aspects to the church but it is, nevertheless, the visible company of believers gathered together under Christ.[10]

3 The local *ekklēsia* is a governed church

R. B. Kuyper rightly affirms that no aspect of Christ's relationship to the church looms larger in the Bible than the fact that Christ is its head.[11] Christ is the federal head of the church as well as the organic head in whom believers are sustained and united. It is the aspect of Christ's ruling headship which is immediately relevant to this discussion. The Lord rules his people by the infallible word of God and the Holy Spirit; he is also pleased to appoint pastors/elders to teach and rule in accordance with the Bible. Christ does not transfer his authority to these men; rather, he continues to govern the church by the word and through the men he calls and equips to preach and apply this word.

Many connectionalists argue that independency weakens rather than honours the principle of Christ's headship over the church. For example, they say, does not independency encourage democracy in church government instead of theocracy?

The formulation of the disagreement in this way is not particularly helpful for it is unfair, imprecise and, in addition, conceals some of the difficulties inherent within both independency and connectionalism. Strictly, the issue is not between democracy or theocracy but rather how the theocratic rule of Christ over churches through the word and elders is to be related to the membership of the local church. More briefly, what is the relationship of elders to the members and to the church members' meeting?

Traditionally, congregationalism has tended to favour a more 'democratic' form of church government where members in their church business meeting decide all matters relating to the life of their local church. For some, like R. W. Dale, this is expressed theologically in the principle that all the members are directly responsible to Christ their head for the maintenance of his authority in their local church.[12] A Baptist theologian, A. H. Strong, agrees but insists there is no contradiction between theocracy and democracy in church government:

> While Christ is the sole king . . . the government of the church . . . is an absolute democracy, in which the whole body of members is entrusted with the responsibility of carrying out the laws of Christ as expressed in his Word.

Both Dale and Strong insist on Christ's government of the church although they relate it directly to members rather than exclusively to elders. For them, elders are delegated representatives approved by, and accountable to, the church members' meeting.

But connectionalists such as presbyterians have their difficulties too. Although they advocate a theocracy, that is, Christ's rule through elders, they are often in danger of ignoring the role and responsibility of church members. James Bannerman is one of several presbyterian theologians who acknowledges this tendency in presbyterian church polity and he is prepared to make concessions to the independent position. He warns, for example, that the authority of elders is not an arbitrary one and that both elders and members are 'entitled to give as well as receive counsel'. In an interesting and almost tantalizing statement, Bannerman insists that elders should 'secure the concurrence of members by instruction and conviction'.[13] I agree but in practice some presbyterian elderships govern in a remote, insensitive way without obtaining the concurrence of members.

To recap briefly, I have attempted a more precise formulation of the disagreement between independency and connectionalism concerning Christ's government of the church. Avoiding the simplistic and imprecise, not to mention emotive, formulation in terms of democracy or theocracy, I have focused on the relationship of elders to the members in the local church. Now I want to define and describe this relationship; in doing so, I will argue for an independent position where elders rule under Christ but with the concurrence, respect and support of the local church membership. I believe this is a more biblical position which honours Christ's rule through both elders and members.

My contention is that elders exercise a delegated authority which is two-dimensional. First and foremost, there is the dimension of Christ the head of the church who calls men into office and gives them authority in so far as they teach the Bible. The second dimension is that of Christ's church which is in a most intimate spiritual relationship with Christ and in submission to him as its head. This first dimension is foundational yet incomplete without the body of Christ, the church, also delegating authority to elders in a confirmatory sense. Independency has stressed the second dimension but in different ways, thus making elders and deacons accountable to the church members' meeting. On the other hand, presbyterians have underlined the dimension of Christ's authority delegated to elders; rather than decide all matters of church polity and business, members are to be ruled by elders.

Are we justified biblically in understanding the delegated authority of elders only in a one-dimensional way, where the independent/presbyterian positions are regarded as being mutually exclusive? I will answer this question by referring to the either-or position reflected in the writings of John Murray.[14] He contrasts elders as 'delegated representatives of the people' within both a defective presbyterianism and independency, with those in true presbyterianism who have the delegated authority of Christ. The former are church representatives only, while the latter are church rulers. This sharp contrast drawn by Murray is questionable for it polarizes what are really two complementary truths.

Unquestionably elders must 'rule' and not merely represent members or carry out their wishes (see e.g. Heb. 13:17; 1 Thes. 5:12; *cf*. 1 Tim. 3:5). Elders have a strong leadership role to fulfil and it is a role related to the headship of Christ over his church (Acts 20:28; Eph. 4:11–13). Murray is correct, therefore, in underlining the dimension of Christ's delegated authority to elders, but an increasing number of independent evangelical churches today now recognize this biblical view of elders. However, independents insist that as Christ's headship extends over individual believers and, consequently, over the local church this has implications for the relationship of elders and members. Individual church members seek to maintain Christ's rule in the church through personal attendance, involvement, and obedience as well as maintaining the church's purity of doctrine and life. Members then, as well as elders, acknowledge and maintain Christ's headship in the local church. Furthermore, members recognize Christ's call and equipping of certain men for the office of elder. Their godliness and aptitude to teach are apparent to church members and, whichever method is used to nominate men to eldership, it is the membership which confirms and accepts them to function in their church as elders. Again, elders will gain the respect of members for fidelity to the Bible, godliness and the faithful discharge of their duties (1 Thes. 5:12–13). Members will want such men to lead the church and one or more will be supported financially (1 Tim. 5:17). Provided elders fulfil these biblical requirements and are gracious and wise in their use of authority, members will submit to elders as those who 'are over you in the Lord' (1 Thes. 5:12). The delegated authority of elders, therefore, is two-dimensional. There is a tension here, of course, and there will be failures in practice at times by elders or church members, but elders need not fear the members' meeting. The elders' rule of the church by the word of God needs to be regularly considered, confirmed, complemented and prayed over by members as part of their submission to Christ and concern for his church. While the word is infallible, elders can be notoriously fallible in their teaching and application of the word, so the church members' meeting fuses the two aspects of delegated authority into an harmonious, beautiful relationship in Christ between members and elders.

4 The local *ekklēsia* is the God-given unit for fellowship, instruction and mission

Not only is the church God's creation, subject to the headship of Christ, but it is also the unit established by the Lord where believers are to have fellowship and serve him. Christ, the only head of the church, has instituted the preaching of the word, baptism, the Lord's Supper, prayer, godly conversation and fellowship as means whereby he strengthens, instructs, sanctifies, preserves and revives his people. The Lord has provided a ministry of the word by pastors/elders who 'feed the church of God' (Acts 20:28; Eph. 4:11–16). The church, therefore, is central in God's purpose. Mission, too, is rooted in the local church (Acts 13:2–4; 1 Thes. 1:8); the church supervises and supports evangelistic work while missionaries report back to their local church (Acts 14:26–27). All gospel work should be undertaken through the church and evangelism must be geared to the strengthening or establishing of churches where converts can be nurtured in the Bible and fellowship.

Undoubtedly, 'one of the critical issues with which we need to struggle'[15] today is the relationship between the local church and para-church organizations. Although there has been a proliferation of such organizations since the late 1960s, they have a long, interesting history.

Some historians trace their origins to 1701 and the founding of the Society for the Propagation of the Gospel in Foreign Parts, or to 1792 when Baptist missionary work was launched in earnest through William Carey. Historically, it was the census of 1851 in England which stirred some Christians and churches into action. The census revealed that only half the population had any kind of involvement with Christian churches and almost immediately there was a determined effort by some denominations to reach the unchurched.[16] While para-church organizations emerged in increasing numbers after 1851, it is during the last twenty years that we have seen such a multiplication of these groupings that the local church is being squeezed into second place for many Christians.[17]

There is a three-fold challenge here if the God-given unit of the local church is to be honoured.

First of all, there is a challenge to individual Christians to major on church involvement rather than para-church activities. For example, college students can find all their fellowship and instruction within a Christian Union so that they feel little need to attend church services or be involved in church life. Youth movements can unsettle youngsters in local churches while the strong charismatic emphasis of at least one association can adversely affect church loyalty. Even worthy evangelical causes can divert desperately needed monies from churches for what they perceive as priorities. Para-church weekend conferences also serve to distract Christians from their own churches. There are encouraging signs that some organizations recognize their subordination to the local church but Christians themselves need to honour this God-given unit.

Secondly, there is a challenge to churches. Undoubtedly, the failure and indifference of churches have contributed to the emergence of many para-church organizations and also to a sense of disillusionment on the part of Christians towards churches. In addition, many churches have neglected to teach ecclesiology partly due to an excessive emphasis on individualism, pietism and a low estimate of the church. Elders and pastors have a major task, therefore, in teaching and challenging their people to a wholehearted commitment to the church and its world-wide mission.

Thirdly, there is a challenge concerning the legitimacy of para-church organizations. The word *para* means that these organizations should, ideally, stand alongside the local church as 'helpers' or agencies providing specialist knowledge or gifts enabling the church to fulfil its God-given responsibilities. Only within this framework can local churches recognize the legitimacy and usefulness of para-church organizations.

Local churches are interrelated

Ekklēsia

As we have seen, the word *ekklēsia* is used in the New Testament predominantly to refer to the local assembly of believers; in fact, 90 out of 140 references in the New Testament are to the local church. However, *ekklēsia* is also used more widely on occasions and here disagreement creeps in. Is *ekklēsia* used in two or three ways in the New Testament? Are we to think only of the universal and local church or is there a third use where *ekklēsia* is used in the singular to designate a collective unity of churches?

The universal church, for example, is generally

regarded as comprising the elect of every age who are redeemed and sanctified in Christ.[18] References like Matthew 16:18; Ephesians 1:22; 3:10; 5:23 and Hebrews 12:22–23 indicate the generic, comprehensive use of the term and local churches are manifestations of this universal church. An independent like John Owen prefers to distinguish between the church in its three aspects, firstly, the mystical body of Christ, secondly, the world-wide church of believers who profess and obey the gospel and, thirdly, the local church.[19] This is helpful for it recognizes the rich biblical use of *ekklēsia*, yet Owen rejects the connectionalist argument. James Bannerman, a presbyterian, adopts Owen's three-fold use of *ekklēsia* and adds a further use, namely, a number of congregations associating together under a common government of elders.[20] John Murray is a modern exponent of this further use of *ekklēsia* in the New Testament, a use which he believes justifies connectionalism. Murray believes that *ekklēsia* is used in the singular to designate 'churches' in their collective unity. His arguments, briefly, are these.

From the statement in Acts 8:3, 'Saul began to destroy the church', Murray thinks the reference extends beyond the Jerusalem church. But this is inconclusive for the opening verse of the chapter refers to this Jerusalem church (see also Gal. 1:13).

He then refers to Acts 9:31, 'Then the church throughout Judea, Galilee and Samaria enjoyed a time of peace', arguing there is 'no question about the inclusive use' of *ekklēsia* here and taking 'church' to refer to the churches in the provinces of Judea, Samaria and Galilee.[21] (The plural 'churches' (AV) does not have the support of the best Greek manuscripts and the singular 'church' is probably the correct translation.) Are many local churches, therefore, regarded here as a collective unity? Does this suggest or even prove connectionalism? I do not think so and I submit three arguments. First of all, Acts 9:31 is the only verse in the New Testament where *ekklēsia* is used in the singular to designate a number of local churches. For this reason alone caution should be exercised in using the text to support connectionalism. Another significant consideration is that there are two occasions when the apostle Paul uses the plural 'churches' to refer to the same group of churches mentioned in Acts 9:31 (see Gal. 1:22; 1 Thes. 2:14). Thirdly, it was the believers of the Jerusalem church who were persecuted and compelled to settle in the regions of Judea and Samaria (Acts 8:1) so that the numerous independent churches in these regions had originally been part of the one Jerusalem church. Is the singular 'church' in Acts 9:31, therefore, a reference to the original Jerusalem church now divided and settled in these areas?

Corporate church government

Together with many connectionalist writers, including J. H. Thornwell and James Bannerman, John Murray argues that the unity of the church is expressed visibly and practically in unity of government. The biblical model of the body (1 Cor. 12:12–28), the oneness of faith (Eph. 4:5), Christian fellowship (Eph. 4:3–4, 11–16; Phil. 2:2–3; 4:2), the ethnic universalism of the gospel (Gal. 3:28; Col. 3:11) and the Lord's prayer for unity (Jn. 17:20–21) all serve to underline the profound spiritual unity which obtains between believers and churches. Do these facts, however, point as Murray suggests, 'to the necessity of unity in government'? I will now briefly consider three of Murray's arguments.

Murray argues that Christ's ecumenical headship is expressed in the corporate government of his churches.[22] Independents reply that the Lord's ecumenical headship operates through a great number of local churches in many countries where Christ rules by his word and Spirit. This does not entail a 'corporate government' over all churches but rather a submission by each church to Christ and his word.

Secondly, John Murray appeals to the unique authority of the apostles in the New Testament church which 'exemplifies the ecumenical principle in government'. He adds further, 'the government of the church is one under the auspices and direction of the apostolic witness'.[23]

Two arguments are then used from this principle of the apostolate to justify presbyterian church government. One argument refers to an institution intermediate between the apostolate and the presbyterate expressed through the work of men like Timothy and Titus. Were they evangelists (Eph. 4:11; 2 Tim. 4:5)? Possibly, but they often accompanied the apostles and were delegated work by the apostles.[24] Timothy and Titus were not confined to one local church, so they could have been 'delegates of the apostles'. What this establishes, however, is not connectionalism but the need for the apostles to be assisted in their onerous work and also it shows the importance of training church workers. Without arguing for a specific office, are there not men today who, while anchored in a local church situation, exercise a wider, fruitful ministry to the churches yet without a centralized denominational structure? Another supporting argument by Murray is that elders were ordained concurrently with the ministry of the apostle. One fascinating example is Acts 14:23, but what this demonstrates is the importance which the apostles attached to the permanent office of elders by supervising their appointment and encouraging them in their work.

Is it conceivable, however, asks Murray, that 'corporate government no longer exists' after the death of the apostles? 'Are we to suppose that every unit of the church of Christ exists governmentally in complete independence of all other units?'[25]

These questions, however, are somewhat emotive and a phrase like 'complete independence' is misleading. For example, self-governing churches are not independent of each other. How can they be? They are joined to Christ and consequently to one another in a vital, spiritual way. Such churches owe a common allegiance to the Bible, in believing and teaching its doctrines. In varying degrees, local churches are also aware of other churches worldwide and contribute financially to their needs (Acts 11:29–30; 2 Cor. 8:1–5). Inter-church fellowship is expressed through greetings (Rom. 16:23; 1 Cor. 16:19), mutual prayer and consultation (Acts 15), reports and

visits by pastors/elders of other churches. In the words of
John Owen, 'churches are obliged unto mutual communion among themselves. This communion is incumbent on every church with respect to all other churches of
Christ in the world equally'[26] and this mutual communion majors on adherence to the word of God.

Another argument used by Murray is 'the example of
the Jerusalem Council' in Acts 15 which he sees as providing 'a pattern of consultation and adjudication'.[27] I
submit, however, that the council was advisory and I offer
two lines of evidence. First of all, the *calling* of the council. It was the younger church at Antioch which took the
initiative in sending its leaders to confer with the apostles
and elders of the Jerusalem church (v. 2) and this was an
expression of fellowship and co-operation between two
churches (vv. 3–4). Why consult with the Jerusalem
church? One obvious reason was that the Jewish teachers
perverting the gospel message in the Antioch area had
originated from Jerusalem. Another reason was the
experience and maturity of the Jerusalem church which
was blessed with the presence of apostles as well as
elders. The leaders of the Jerusalem and Antioch churches
met, therefore, as representatives of two independent
local churches in order to safeguard the purity of the
gospel and give guidance to Gentile converts concerning
Jewish ceremonial regulations.

Consider next the *decision* of the council. After initial
discussions, Peter (vv. 7–12) then Barnabas and Paul (v.
12) made important speeches which were confirmed by
James (vv. 13–21). The latter added his personal judgment
(v. 19) that Gentile converts should be asked only to
abstain 'from food polluted by idols, from sexual
immorality, from the meat of strangled animals and from
blood' (v. 20) and this in order to avoid unnecessary
offence to the Jews (v. 21). James' statement was considered and approved by the officers of the two churches
and it was then agreed to send a delegation from Jerusalem to the Antioch church (v. 22) with a written message commending the decisions of their leaders (vv.
23–29). Interestingly, there are no verbs of command in

verses 19–20 and the decision was not forced universally on all the churches. Only the Antioch church is in view together with the neighbouring areas of Syria and Cilicia (v. 23). Gresham Machen remarks that

> Paul entered into no obligation whatsoever to impose the decree upon the Gentile church generally. Apparently he chose to do so in some of the churches of S. Galatia (Acts 16:4) but it is evident from the epistles that the decree was of limited range.[28]

The example of Acts 15 establishes the principle that the officers of local churches can meet together to seek advice and assistance. Independency both encourages and practises this practical communion between local churches for the purpose of mutual edification. However, independents reject the connectional claim that such communion/unity entails corporate government of all churches.

Denominations

If connectionalism is not established from Acts 15 or other New Testament references, the validity of church denominations must be seriously questioned. Surprisingly, there has been little theological study of denominationalism[29] and a thorough appraisal of this subject is long overdue. Not only ecumenists but house church leaders are sometimes vociferous in declaring both the sinfulness of denominations and the scandal of division. In the latter group, Terry Virgo and Gerald Coates condemn denominations for at least six reasons. They argue that the Greek word *ekklēsia* refers to the local/universal church only; that unity is spiritual, not structural or organizational as in denominations; that the New Testament churches did not separate from one another over a particular doctrinal emphasis; that it is unbiblical for one church to impose its authority on other churches and that denominationalism is heresy in the sense that people have their own way and display wrong attitudes. Finally, they say, all Christians need each other's fellowship, help, gifts and prayer.[30] I concur with many of these points but it would be simplistic to stop here, for denominationalism is a complex subject particularly when one attempts to understand the historical phenomenon of denominations.

One major reason for denominational diversity is the apostasy of major church groupings. For this reason significant numbers of Christians have felt that separation from the Roman Catholic Church in the sixteenth century, or from the established church in the eighteenth century, or from major Protestant denominations in the twentieth century, has been necessary for the preservation of biblical truth. A second major reason for denominational divisions is 'hermeneutical failure'. Professor Edmund Clowney, for example, gives one illustration of this in relation to

> isolated and distorted models of the church ... the sacramentalist and hierarchical model of the Middle Ages ... the universalist 'servant-church' of ecumenical theology. So long as one metaphor is isolated and made a model, men are free to tailor the church to their errors and prejudices.[31]

A further reason for denominations arises 'from differences of ethnic identity, cultural background and historical circumstances'.[32]

These historical reasons are important and demand separate study but there are several pointers which suggest that the perpetuation of denominationalism is unacceptable.

One such pointer is that denominations cannot be justified biblically. John Murray expresses this point admirably:

> There is no evidence in the New Testament for the diversification of distinct denominations, and anything tending to such diversification

was condemned (1 Corinthians 1:10–13). The emphasis falls upon the oneness of faith (Ephesians 4:5) and the oneness of the fellowship of the saints (Ephesians 4:2–4, 11–16; Philippians 2:2–3; 4:2).[33]

A second pointer is that denominations restrict their fellowship, in a large measure, to churches within their own grouping; such unity is at best only partial and selective. By contrast, independent churches are often more inclusive in their relationships. Is this not a more scriptural pattern? Thirdly, the departure of most denominations from biblical truth has had a disastrous effect upon churches at a local level where the light of the gospel has often been extinguished. Rather than propagating the truth, denominations have usually compromised and then reinterpreted mission in more humanitarian and secular terms.

But this discussion can even transcend the connectionalist/independency divide. Peter Hocken, for example, thinks there is a 'third way' which neither disposes of denominations as they are nor absolutizes them. Writing within the context of the charismatic renewal, Hocken argues that the ultimate distinctive of each denomination or local church is its witness to Christ and it is this witness supremely which the Holy Spirit honours. For some denominations this means, 'clarifying the centre, bringing basic truths to their rightful centrality, throwing light from the centre on the periphery. It means uncluttering the inheritance.[34]

I do not share Hocken's optimism that denominations can be reformed for, despite the charismatic movement, there is no evidence that denominations are becoming more biblical and Christ-centred. On the other hand, local churches which have seceded from doctrinally mixed denominations value independency as a more scriptural way of preserving and propagating the word of God and of expressing their spiritual union with other Christian churches.

Local churches are interdependent

Trusting the same Saviour, believing and teaching the one inerrant word of God, indwelt by the one Holy Spirit, ruled over by Jesus Christ the only head of the church and facing the same enemy, local churches need each other. Some churches are young and need to discuss their problems with more experienced churches, as in Acts 15. An association or synod or conference can then be called in order to facilitate such discussion and fellowship. Other churches may be facing serious poverty or famine and are dependent on local churches in other areas or countries to provide practical support (Acts 11:29–30; 2 Cor. 8:1–5). Circumstances vary from church to church (Rev. 2 – 3) and from country to country; smaller or persecuted churches may feel more keenly their need of help from other churches. Also letters of commendation (Rom. 16:1–16; 1 Cor. 16:15–21, *etc*.) and introduction may be exchanged between churches, and pastors mutually recognized. Another important area where the interdependence of local churches is expressed is in the training of men for the Christian ministry. Yes, independent local churches are interrelated and interdependent; they need one another and co-operate together but they do so without the structure and inhibitions of connectionalism.

Response to Eryl Davies

Harry Uprichard

Eryl Davies presents the case for independency in a clear, balanced and lucid manner. His introductory observations are most helpful in promoting understanding and clarifying the issue. His method of procedure rightly stresses the normative position of Scripture in the debate. The unfolding argument – local churches are independent, interrelated and interdependent – forcefully develops the thesis in a quietly persuasive way. One fears in all our discussion any kind of acrimony which scandalizes the church before the world. Both in what he says and how he says it, Eryl promotes nothing but stimulating thought. My response will hopefully be along similar lines.

The regulative import of Scripture is common to both sides of our debate. On both sides 'all our cherished traditions and practices need to be radically reappraised at the bar of Scripture' (p. 74). Eryl's exegesis of Scripture is fair, objective, reasonable and well presented even to those who take a different interpretation or viewpoint. His criticisms of the excesses of denominationalism, and of crass authoritarianism on the connectional side, as well as his willingness to turn that judgment on certain forms of independency, are commendable and right. However, the 'light of nature and Christian prudence' to which John Murray appeals as justification for aspects of presbyterian polity would hardly extend to the entire ethos of presbyterianism, even in his own view. Here, both sides of the discussion would allow the normative influence of scriptural *principle* and Murray, rightly or wrongly, would seem to argue from scriptural principle.

Eryl's portrayal of the local church as genuine, gathered, governed and a God-given unit for fellowship, instruction and mission is clear and well proofed biblically. It recalls the same incisive force as reading John Owen on the subject. One is left with a vital impression of the completeness of the local church. However, when the New Testament view of the visibility of the entire church is appreciated and when this is set against the background of the unified Old Testament *qāhāl*, the completeness resembles microcosm rather than independency.

Connectionalists who 'argue that independency weakens rather than honours the principle of Christ's headship over the church' (p. 77), are certainly wrong if they pitch the issue on democracy versus theocracy. But they are not wrong to question whether the church members' meeting as an independent unit should take precedence over Christ's government of his church by the word through the delegated authority given to pastors and elders, an authority clearly evident in the Bible, with its stressed apostolic imprimatur.

Indeed, it is at the point of the elder's authority that I find a significant distance between Eryl and myself. Without doubt, such authority must never be dictatorial nor censorious. Scripture's analogy of the husband and father's caring headship over marriage and family is helpful here. But authority there is, and it does not seem to be an authority delegated to the elder by the church members' meeting. In pleading for such delegated authority there seem to be insufficient biblical grounds for substantiating Eryl's 'second dimension' in respect of this delegated authority (pp. 78–80). 1 Thessalonians 5:12–13 and 1 Timothy 5:17, while indicating that eldership ought not to be dictatorial and is to be respected for its inherent worth, do not seem to imply 'the body of Christ, the church, also delegating authority to elders', even in a 'confirmatory' sense.

Eryl provides excellent word-study material on the use of *ekklēsia* and gives helpful summaries of leading theologians' views of this data relevant to our discussion. His excursus on some of John Murray's arguments for presbyterianism, in the sense of elders' government beyond the local fellowship, again brings us to the heart of the debate.

I believe Eryl, however, undervalues the significance of Murray's arguments as based on the general visibility of the church universal, and on Christ's ecumenical headship over the church. Murray's thesis rests strongly on this foundation. The intermediate nature of the 'evangelists' and the concurrent appointment of elders on apostolic authority, seems to imply much more than an overworked apostolate needing assistance and a general appreciation of the practical importance of a presbyterate. Certainly, based on Murray's basic presuppositions, it implies more. It stresses a continuity of Christ's rule over the entire church which Murray understandably feels is vitiated if presbyterial rule is limited to the local fellowship.

Eryl's perception of the Jerusalem council is in terms of a purely advisory function. His exposition of both the calling and the decision of the council makes this clear. He stresses the inexperience of the younger Antiochan church seeking the guidance of the Jerusalem church, who by their attitude may have been compounding the problem. He emphasizes the limited nature of the imposition of the decrees. But the part played by the apostles in conjunction with the elders in deliberating and deciding the issue is significant. Furthermore, whatever the terms of reference, appeal was made, a decision was taken, decrees were drawn up and, however limited in application, it was expected that these decrees would be complied with. Both the importance of the elders alongside the apostles, and the authority of the council generally, seem basic to the account and these features tend to support a connectional view of the council as exemplifying an assembly of elders in church government exercising authority over more than a local fellowship.

Eryl's observations on the para-church movement I found to be excellent and most pertinent to the present situation. While due appreciation must be given to the sincerity and practical Christian work carried out under the banner of para-church activities, such groupings must face up to the challenge and demands of the doctrine of the church as represented in Scripture.

Eryl's censures of denominationalism are in many cases valid and those adhering to connectionalism must take them seriously. However, there was, in my opinion, at times too bald an equation between connectionalism and denominationalism. While connectionalism is historically and, no doubt, inevitably closely related to denominationalism, independency as represented in congregationalism might also be seen as a denomination. The important thing is that, whatever our view on connectionalism or independency, it ought not to lead to a narrow exclusive denominationalism mindless of the biblical ecumenicity of the church of Christ in visible form. A true independency or a true connectionalism can avoid the excesses of an unduly rigid or improperly loose denominationalism.

Our discussion, however, will not be without positive results if it helps produce a polity based on scriptural principle, a leadership reflecting New Testament process, and a doctrine of the church and its fellowship which is biblical, visible and, to some degree at least, attainable. If it helps the church to manifest to principalities and powers in heavenly realms, as well as to an unbelieving world around us, the manifold wisdom of God which he accomplished in Jesus Christ our Lord (Eph. 3:10), then our debate will have been worthwhile. We pray that both the content and spirit of this interface will produce this result, as a stimulus and encouragement to the body of Christ, God's church on earth, to his great and eternal glory.

Connectionalism

Harry Uprichard

The 'regulative principle' • A principle of
development • The historical debate between
connectionalism and independency • The concept of the church • The concept of the
eldership • The concept of connectionalism •
The principles of connectionalism • Some
questions

'Connectionalism' describes a form of church government
where individual churches or congregations associate in
nature, witness and mission. It embraces both the looser
fellowships (where congregationalist or independent
churches combine in association) and the firmer bonds
characterizing national churches or denominations (such
as Anglicans, Presbyterians and Methodists). 'Independency', on the other hand, stresses the autonomy of each
individual congregation. Each congregation is perfectly
sufficient and adequate as a church in and of itself. The
congregation is, in fact, a complete church. Encouragement
and benefit may come from mutual fellowship with other
churches, but this is not a necessity. Certainly, in the
concept of independency no one individual church is
subject to any authority outside itself.

The 'regulative principle'

Both connectionalism and independency presuppose that a form of church government is possible, and that it is discernible from Scripture. The term 'regulative principle' is one expression used to describe this contention. By this is meant that it is possible to uncover at least the basic principles on which church polity ought to rest – the details and practicalities are to be worked out in the light of human reason.[1] It is not that Scripture provides an unalterable pattern or blueprint for church government, but rather that it contains the underlying concept or concepts from which church government might be formulated. Certainly nothing contrary to Scripture, nor anything which could not be reasonably construed of as arising from scriptural principle, ought to be part of any form of church government purporting to be Christian.

While evangelicals commend the contention of the regulative principle, many would not support it. Some maintain that the situation, as far as church government in the New Testament is concerned, was so fluid, unformed, varied and even mutually conflicting, that it is impossible even to ascertain principles for guidance, let alone formulate any tentative scheme of polity.[2] Others react quite differently. They feel that for far too long the institutional church has been hidebound by its form of government, and has claimed scriptural principle for its particular form of government, when in fact it rests on historical tradition. What is needed is a fresh breath of God's Spirit, where structures and discipline will be relatively unimportant, and where the church will be occupied with more vital priorities such as evangelization and mission. Yet others bemoan the ongoing 'scandal' of our denominational disunity, and wonder if we are going to get our act even remotely together, ecumenically speaking, as the church enters the twenty-first century.[3] The growth of house churches and para-church groups, and the declension in the institutional church, are surely sufficient warning that we have little time to spend on the luxury of denominational hair-splitting and arguing over issues centuries old.

Neither the idea of a form of church government arising from Scripture, nor the concept of denomination, however, can be so lightly dismissed. Those who take Scripture seriously will be concerned to discover, however difficult the task, at least principles to guide them towards a biblical polity. This is a distinct possibility. The regulative principle is viable for Bible-believing Christians. It is also practicable. Discipline, structure and order were part of the New Testament church. While institutionalism is rightly condemned, institution is not evil in and of itself. There was outer form and structure to the New Testament church – institution in that sense – and this alone predisposes us to consider it within our view of the church today. Parachurch reaction against institutionalism in the church is understandable, but the pursuit of discipline, structure and order in the church is legitimate for evangelicals, because evangelicals take everything Scripture says seriously, including what it says about the church and its government.

A principle of development

Alongside the regulative principle there is another aspect which ought to inform our discussion on the issue of denomination. It is the possibility that within the New Testament data on church government there may be growth and development, a 'developing principle'.[4] Rather than presenting us with a picture of fluid, unformed and even disparate polities, it may well be possible to trace in the New Testament, in principle at least, a maturing progression of form and order in the church, somewhat clearer in the later New Testament writings than in the earlier. Of course, much will depend on the dating of the New Testament documents. It might also be argued that variation in terms of progression may not reflect time-scale at all but simply, for example, the intention of a New Testament letter like 1 Corinthians to grapple with specific problems within the church while 1 Timothy majors on matters of church organization. It is at least viable, however, to consider the possibility of progression and growth in polity and expression of church government.

This brings us to the nub of our discussion, the debate between connectionalism and independency.[5] Is any kind of disciplined structure needed to enable churches to fulfil their positive mission in the world? Does such co-operation restrict or enhance the local church in its relationship to Christ as its head? If they do exist should denominational labels be ignored in favour of para-church co-operation? Above all, does the Bible in general, and the New Testament in particular, suggest principles of connectionalism or independency on which our view of church polity ought to rest?

The historical debate between connectionalism and independency

Historically the debate found vivid expression during the Reformation era. It came to decisive significance during the discussions of the Westminster Assembly – a group of ministers called in 1643 for the specific purpose of formulating a doctrinal structure and form of church government for the Reformed church in the British Isles. There was division over the matter of church government. A number dissented from the general 'presbyterian' view of polity on 'independent' or 'congregationalist' principles. It seems fair to comment that, at that point of time, the objections were as much against the rigidity and legalism of presbyterianism as against its principles of polity. John Owen, for example, commended occasional gatherings of church synods for mutual encouragement and discussion but with no governmental or legal status. These views are clearly expressed in the Cambridge Platform of 1648 and in the Savoy Platform of 1658 which can be compared with the view of the Westminster divines in The Form of Presbyterial Church Government of 1645.[6]

While presbyterianism has generally followed those Westminster guidelines quite rigidly, with some variations on the continent and the USA, the history of congregationalism and independency seems to indicate more variation. This is evident in both the terms used to describe the polity. Congregationalism stresses the right of each particular church to govern itself in a fashion reflecting the will of Christ discerned by the whole gathered congregation, the officers of the church being ultimately subject to the authority of the corporate membership. Independency has majored on the facet where each particular church has the right to order its business without any interference whatsoever from outside. Presbyterianism is, strictly speaking, government of the church by presbyters, elders or bishops, titles which are generally regarded as indicating one office and as the authoritative mode of oversight within the church. This oversight is further structured in church courts in ascending gradation – Kirk Session at congregational level, Classis or Presbytery comprising a number of congregations in an area, and Assembly or Synod usually on a national or provincial basis. Episcopalianism and Methodism share a connectional form of church government with Presbyterianism as distinct from independency. They differ, however, in respect of the particular expression of the polity. Episcopalianism preserves the personal authority of a bishop over a number of individual churches in a diocesan area. Methodism develops a superintendency on both personal and corporate bases. Episcopalianism and Methodism along with Presbyterianism organize oversight over a national or provincial area which emphasizes their denominational character.

In proposing connectionalism rather than independency as a polity arising from biblical principles certain areas of reflection naturally present themselves.

The concept of the church

It is a basic contention of independency that the church visible, as perceived from Scripture, is evident in 'particular churches'.

> Those thus called [through the ministry of the
> Word by his Spirit] he commendeth to walk
> together in particular societies or churches, for
> their mutual edification, and the due perform-
> ance of that public worship which he requireth
> of them in the world.[7]

Indeed, the particular church and the profession of the
individual's faith are the only expressions of the universal
visible church.[8]

The pattern of particular churches is evident in the New
Testament. There was the church at Jerusalem (Acts 8:1;
11:22), at Antioch (Acts 11:26; 14:27; 15:3), at Ephesus
(Acts 20:17, 28), at Cenchrea (Rom. 16:1), at Corinth (1 Cor.
1:2), at Laodicea (Col. 4:16), at Thessalonica (1 Thes. 1:1) as
well as those mentioned in Rev. 2:1, 8, 12, 18; 3:1, 7, 14. The
usage of *ekklēsia* in the plural further confirms this.[9] There
were the churches in Cilicia (Acts 15:41), the churches of
Galatia (1 Cor. 16:1; Gal. 1:2), the churches of Macedonia (2
Cor. 8:1) and the churches of Judea (Gal. 1:22; 1 Thes. 2:14).
There is sometimes an inclusive reference which amplifies
the description, for example 'all the churches of the Gentiles' (Rom. 16:4), 'all the churches of Christ' (Rom. 16:16)
and 'all the congregations of the saints' (1 Cor. 14:33).

This data substantiates the claim that the existence of
particular churches in various places described individually or inclusively was the norm in the New Testament.
What it does not seem to imply, however, is that this was
the only concept of the church, or the only expression of
the visible church, in the New Testament period. Certain
factors tend against this presumption.

There is also a view of the church in Scripture, both in
the expression used and in the concept defined, which is
singular, inclusive and all-embracive, indicating that the
church may properly be seen as a unity wider than, and
comprising, all particular churches.

Jesus' words recorded in Mt. 16:13–19 and Mt. 18:15–20
are important here. While it is arguable from Mt. 18:15–17,
and especially from the words, 'tell it to the church' (v. 17),
that a particular church is contemplated here, Mt. 16:13–19

will only bear such a particularistic interpretation with great difficulty. The massive and general nature of Peter's faith upon which Christ's church is to be built, the parallel between this church and the 'kingdom of heaven' and the remit of binding and loosing in universal terms both on earth and in heaven in Matthew 16:13–19 requires a much wider reference. It is surely the church on a world-wide basis as a development and continuum of the unitary 'congregation of the Lord' of the Old Testament which Jesus has in view here. It seems too general a representation to appear otherwise.

The book of Acts also makes a contribution to this understanding of the church. While there are numerous references in Acts to 'churches' at various places, and while the singular significance of 'church' in the early chapters may denote simply the Jerusalem church, Saul is, nonetheless, introduced as beginning 'to destroy the church' (8:3). This *may* refer to the Jerusalem church (8:1), but the fact of the dispersion throughout Judea and Samaria (8:1) and Saul's plain intention to extend the parameters of persecution to Damascus (9:2), could indicate a wider context to this persecution than Jerusalem alone. This seems all the more significant when viewed in the light of the conclusion of the phase. 'The church' in the singular throughout Judea, Galilee and Samaria, is described as enjoying a time of peace after Saul's conversion (9:31), albeit a reading open to dispute. The reference to 'Judea, Galilee and Samaria' reflects not only the area of dispersion (8:1) but also the predicted extension of the church (1:8). The implied unity of area may well be significant in interpreting 'the church' at 9:31.

The Westminster fathers contended that there were a number of congregations at Jerusalem and Ephesus.[10] They did so on various grounds. The large number of converts would be excessive for one congregation. There were too many apostles and evangelists to envisage working in one particular church. The difference of language, Greek and Hebrew, would suggest at least two separate groupings. The 'church' that met at the house of Priscilla and Aquila in Ephesus (1 Cor. 16:19) implies a multiplicity of assemblies.

Against this, the congregationalist dissenters in the West-minster Assembly pitted terms suggesting one meeting place with all the church gathered there, and a reduction in the number of converts both after the Pentecost festival and certainly at the dispersion. While the arguments on both sides too often have the air of special pleading, and for that reason cannot be proven, the possibility at least exists of a number of congregations rather than one particular church at Jerusalem and Ephesus.[11]

It is when we consider Paul's letters, however, that the strongest evidence emerges for the singular inclusive expression and concept of the church. Paul envisaged himself as persecuting 'the church' in the singular (1 Cor. 15:9; Gal. 1:13, *cf.* 22; Phil. 3:6). He perceived the church as the body of Christ into which all believers were Spirit-baptized, regardless of ethnic distinction or social condition (Rom. 12:4–6; 1 Cor. 12:12–13), as one loaf of which all partook (1 Cor. 10:17). The church at Corinth, for example, was but one manifestation of an aggregate community experiencing unity with one Lord – Paul wrote, 'To the church of God in Corinth, to those sanctified in Christ Jesus and called to be holy, together with all those everywhere who call on the name of our Lord Jesus Christ – their Lord and ours' (1 Cor. 1:2).

Now it is possible to regard all of this as focusing upon the particular church, but the imagery of analogy with Christ in his oneness would tend against this view. This is especially the case when we consider Paul's view of the church in singularity as administered in plurality by apostles, prophets, teachers, workers of miracles, healers, helpers and those speaking in tongues (1 Cor. 12:28) and when we contemplate his description of 'the church of the living God, the pillar and foundation of the truth' (1 Tim. 3:15). Here Paul surely goes beyond particularity and locality and embraces universality of time and place.

This seems patently obvious in Ephesians and Colossians. Such descriptions of Christ as 'head over everything for the church which is his body' (Eph. 1:22–23) and 'head of the church, his body' (Eph. 5:23), and the statement that he 'loved the church and gave himself up for her' (Eph.

5:25; *cf.* 3:10; 5:24–32; Col. 1:18, 24) transcend the particular. They envisage the church, Christ's body, Christ's bride, in an embracive unity of life and love with him beyond race, time or place, much broader than particular churches can express.

Should those scriptures, however, which appear to stress this singular, inclusive and all-embracive aspect of the church, be viewed as pertaining only to the church invisible, and not to the church visible? Do they refer to the church triumphant rather than to the church militant? Is it competent to apply them at all to the visible church? We would suggest that it is possible and right to do so.

The import of Jesus' words in Matthew 16 certainly seems to point in this direction. Jesus' words to Peter concerning binding and loosing are specifically to the end that the visible expression of the kingdom of heaven on earth may be demonstrated. The binding and loosing metaphors lose all their meaning if they are not lodged in the church's visibility.

The body and loaf symbolism used of the Roman and Corinthian Christians is of the same nature. The body into which they are Spirit-baptized, the loaf which they share, the gifts which extend in variety over the church are only vital if the unity, nourishment and service they specify are exemplified in the church visible at Rome and at Corinth.

The imagery of Ephesians and Colossians completes the picture. While there are invisible and eschatological aspects to the church as portrayed in Ephesians and Colossians they are not in terms of transcendental mystery but of visible glory, in space and time. The church is ruled over by Christ its head, who is invested with government at the point of his exaltation to the mediatorial role and not before it (Eph. 1:22–23). The church is nourished by Christ its bridegroom, and can only meaningfully benefit from that care if the analogy of marriage is fulfilled in the visibility of experience (Eph. 5:24). The church is administered through the gifted offices of the ascended Christ towards the end of growth in knowledge and maturity of a church militant here and now. The situation at Corinth is the same (Eph. 4:11; *cf.* 1 Cor. 12:28). The church witnesses the manifold nature of God's grace to principalities and powers *now* in the present not in the hereafter (Eph. 3:10).

The visibility of the church is at all points evident. Believers at Ephesus and Colosse were subject to the same Christ, and followed the same apostolic instructions for their growth in grace as those at Corinth or Rome. They belonged to the same church in this sense – one Lord, one faith, one baptism. We should not abstract the data of Ephesians and Colossians into transcendental mysticism, for it was not meant for that. Strictly speaking, the church is only 'invisible' in those aspects which are known to God alone. The specifications of a singular, inclusive, all-embracive church are visible. The Form of Presbyterial Church Government rightly affirms, 'There is one general church visible held forth in the New Testament.'[12] The congregationalist and independent view of the church visible seems deficient at base, and it is a deficiency which affects every aspect of the polity.

The concept of the eldership

A second consideration which is relevant to our discussion on connectionalism or independency is the concept of the eldership. The primary importance of the elder within the government of the New Testament church strengthens the case of connectionalism against the congregationalist polity.

There can be little doubt as to the significance of the elder within the order of the church in Scripture. It is an office basic to the government of God's people in both Old and New Testaments. There were elders in the Old Testament both locally over individual synagogues and provincially over the whole people of God. 'Elders of the people' figured prominently in the opposition to Jesus during his ministry. The elders of the church in Judea received gifts from the church at Antioch during the days of famine (Acts 11:30). Returning to the churches at Lystra, Iconium and Antioch, Paul and Barnabas appointed elders in each church (Acts 14:23). Elders joined with the apostles in the deliberations and decisions at the Jerusalem Council (Acts 15). Paul summoned the elders from Ephesus and addressed them on their duties at Miletus (Acts 20:17f.). Paul gave Timothy instructions about elders' privileges and responsibilities and enjoined Titus to appoint elders in every town in Crete (1 Tim. 5:1, 17, 19; Tit. 1:5). Peter directed remarks in his letter specifically to the elders of the churches in Asia Minor (1 Pet. 5:1f.). James outlined the meaningful involvement of elders in the life of the church or churches to which he wrote (Jas. 5:13–15). Two letters in the New Testament purport to have been written by John 'the elder' (2 Jn. 1; 3 Jn. 1). Quite clearly, the position of the elder was as pivotal in the New Testament church as in the Old.

Rule and authority were an integral part of the function of eldership in the New Testament. This is quite explicitly mentioned in 1 Timothy 5:17, where the strong verb *prohistēmi*, expressive of precedence, is used: 'The elders who direct the affairs of the church well are worthy of double honour, especially those whose work is preaching and teaching.' It is obvious in the emerging pattern of authority of the eldership both in Acts and the letters. The appointment of elders was associated with the strengthening and maturing ministry begun by the apostles in Asia Minor and Crete (Acts 14:23; Tit. 1:5), and elders, together with apostles, determined the terms of Gentile admission to the church (Acts 15:6; 16:4). This role is also clear in the kind of descriptive functions ascribed to the eldership, such as ruling, teaching, shepherding, oversight. Peter's warning against the abuse of elders' power is meaningless if such power were not presumed to exist in the first place – 'not lording it over those entrusted to you, but being examples to the flock' (1 Pet. 5:3). It can also be seen in the requirement of respect due from believers towards elders (1 Tim. 5:1, 17, 19). Even where elders are not mentioned by name, the authority structure appears normative: 'Obey your leaders and submit to their authority' (Heb. 13:17); 'Now we ask you, brothers, to respect those who work hard among you, who are over you [*prohistēmi*] in the Lord and who admonish you. Hold them in the highest regard in love because of their work' (1 Thes. 5:12–13); 'Those with gifts of administration' (1 Cor. 12:28); 'If it is leadership [*prohis-tēmi*], let him govern diligently' (Rom. 12:8).

Elders in the New Testament had authority. It was neither absolute nor dictatorial power. It was not to be abused. It was for 'ministerial' purposes of shepherding the flock. But it was authority, nonetheless, to be received, respected and obeyed.

Another feature of New Testament eldership relevant to our discussion is that it represented an office immediately below the extraordinary status of apostle, prophet and evangelist and was of prime and continuing importance in the church. It seems only fair to note at this point, however, that while for years the received interpretation of Reformed theologians was that the offices of apostle, prophet and evangelist were extraordinary and ceased with the closure of the New Testament canon, and that those of elder, pastor, teacher and deacon were perpetual and continue in the church, this is not the only interpretation held by evangelicals today. Hywel Jones, for example, while denying the claims made by some charismatics for apostles within the contemporary church, discerns a third category of 'apostle' besides the Twelve and Paul in the New Testament which allows for the use of 'apostle' in a particular sense today, 'that is church-appointed men and women who devote themselves to the work of the gospel. These can be better described as pastors, teachers, preachers, evangelists, or missionaries.'[13] Roy Clements, following Wayne Grudem, has argued for a continuing gift of prophecy, similar to that mentioned in 1 Corinthians 14 but quite distinct from scriptural prophecy, as something we ought to anticipate and indeed encourage in today's church.[14] For some time the New Testament office of evangelist has been a moot point and if understood as a 'delegate' of the apostles might be paralleled in the present peripatetic evangelist of the global church as for example, Dr Billy Graham.

Even allowing for such views, however, the office of elder as immediately below the status of apostle, prophet and evangelist is evident from a number of considerations. Firstly, it is anticipated in the equation of the New Testament office of elder or presbyter with bishop. Both presbyterians and independents are in agreement on this point. The following reasons are usually adduced for this contention. Paul summoned the Ephesian elders (*presbuterous*, Acts 20:17) to meet him in Miletus and when they arrived, he addressed them as 'bishops' (*episkopous*, v. 28). Paul mentions elders, bishops and deacons in 1 Timothy, but the strong similarity of function in respect of rule in 1 Timothy 3:4–7 and 1 Timothy 5:17 suggests that elder and bishop were one and the same office. Paul required Titus to appoint elders in Crete and immediately followed this with the qualifications for a bishop in such a way as to make the equation of offices the most natural interpretation of the data (Tit. 1:5–7).

Secondly, it seems a reasonable deduction from the appointment of elders by apostolic authority and their appointment to a work involving a continuance of that begun by the apostles. Paul and Barnabas appointed elders in every city, having previously strengthened the believers (Acts 14:23). The reason Paul left Titus in Crete was to 'straighten out what was left unfinished and appoint elders in every town' (Tit. 1:5).

Thirdly, it is well illustrated at the Jerusalem Council where the elders are coupled with the apostles not only in debate but in authoritative decision (Acts 15:6; 16:4).

Fourthly, it is hinted at in the placement of 'pastors and teachers' immediately after apostles, prophets, evangelists (Eph. 4:11) and in the order and discrimination between the offices of 'bishop' and 'deacon' (Phil. 1:1; 1 Tim. 3:1, 8; *cf.* 1 Pet. 4:11), though the lists at Romans 12:6–8 and 1 Corinthians 12:28–31 would not necessarily bear the same implication.

There is not the slightest hint of hierarchy among the elders of the New Testament. A signal reference to the collectivity of the presbyterate and to their collective function is found in Paul's words to Timothy, 'Do not neglect your gift, which was given you through a prophetic message when the body of elders [*presbyterion*] laid their hands on you' (1 Tim. 4:14). There is a greater likelihood that *presbyterion* refers to a 'body of elders' rather than to

the office of elder on account of the use of the same word at
Luke 22:66 and Acts 22:5 for the Jewish council of elders.

These considerations have led John Murray to conclude:

> Rule by elders is the apostolic institution for the
> government of the local congregation and this
> involves the principles of plurality and parity.
> The inference is inescapable that this is the
> permanent provision for the government of the
> churches. Since the apostolate is not per-
> manent, and since there is in the New Testament
> no other provision for the government of the
> local congregation, we must conclude that the
> council of elders is the only abiding institution
> for the government of the Church of Christ
> according to the New Testament.[15]

With much of this those holding an independent polity
could agree. The problem arises when we relate the elder's
oversight not to the local congregation but to the wider
church. One inconsistency the dissenting congregationalists at the Westminster Assembly objected to concerning presbyterian polity was that ministers normally exercised preaching oversight within a local congregation but
ruled within a wider area, namely the Classis or Presbytery.[16]

As congregationalist polity developed, and particularly
by the nineteenth and early twentieth centuries, it tended
to produce within each particular church one preaching
elder surrounded by a group of deacons who, to all intents
and purposes, acted as New Testament elders.[17] However,
the early congregationalists, the dissenters and their heirs,
held a strong view of eldership both teaching and ruling
but limited their oversight to the local church. In their view
a congregational presbytery, a Kirk Session, is the only
form of presbytery drawing authority from Scripture.[18] It is
interesting to note that today among some evangelicals,
including those of a congregationalist polity, there is a
return to plurality of elders. This is to be encouraged. It
certainly reflects the principles of the founding fathers of
congregationalism.

Where the problem more precisely arose with regard to the eldership was the relative authority of the elders and the church as a corporate membership. The Cambridge Platform expresses the distinction like this:

> Ordinary church power, is either the power of office, that is such as is proper to the eldership: or, power of privilege, such as belongs unto the brotherhood. The latter is in the brethren formally, and immediately from Christ, that is, so as it may according to order be acted or exercised immediately by themselves. The former is not in them formally or immediately, and therefore cannot be acted or exercised immediately by them, but is said to be in them, in that they design the persons unto office, who only are to act, or to exercise this power.[19]

The practical effect of this was that ultimately the elders were subject to the church members and ruled in delegated authority from them.

Congregationalists tend to locate this immediate 'power of privilege' from Christ to the church as 'brotherhood' in three particular areas of Scripture.[20] Christ granted this power to the church in a context of discipline (Mt. 18:15–19). The power was that of binding and loosing. The church were the two or three gathered in Christ's name. The Corinthian church exercised this power against the 'immoral brother' (1 Cor. 5). The church, not the leadership, were charged with the responsibility for discipline. The church as 'assembled in the name of our Lord Jesus' were to act judicially. The Jerusalem church exemplified this power in choosing an apostle and the Seven and in their participation in the Jerusalem Council (Acts 1:23–26; 6:2–6; 15:4–29).

Basic to the congregationalist interpretation is the understanding of the church only as 'the brotherhood', not in any organized form, nor represented by its leadership. Any view of the church other than 'the brotherhood' is regarded as vitiating the immediacy of Christ's power and presence with those gathered in his name. With this perception a number of reservations might be expressed.

Firstly, the whole congregation of the Lord in the Old Testament is represented as present and acting when the elders act on its behalf (Ex. 12:3, 21; Nu. 35:12, 24; Jos. 20:4). The elders are thus identified with the congregation. Of particular relevance to Matthew 18:15–19 and 1 Corinthians 5 is Deuteronomy 19:15–19.[21] In the necessary requirement for 'two or three witnesses' (*cf.* Mt. 18:16), where a malicious witness appears, the two men involved in the dispute must stand in the presence of the Lord 'before the priests and judges who are in office at the time' (Dt. 19:17). After the judges have made a thorough investigation of the matter, if the testimony is found false, the witness is to be punished. 'You must purge the evil from among you' (Dt. 19:19; *cf.* 1 Cor. 5:13). In the light of the relevance of Deuteronomy 19:15 to Matthew 18:15 and 1 Corinthians 5, where this Old Testament passage seems to be in the mind of both Jesus and Paul, the interpretation of 'the church' in the sense of 'the brotherhood' as the residuum of immediate power would be a signal, and probably intentional, departure from Old Testament procedure.

Secondly, Christ initially granted the power of the keys to Peter on the grounds of his confession (Mt. 16:19). It seems reasonable to assume that this was granted not to Peter personally but to him as representative of the apostles, since it was to the disciples specifically that Christ later gave authority to remit and retain sins (Jn. 20:23). In Matthew 18:1 the disciples are again particularly addressed. Christ's statement about answered prayer, associated with that concerning the two or three gathered in his name, stresses his presence and authority among the smallest group of those so assembled. It need not necessarily indicate judicial procedure nor be a qualifying interpretation of 'the church' in verse 17. The presence of God indwelt the congregation of the Lord in the Old Testament and the immediacy of God was in no way inhibited by the judicial process of those in office at the time acting as representatives of the whole congregation. It seems admissible to refer the power of binding and loosing in Matthew 18:16 to the apostles as those in office in Christ's church at that time and to interpret 'the church' in verse 17 as represented in its judicial process by them and not in the more general sense of 'the brotherhood'.

Thirdly, the church as the body of Christ possessed gifts of rulership (Rom. 12:8) and government (1 Cor. 12:28). The exalted Christ as the head of the church bestowed gifts for the perfecting of the body, the church (Eph. 4:4–13). Rule in the church appears to have been vested in the eldership by apostolic injunction under Christ's institution (Acts 14:23; 1 Tim. 5:17).

Fourthly, the absence of any reference to elders in 1 Corinthians 5 is not an insuperable problem.[22] It might be mooted that because of the early founding of the Corinthian church in a Greek society eldership was still at an early stage of development.[23] The later more settled state of eldership in the pastoral epistles could be seen as the norm of rule in the New Testament church.

Fifthly, there is no ultimate difference of opinion between connectionalists and congregationalists on the issue of 'the brotherhood' choosing its officers.

Finally, the Council of Jerusalem in Acts 15 offers a good example of the respective participation of congregation and eldership in relative terms of authority.[24] The delegation from Antioch went specifically to see the apostles and elders at Jerusalem about the matter in question (v. 2). On arrival, they were welcomed by the church, apostles and elders, and some believers of the party of the Pharisees vouchsafed an opinion (v. 5). The apostles and elders met, considered and decided the question (vv. 6–21). The apostles and elders 'with the whole church' chose men to accompany Paul and Barnabas to Antioch (v. 22). The Council letter and decrees were addressed in the name of the apostles and elders (v. 23; 16:4). It seems reasonably clear from this that the deliberative and deciding aspects were the responsibility of the apostles and elders. The church concurred in the decision and chose representatives to deliver the decrees. Rule and government were with the apostles and elders, not with the brotherhood.

It seems unnecessary, then, to postulate from this data – Matthew 18:15–19; 1 Corinthians 5; Acts 1, 6 and 15 – that immediate 'power of privilege' lay with the brotherhood. It is possible to understand these features, within the developing process of rule by eldership, on the basis of Christ's own institution to the apostles and mediately through them to the eldership. The immediacy of Christ among his people is in no way harmed by what he himself originally instituted and, through his representatives the apostles, conferred.

The concept of connectionalism

If, according to regulative principle, the visible church extends to all those who in every place call upon the name of Christ, and if the continuing means for teaching and ruling the church, following the demise of the apostolate, is the eldership, the ground is prepared for a connectionalism of presbyterial teaching and rule over a world-wide church. According to the developing principle, the church matures in its unity so that it is seen as the body of Christ, of which he is the head. It progresses in its rule from the incipient gifts of government and administration of 1 Corinthians 12:28 and Romans 12:8 to the more settled presbyterate of 1 Timothy 4:14, and the teaching/ruling eldership of 1 Timothy 5:17. If this is so, a connectionalism of teaching and rule over the body of Christ, visibly extended as a unified church throughout the world, is anticipated at least in principle. Does Scripture, however, provide any evidence of this connectionalism in general or of a connectionalism in church government in particular?

Connectionalism was evident in the Old Testament in the unified nature of the congregation of the Lord; in the annual appearance of God's people at assemblies and feasts; and in the leadership appointed by God representatively for his people. Indeed, the concept of *qāhāl* in the Old Testament, as the whole people of God called together before him at specific times during the year, is a feature which has weighed heavily with connectionalists. This unified nature is nowhere more evident than in the obvious detestation with which rival cults were deemed false at the time of the divided monarchy, or in the bitterness with which the claims of Samaritanism were viewed at a later date. The precedence of this unity of God's people over any local manifestations of the Jewish faith is significant. It is true that church and state were fused in a theocracy during the old dispensation. Nevertheless, for connectionalists the oneness evident in the polity of the Old Testament 'church', anticipates a unity in the polity of the church in the New Testament and hence in the church today.

Connectionalism, in the form of unity of teaching, marked the New Testament church both in content and method of instruction. The faith of a common salvation was once for all delivered to the saints (Jude 3). The pattern of sound teaching was a deposit to be kept intact (2 Tim. 1:13–14). Reliable men qualified to teach were responsible for its transmission (2 Tim. 2:2). Fellowship itself was a high-point of connectionalism in the New Testament church. Mutual care characterized the Jerusalem church or churches (Acts 2:42–47). Apostolic instruction and pastoral care were the common coinage of more than one group of believers (1 Cor. 1:2; 1 Pet. 1:2; 5:1–4). Unity was co-extensive with all God's people (1 Cor. 12:26; Eph. 4:5–6). Prayer was to interlace the whole family of God (Eph. 6:18; Phil. 1:3–5). Financial support came from the church at Antioch to Judea and from the Macedonian Christians to others (Acts 11:30; 2 Cor. 8:9). Apostolic mission embraced the whole people of God and expressed itself in division of labour, determining of purpose, discussion of policy, difference of opinion and resultant spread of witness.[25] There was connectionalism in teaching, in fellowship and in mission in the apostolic church. It was a unified effort and certainly viewed by the apostles as such.

The Council of Jerusalem above all, however, evinces connectionalism in polity in the New Testament church. A number of features are particularly salient. Delegates came from the church at Antioch to seek advice from the apostles and elders at Jerusalem (Acts 15:2). The matter in question was discussed and a decision was taken by the assembled apostles and elders (Acts 15:6–19, 22). In this capacity, the apostles appear to have acted as elders. They joined in the normal process of debate and deliberation rather than giving a definitive pronouncement with apostolic authority (Acts 15:6–19). The council's letter was issued in the name of the apostles and elders (the word 'brothers' at Acts 15:23 [*cf.* v. 22; 16:4] was probably Aramaic idiom in apposition to 'apostles and elders' and does not refer to the whole church).[26] The decision reached was obviously regarded as binding, being described within the council's letter as 'requirements' and later as 'decisions' (*dogmata*, a word used for imperial decrees at Acts 17:7; Lk. 2:1) reached by the apostles and elders in Jerusalem for the people to obey (Acts 15:28; 16:4).

G. W. Knight pertinently comments:

> The interrelationships of the churches seen in Paul's letters and the council of Acts 15 and its resultant decree, as evidenced in Acts 16:4, show that the mutual submission extends to an interrelationship not only among members in a local congregation but also among congregations.[27]

Principles of connectionalism

From these considerations two important principles of connectional polity arise. The first is the principle of the authority of ruling officers in matters of government within the church, an authority which extends over other particular churches. The second is the principle of appeal to ruling officers in matters of government within the church with due acquiescence to their considered opinion. Since the apostolate has ceased within the church, and the office associated with the apostolate in rule within the New Testament church was the eldership, presbyterians, among the connectional family, regard authority of government within the church as vested in the eldership. The principles of authority and appeal constitute the ground of their reasoning. From these principles presbyterians order government by elders within the church in ascending courts of authority and appeal – congregational (Kirk Session), regional (Presbytery or Classis) and provincial (Synod or Assembly), the details of which 'are to be ordered by the light of nature and Christian prudence, according to the general rules of the Word, which are always to be observed'.[28]

Congregationalists have objected on a number of grounds to this thesis. They maintain that the participation of the whole church at the Council of Jerusalem has been undervalued. Those from Antioch were welcomed by the Jerusalem church as well as by the apostles and elders and reported to the same body (Acts 15:4). Believers from the party of the Pharisees were permitted to contribute to the discussion (Acts 15:5). The concurrence of the Jerusalem church was involved in the final determination and the church as a body chose representatives to accompany Paul and Barnabas to Antioch (Acts 15:22–28).

As previously noted, however, it was the apostles and elders to whom the matter was directly referred. They deliberated, decided and issued the decrees on their authority. It is only with great difficulty that the data of Acts 15 can be interpreted as demonstrating the inherent church-power of the Jerusalem church.

Congregationalists claim that there is no true analogy between the Jerusalem Council and presbyterian 'church-courts'. The Jerusalem Council dealt with a specific issue, an appeal from the Antioch church to the Jerusalem church. Representatives were not called from various churches over a regional area to discuss business. The whole gathering was an occasional affair, not a fixed regular occurrence dealing with a continuum of church business.

While there are these differences, the principles of authority and appeal remain. There was some degree of representation. A matter of difficulty was discussed and resolved. A judgment was given to be observed. The application of these principles to an on-going progression of church government on a regular basis simply exemplifies the biblical principle of carrying out affairs decently and in order. There is no necessity or principle involved in the council's 'occasional' nature.

By far the most severe criticism of the connectionalist interpretation of Acts 15 is that it contravenes the principle of church-power. The Cambridge Platform, after listing numerous ways in which churches may share communion with one another, cites the calling of synods on the analogy of Acts 15 for resolving disputes within the church.[29] The Savoy Platform similarly permits occasional synods for dealing with difficulties or differences among churches or believers.[30] Where both statements draw the line is in denying such synods any 'church power, authority or jurisdiction'. This arises logically from their perception that the seat of such power resides in the brotherhood of the particular church.

The general contention, however, that primacy of government within the church is vested in the presbyterate and not the brotherhood, and the particular instance of presbyterial government of the Jerusalem Council exercising authoritative jurisdiction over other churches, are the decisive factors for the connectionalist viewpoint. Connectionalists understand this to be the precise implication of Acts 15 and, therefore, it is fundamental to their position.

The concept of the visible church as the body of Christ on a world-wide and unified basis, the perception of the eldership as the gift of Christ's headship for the government of his church on earth, and the appearance of connectionalism not only as generally characterizing the New Testament church but as a particular expression of New Testament church government, are three vital aspects undergirding a connectionalist polity of the church of Christ. Read against the background of a regulative and, perhaps also, of a developing principle of Scripture, these elucidate connectionalism in general and presbyterianism in particular as a viable biblical polity.

Some questions

The implications of connectionalism might, in conclusion, be pursued in responding to some questions posed earlier in our discussion.

Is any kind of disciplined structure needed to enable churches to fulfil their positive mission in the world?

However varied the perceptions and priorities of the church's mission might be, mission involves, at least minimally, the attempt to win the world to faith in Christ, and the nurturing of those won to that faith. The New Testament represents this in terms of an evangelism through gospel preaching and a nurturing through instruction, fellowship and pastoral care in communities of believers, particularly churches. Some form of disciplined structure marked this process of evangelism and church planting at the local level. The perception of the visible church as the one body of Christ world-wide, the unified purpose and direction of the apostles over this one church conferred on the eldership, and the interrelatedness of apostolic churches in instruction, prayer, fellowship, mission and, however incipiently, in polity, means that such a disciplined structure is not a restrictive intrusion to be avoided, but a natural development of biblical connectionalism to be encouraged.

From a purely pragmatic point of view we have seen the advantages of this aspect of connectionalism in our own area. We live close to a provincial town in a predominantly presbyterian and relatively peaceful part of Northern Ireland and we were greatly excited at the influx of fresh population, and the speedy growth of new housing developments in the district. Under our General Assembly's Church Extension Committee, and our local Presbytery's supervision and assistance, three 'Church Extension charges' were monitored, erected to congregational status and now provide flourishing congregations with valuable outreach of witness, mission and teaching for the increased population. The entire process was facilitated in large measure through the on-going means of a connectional polity. This can be seen in the way the work was introduced, leadership afforded by 'interim Kirk Sessions' comprising elders from surrounding congregations and spiritual and financial help directed through central Assembly Committee and local Presbytery. It is easy to conceive how much more difficult this would have been in a context of independency. This pattern, which we have experienced in our locality, has been repeated in other similar situations within our denomination's work in the province. A connectional polity has certainly been of great practical benefit in this case and our circumstances reflect what is happening in even larger urban areas both here and on the mainland.

Does such co-operation restrict or enhance the local church in its relationship to Christ as its head?

If we begin with the premise that Christ has given elders in each local church for government, who in no way vitiate the immediacy of Christ with his people, it seems no more injurious to the local church's relationship to Christ if such corporate oversight by eldership is extended over a number of churches. This is not a centralized bureaucracy, robbing individual churches of their rights in Christ, but a helpful, biblical oversight channelling and unifying the energies and vision of the whole people of God. As such, it enhances rather than restricts the local church in its relationship to Christ its head.

Dr Robert Runcie struck a very different note in an address opening the Lambeth Conference of 1988. He raised the issue of a reformed papacy as a focus for the unity of the church catholic. Alluding to Canterbury and Roman primacy he went on to comment, 'But could not all Christians come to reconsider the kind of primacy exercised within the early Church, a "presiding in love" for the sake of the unity of the Churches?'[31]

Evangelicals would want to question the very existence

of any kind of primacy, certainly within the church of the New Testament. Whatever position, if any, appears to be occupied by James in the Council of Jerusalem it is a far cry from the precedence of the see of Rome or Canterbury. The forthrightness of Paul, who opposed Peter to his face because he was clearly in the wrong (Gal. 2:11), indicates that there was little consciousness of such primacy among the apostles themselves in the conduct of church business. There is no primacy as such in the New Testament but every indication of plurality and parity among the leadership. This form of leadership, arising naturally from the ordinance of Christ, in no way restricts the local church in its relationship to him as its head, whereas primacy, by its very nature, injures this relationship.

If they do exist, should denominational labels be ignored in favour of para-church co-operation?

The para-church movement has certainly some important lessons to teach us. The enthusiasm and sincerity of its members are impressive. The naturalness and spontaneity of their religion condemns the frequent formalism and frigidity of the institutional church. They pitch their witness and amplify their influence on a global scale with remarkable success. Their weakness lies in their lack of biblical parameters. This means that their enthusiasm is often misdirected and there is an air of unreality about their procedures as they face difficulties or disciplinary matters within church life. The root problem is that they fail to recognize the visibility of the church or, at least, fail to give it proper recognition. If we could learn from their strengths, and they from their weaknesses, co-operation would benefit the Christian church as a whole.

Our response, however, to the question posed above will also largely depend on our perception of denomination. If we regard this merely as historical tradition, denomination is evidently expendable. If, however, for us, denomination reflects biblical norms of doctrine and polity, we shall rightly be jealous to guard it. This will not necessarily mean unbending rigidity on our part, but it will certainly not lead us to throw out denomination or its label unthinkingly in favour of para-church co-operation. It will, indeed, not be so much an either/or situation. Rather, working within the clearly but reasonably defined biblical parameters of denomination, both in doctrine and polity, we will seek as best we can to co-operate with those of kindred mind on fundamentals, but who differ from us on details. We shall pursue this course, seeking the visible unity of Christ's church militant. If the church of Christ treads warily in this direction as she enters the twenty-first century, far from perpetuating the 'scandal of disunity', or the deadness of mere historical tradition, she will hopefully anticipate a truly biblical ecumenism, the answer to her Lord's earnest longing:

> 'My prayer is not for them alone. I pray also for those who will believe in me through their message, that all of them may be one, Father, just as you are in me and I am in you. May they also be in us so that the world may believe that you have sent me' (Jn. 17:20–21).

Response to Harry Uprichard

Eryl Davies

I feel like a housewife whose time in the kitchen is restricted to thirty minutes but who has all the ingredients and enthusiasm to bake a fruit cake which would take three hours to finish. Reluctantly, she settles for scones which will be ready within the allotted time. Similarly, I would like to comment in detail but limitations of space rather than time have been imposed upon me. However, I prefer fruit cake to scones!

Much of what Harry Uprichard writes, I agree with. To be more precise, the regulative principle, the development of church polity in the New Testament, the importance and authority of elders, the Old Testament background to *ekklēsia* and elders as well as inconsistencies in some forms of presbyterianism and independency are all points on which I agree. But there are disagreements. I confine my attention to two areas of disagreement; the way in which wrong inferences are drawn from valid principles and the questionable way certain scriptures are interpreted.

Under the sub-title, 'The concept of the church', Harry's denominational interpretation of Matthew 16:13–19, Acts 8:3 and 9:2, 31 is not established and I refer readers to my original discussion of these passages. Further, what is supposed to strengthen 'the case of connectionalism against the congregationalist polity' is the concept of eldership. I disagree. All that is established is the authority and parity of elders within a local church, not connectionalism. While he acknowledges this as one important difference between us, his own arguments and inferences must be challenged.

Let me take one example. Harry claims that 'a connectionalism of teaching and rule over the body of Christ . . . is anticipated at least in principle' (p. 112). The language is cautious but the conclusion and inference are unwarranted. Now one of his arguments is that the unified nature of the congregation of the Lord in the Old Testament establishes connectionalism. Again, I disagree. For one reason, we have the vexed question of the church/state relationship in the Old Testament which complicates the discussion. Harry does not indicate the ways in which the one, eternal covenant in both the Old and New Testaments has a different administration in the New Testament. Is not this 'corporate unity' expressed in the New Testament through inter-church fellowship, synods and apostolic doctrine rather than connectionalism? Harry also needs to allow for greater variation on the part of independents/ congregationalists in understanding and applying the distinction between 'power of office' and 'power of privilege' (p. 109). As he is aware, an increasing number of such churches insist that elders rule but with the respect and confirmation of the church through members' meetings. Admittedly, it is a sensitive area and one that is abused in both independent and presbyterian contexts.

Another of his arguments concerns the Council of Jerusalem in Acts 15, but the interpretation is questionable. Harry thinks that this council 'above all, evinces connectionalism in polity' (p. 113). In addition to what I have written in my article on this subject, these further points are offered in order to reach a more fair interpretation of Acts 15.

There were no other churches involved besides the two churches of Jerusalem and Antioch (vv. 3–4). This is not connectionalism or classic presbyterianism but two local churches conferring on a common problem. The 'judgment' by James in verse 19 was a personal one which was discussed and then approved by the 'apostles and elders, *with the whole church*' (v. 22). Notice that there is no verb of command here at all. Furthermore, this was not a major church decision imposed upon all the churches but rather a reply to the church of Antioch; the decision was also shared with the churches of Syria and Cilicia (15:41; 16:4). The decision was limited in its range and application while Philippians 3:2–3 implies it was not accepted universally. Then there is the question of interpreting the 'decisions' (*dogmata*) in Acts 16:4. Harry is right in saying the same word is used with reference to the decrees of rulers in Luke 2:1 and Acts 17:7, but it does not mean it is used in exactly the same way in Acts 16:4. As Lenski observes, the verb means 'it was resolved', not 'decreed' and *dogmata* is the corresponding noun meaning 'resolutions'. Notice, too, that the decision by the apostles and elders (16:4) was in the context of the 'whole church' (15:22).

One final practical point. Harry refers to the advantages of connectionalism in his area with regard to church planting. I rejoice in the way in which three 'flourishing congregations' have been established through his own denomination. This is good and encouraging. But there is a bite in the tail from my friend when he writes: 'It is easy to conceive how much more difficult this would have been in a context of independency' (p. 118). To be fair, I think there are advantages and disadvantages for both connectional and independent churches with regard to church planting. A connectional church is often frustrated waiting for committees and church courts to give authorization and allocate resources whereas independent churches can sometimes lack resources and vision.

Allow me to end on a personal note. My second pastorate was in north-west Wales in a small independent church with sixteen members. Our membership increased to forty-five but our congregations were much larger. For a radius of twenty to twenty-five miles in several directions there was no other Bible-teaching church. Within seven years, that small church was enabled of God to plant two other churches and help in establishing a third besides sending men as pastors/elders to churches further afield. We were not hindered by committees or denominational hierarchies but prayerfully supported by other independent churches. Now in Wales about fifty independent evangelical churches have formed the Associating Evangelical Churches of Wales (AECW) for purposes of inter-church fellowship and church planting. New areas and churches are being opened up by these independent churches in fellowship and without the cumbersome machinery of connectionalism. Here is New Testament independency in action!

Part 3

The issue of doctrinal purity

Gordon W. Kuhrt
and Graham Harrison

- Should churches be doctrinally comprehensive or entirely separated from error?
- How far can a gathered church, seeking to maintain a realistically pure membership, enjoy fellowship with another local church which seems to accept a more mixed membership?
- Does it make any essential difference if that other local church itself maintains a vigorous evangelical testimony within a denomination in which other churches do not?
- Is the lack of clarity in a mixed body too high a price to pay?

Principled comprehensiveness

Gordon W. Kuhrt

The issue ● Can evangelicals be 'unbiblical'? ●
Some models of ecclesiology ● Evangelical
problems with ecclesiology ● The biblical doctrine of the church ● The importance of truth ●
The biblical response to false teaching ● Other
factors to bear in mind ● The situation today ●
In conclusion

The issue

The Bible speaks of the church in two ways. Firstly, there
is the universal church which is God's people in every
place throughout time and eternity (e.g. Col. 1:18).
Secondly, there is the local church which is always described in a territorial way – of a city, town or district (e.g.
1 Cor. 1:2; Rev. 2; 3). There is no approval of Christians in
a locality separating into denominations. The local
church consists of *all* the Christians in the area.

Unfortunately, church life has been marred over the
centuries by some Christians not holding to fundamental
doctrines of the faith. This has sometimes led to others
separating into new churches where particular teachings
of belief or behaviour are especially emphasized. It is

often a sad story – not only of doctrinal and moral indifference but also of continual splintering and division, of personality cults, of spiritual pride and lack of love.

We come to this subject from very different backgrounds. We have knowledge and experience of churches which are more or less comprehensive (in a principled or unprincipled way) or more or less separatist (in a principled or unprincipled way). I wish to argue for the principled comprehensiveness of all the Christians in a locality being the church – not on the basis of history or tradition but on the basis of the Bible's doctrine. But all the contributors to this book are evangelicals, and claim to submit to biblical teaching. So we have to ask whether the Bible is confused and contradictory on this issue.

Can evangelicals be 'unbiblical'?

This is a complex question because it can quite rightly be answered 'no' and 'yes'. 'No' can be the answer because, when evangelicals are found to be 'unbiblical', they are only true to themselves as evangelicals when they reform themselves in the light of Scripture, and at that point become biblical. Evangelicals, by definition, are to be open to reform in submission to the Bible's authority. But the question can be answered 'Yes' – because evangelical movements have not always been true to themselves or to the Scriptures. They have often been imprisoned by human traditions, and improper interpretation of the Bible. Thus evangelicalism as a 'theological model' is, in principle, biblical. However, evangelicalism as a 'historic tradition' is, in practice, often unbiblical. This is particularly, and sadly, so in the area of ecclesiology. Before we look at some examples of that, we shall consider some models.

Some models of ecclesiology

It would be impractical and unhelpful to think only in theoretical terms. The theory and the doctrine are, for all of us, embodied and experienced in actual historical church institutions and structures. Some main models we meet in Britain are:

1. *Jurisdictional catholicity*. The Roman Catholic Church sees itself as having world-wide authority over all Christians who are called to submit to its jurisdiction.

2. *Unprincipled comprehensiveness*. Those who are theologically liberal in various churches urge that all Christians should be in a united church, but often give the impression that matters of belief and behaviour are of little significance and that unity is all.

3. *Principled comprehensiveness (catholicity)*. The Reformed Anglican and Presbyterian Church of Scotland position is that, in principle, all true Christians in each locality constitute the church in that place. I am arguing that this is the biblical doctrine.

4. *Separatism*. Various groups of Christians have, over the years, separated (or seceded, or felt themselves expelled) from the parent body. The issue might be a matter of doctrine, church order or leadership. Some denominations that were separatist in origin (e.g. Baptists, Methodists) are now, in varying degrees, comprehensive. Separatist churches today include the Brethren, the Pentecostals and the Independent Evangelical churches. The most recent 'separatist' development has been the formation of the house churches or restorationist groups, the 'new churches'. Many of them believe that God is 'restoring his kingdom' in this generation, and that because all other churches are unspiritual, the restoration is to be accomplished only in and through these new charismatic groups. While they must be in the 'separatist' model, many of them are linked to strongly organized and authoritarian hierarchies.[1] The present debate is about the third and fourth models.

Evangelical problems with ecclesiology

Many evangelicals have been unbiblical about the nature and unity of the church because of their individualism and subjectivism. In reacting to the authority of the Pope or the Catholic Church they have elevated other 'popes' or traditions to authority. In reacting to rationalist or liberal biblical criticism, some have assented to uninformed patterns of biblical interpretation. Evangelicals have often so emphasized the word and its ministry that they have failed to see the emphasis in that word on the sacraments of baptism and the Lord's Supper.

Too often evangelicals have understood church membership as a voluntary and optional sequel to a personal, individual and subjective experience of conversion to Christ, salvation from sin and renewal through the Spirit. Too often evangelicals have shopped around for a church that suits them, left one church to join another that suits them better, or shared in starting new churches where other Christian churches already exist. There is no biblical justification for this sort of behaviour. It is a far cry from the teaching or practice in the New Testament. So what does the Bible teach?

The biblical doctrine of the church

The biblical question is not who is Church of England or Baptist or whatever, but 'who is a follower of Christ?' The New Testament letters and the Acts of the Apostles indicate without a shadow of doubt that all who were followers of Christ were 'the church' in that place. There is no evidence for any approval of parallel or competing churches in a locality.

There are in the New Testament numerous ways of describing those who follow Jesus Christ. They are the people of God, the baptized in Christ, believers, those who live by the Spirit – and they are God's church. Entry into the church is by conversion, that is, by turning away from sin and unbelief and turning to Christ in trustful submission. God's gift of cleansing, new life in Christ, the Holy Spirit and membership of his church, is signified in baptism. In the New Testament, we see, in principle:

> the believers = the baptized = the church

In the earliest days entry to the church seems to have been simple and immediate. Large crowds were baptized immediately after Peter's sermon on the day of Pentecost when the Spirit came. The Ethiopian government minister and the jailer at Philippi were baptized immediately after they declared belief. No-one really denies that those who professed the faith of Christ were regarded as the church.

There has been a difference of opinion over the place of children in the church. There are Christians who believe that it is God's intention and the biblical pattern for the children in a Christian family to grow up in Christ, to grow up turning away from sin and unbelief and turning to the Lord Jesus Christ. These children need never know a time without the forgiveness of Christ and the new life of the Spirit. Thus, they are baptized and grow up in God's people, his church. Other Christians cannot accept this and argue that one can only be a Christian and member of the church after a personal and credible profession of faith. The age at which such a profession is considered possible and credible is much debated.[2]

However, leaving the issue of believers' or believing children on one side, the New Testament writers clearly and constantly affirm the unity of God's church. This assertion of ecclesiology is no secondary matter for it is linked indissolubly with our understanding of Christ himself, salvation and the Holy Spirit. There is only one Christ, new life is only in him, so all Christians are one in Christ. Again, only Jesus died for our sins on the cross; freedom from the guilt and power of sin is only through that crucified and risen Saviour, so all Christians are united in his death and resurrection. Again, the new life of Jesus is experienced through the Holy Spirit. There is one Spirit of God, so all those who are a new creation in Christ are baptized by one Spirit into the one people of God. Just as God is one, so his people, his church, are one. All this is argued or implied repeatedly, but see especially 1 Corinthians 1 and John 17.

131

In 1 Corinthians 12 Paul argues at length that just as the human body has many parts but is essentially a single entity, so in Christ there are many parts with varying gifts and character, but they are essentially members of the one body of Christ. While recognizing the diversity within the body he goes on, in the following chapter, to underline the supreme role of mutual love. This love will be patient with others and kind. It always protects, trusts, hopes and perseveres. This love never fails. This is the love which in Christ is the common life-blood of the church.

The Nicene Creed reflects this biblical doctrine by describing the church as 'one' and 'catholic' (i.e. with the whole faith and for the whole world). But it asserts the church is also holy (belonging to God alone) and apostolic (dependent on the teaching of Jesus' apostles). Those who have separated to form new churches have often justified their actions on the grounds that the church they have left was not properly concerned for holiness or apostolic truth or (to put it another way) was careless about moral or doctrinal error. The charge is serious, and I wish to assert and agree the biblical emphasis on the truth.

The importance of truth

Firstly, it cannot be asserted too plainly or firmly that the Christian faith is a matter of divine *revelation* and not of human speculation or discovery. Paul made it clear that the world's wisdom cannot know God. Only the Spirit of God reveals God's good news and enables us to understand what God freely gives (1 Cor. 1 – 2). The followers of Jesus 'were included in Christ' when they 'heard the word of truth', the good news of salvation (Eph. 1:13). Jesus is God's supreme revelation, his Word, the light of the word, full of truth. The Holy Spirit is called the spirit of truth. His work is not accepted or recognized by the world which is opposed to God.

Secondly, the truth is vital for Christian *formation* and *growth*. Jesus said that the way of discipleship was to follow his teaching. 'Then you will know the truth, and

132

the truth will set you free' (Jn. 8:32). God's gift of church leaders is so that the body of Christ may be built up towards unity in the faith and maturity in Christ. Then 'speaking the truth in love, we will in all things grow up into him who is the Head, that is, Christ' (Eph. 4:15).

Thirdly, Jesus and the apostles demonstrated their concern for the truth by regularly *arguing against false teaching*. Jesus was by no means 'meek and mild' when it came to ideas that would mislead others about God and his salvation. In his book *Christ the Controversialist*, John Stott expounds the important arguments Jesus engaged in particularly with the Pharisees and Sadducees.[3] Paul engaged in fierce controversy with false teaching in several of his letters, *e.g.* Galations and Colossians.

This leads on to a fuller consideration of such controversy.

The biblical response to false teaching

Firstly, the apostles repeatedly emphasized the importance of standing firm in the truth and holding fast to the gospel tradition. Timothy was urged to guard the truth. The early Christians were warned not to be led astray by strange teaching.[4]

Secondly, the ministry and gift of teaching is very important. The truth is to be preached and taught faithfully, constantly. The gift of prophecy (building others up through the word of God) is of supreme significance, and church leaders should be 'able to teach'. The selection, training and encouragement of new generations of Christian teachers is of great importance – see 2 Timothy 2:2.

Thirdly, just as Jesus himself and Paul the apostle engaged in controversy against false teaching, so church leaders are commanded to fulfil this duty and ministry. They are not only to encourage others with sound doctrine but also to refute those who oppose it (Tit. 1:9). They must watch out for deceivers who do not continue in the teaching of Christ, and contend for the faith (2 Jn. 7–11; Jude 3). Freedom of religion and worship is much to be desired. Witch-hunts, inquisition and religious persecution are to be deplored. Nevertheless, the church's teachers are called to teach God's truth, and to protect Christ's flock from wolves who will bring confusion and destruction.

Fourthly, the New Testament talks about various disciplinary measures aimed at bringing to a better mind those in moral and doctrinal error. These begin with private correction and warning, and may move on to involve other church leaders to establish the case. If unresolved, the controversy may become public, and if there is continuing impenitence and obdurate immorality or heresy, the offender must not be welcomed to Holy Communion or allowed to exercise official Christian ministry. The final step is to declare that such teaching or behaviour is anathema, under the judgment of God.[5]

Any form of church discipline is a difficult and dangerous matter. It must be understood and carried through in the light of other biblical injunctions. Christian leaders are to be humble, gentle and patient, making 'every effort to keep the unity of the Spirit through the bond of peace'. There is one body and one Spirit (Eph. 4:2–6). Paul says that this is a work of restoring gently and is to be done spiritually and with careful self-examination (Gal. 6:1–2). The process of discipline is gradual, patient and loving (Mt. 18:15–17).

It is to be clearly noted that nowhere in the New Testament, by teaching or precedent, are Christians called to leave a church and separate themselves from other Christians. Where separation occurs, either the offenders leave of their own accord (1 Jn. 2:19) or they are excluded by the church's action. The verse that is popularly used to justify 'separation' to a 'purer' church is 2 Corinthians 6:17, '"Therefore come out from them and be separate," says the Lord. "Touch no unclean thing, and I will receive you."' However, a look at the context shows that Paul is not talking about separating from other Christians over immorality or false teaching, he is talking about intimate relationships with non-Christians. The Christian is called to make a decisive break with the old way of life now he or she is 'in Christ'.

Christians must be most wary of appeals to form another 'pure' church, in the light of God's faithfulness towards and patience with Israel in Old Testament times. In spite of much error and disobedience there were always faithful people and there were times of real spiritual revival. Note too, that although in the church at Corinth there were such terrible problems of division, immorality and doctrinal disorder over the resurrection and spiritual gifts, Paul nevertheless addressed them as God's church, sanctified in Christ Jesus and called to be holy. He even thanked God for the many good things God's grace had achieved among them (1 Cor. 1:1–9). There was serious doctrinal and moral disorder in the churches of Galatia, Colosse and Philippi and among the churches of Asia Minor addressed in Revelation 2 and 3. The apostles urged reform and correction in the strongest terms, but never advised Christians to separate into new churches. The biblical pattern of response is quite clear and most important, but, in addition, there are other considerations.

Other factors to bear in mind

Firstly, a distinction must be drawn between churches that formally adopt or approve serious error, and churches which contain individuals who believe or espouse such error. The major Protestant churches have Confessions of Faith, doctrinal bases and sometimes liturgies which clearly state or imply the supreme authority of the Scriptures and the fundamental doctrines of Christianity. For example, the Church of England in its thirty-nine Articles includes one which speaks 'Of the sufficiency of the Holy Scriptures for salvation'. It says:

> Holy Scripture containeth all things necessary to salvation: so that whatsoever is not read therein, nor may be proved thereby, is not to be required of any man, that it should be believed as an article of the faith, or be thought requisite or necessary to salvation.

135

The Roman Catholic Church is in a different situation because it has officially decreed that tradition is to be received with equal veneration to the Sciptures. It has, moreover, decreed that doctrines about the infallibility of the Pope and the immaculate conception and bodily assumption of the Virgin Mary are essential matters of faith.

Secondly, a distinction must be drawn between questions asked and denials asserted. Thoughtful Christians will ask searching questions about complex doctrines such as the mysteries of the Trinity, Christology, providence and the atonement. Theologians will explore and enquire, wishing to integrate Christian doctrine with other areas of knowledge and experience, and to restate Christian truth in the light of each new generation's questions. This is an entirely proper ministry, and in the New Testament itself Paul restates the faith in fresh ways in the light of new challenges and situations (e.g. the Christology in Colossians).

Of course, this task is difficult and dangerous, and throughout the centuries theologians have, on occasions, moved beyond contemporary restatement to reconstruction which, in effect, seems to deny essentials of the faith. There must be constant doctrinal discipline and vigilance. However, the questioning must go on. Is the philosophical category of 'substance' (Nicene Creed) meaningful today? What does the idea of 'two natures without confusion' in the person of Christ (Definition of Chalcedon) say about the reality of human life in the incarnation? To what extent do cultural factors play a part in the different kinds of imagery used to describe the atonement?

Many Christians and churches have been hostile to scientific discoveries and theories in cosmology (e.g. the earth not being the centre of the universe) and biology (e.g. the theory of evolution). Many have been opposed to the research of biblical criticism, enquiring how the books of the Bible came to be written. The issues are not simple. Legitimate research and questioning must be distinguished from presuppositions of a rationalist or humanist type, which, for example, deny the possibility of the miraculous or of divine providence.

Thirdly, there must be an awareness of theological inconsistency or confusion. Many Christians are evangelical in their love of Christ, Bible and gospel, but they shy away from the label 'evangelical' because they feel it involves an anti-intellectual stance towards science and biblical study, or an emotional and individualist view of evangelism, or an inadequate appreciation of church, sacraments, symbol, and the like. Labels mean different things in different situations, and theological categories are slippery matters at the best of times.

The understanding of baptism and communion not only separated Catholic and Protestant, but have also caused several divisions amongst Protestants from the sixteenth century onwards. There have been evangelical Calvinists and Arminians (differing on fundamental issues of grace and faith) as well as evangelical episcopalians, presbyterians and independents (differing on issues of church order). The biblical doctrine of Christian love and unity in the one body of Christ requires far greater attempts at mutual understanding, clarification and dialogue than have frequently been the case between different Christian groups.

In order to consider the situation today we need to keep in mind the biblical doctrine of the church as all the Christians in each place, the biblical approach to false teaching and other significant factors, such as an awareness of theological confusion or inconsistency.

The situation today

Christians today inherit a situation in most towns and cities of several Christian churches more or less co-operating or competing. Some make fairly exclusive claims about the faith, and in varying degrees either ignore or seek to absorb other believers, e.g. the Roman Catholic Church (though this has changed somewhat since the second Vatican Council), the Exclusive Brethren, and some independent and restorationist groups. Other churches acknowledge the brokenness of the visible church of Christ and, with varying degrees of enthusiasm, seek to develop mutual recognition and communion and work towards unity.

The reasons for the emergence of conflicting Christian groups and denominations are exceedingly diverse and often complex. Doctrine, church order, style of worship, personalities of leaders and attitudes to mission have all played their parts. The original reasons are sometimes no longer significant, but different traditions and buildings (and hymn books) exercise a very strong grip. In the last thirty years there have been conflicting developments in Britain. The ecumenical movement has not made much headway in union schemes but has achieved notable progress in mutual goodwill among many churches. The Evangelical Alliance represents an ever-growing number of evangelical churches and bodies in the major denominations and independent groupings.

At the same time, some evangelicals have become more aggressively separatist. They have called on all evangelicals to leave their denominations and form a new association of churches.[6] Some have broken fellowship with the Evangelical Alliance and a few with interdenominational agencies like the Scripture Union, the Universities and Colleges Christian Fellowship and other evangelical missionary societies. There are even some who have refused fellowship with any evangelicals who are involved with the wider ecumenical movement, who do not denounce the theory of evolution, who see any role for the techniques of biblical criticism or who have found blessing in the charismatic movement. There is much debate about such second-degree separation. A spirit of separatism can breed constant division. It happened with Baptists (since the sixteenth century), independent Puritans (seventeenth century), Methodists (eighteenth century), Brethren (nineteenth century), Pentecostals (early twentieth century) and with the restorationist house churches today.

I cannot see that such separatism is either biblical, necessary or right. Evangelicals are stronger (for example) in the Church of England now than for many generations.[7]

There is certainly much doctrinal and moral confusion in that church, as there is in other churches. However, there is a deepening concern for a truly biblical understanding of the church. Many evangelicals (and others) believe strongly in the importance of revealed truth and work hard at teaching truth and refuting error. Thoughtful and biblical responses to current theological and moral issues have been produced by many individuals and agencies, notably the Church of England Evangelical Council and Dr John Stott.[8]

With regard to disciplinary measures, much has been achieved at parish and diocesan levels (often quietly) and in the General Synod and its boards. Bishops do secure or require resignations of misbehaving clergy, but Ecclesiastical Court procedures are difficult and can be counterproductive. In spite of many difficulties, considerable effort is being expended and progress made. There is certainly much more to be done, by God's grace, in the quest for greater doctrinal purity and unity.

In conclusion

We must take the biblical doctrines of the church with great seriousness – the church is to be one, holy, catholic and apostolic. We must not allow temperament, tradition or experience to render insignificant the fact that there is one body of Christ. When we go back to the Bible, we go back to the one church, and (because of whose body it is) we go back to the one Saviour and Lord in whom 'the whole building is joined together and rises to become a holy temple in the Lord' and in whom we 'are being built together to become a dwelling in which God lives by his Spirit' (Eph. 2:21–22). Amen!

Response to
Gordon W. Kuhrt

Graham Harrison

It is very tempting to one who is a nonconformist and a
Baptist to strain at a number of the gnats that swarm in
Gordon Kuhrt's presentation of his case. However, I shall
resist the temptation and instead draw attention to the
more prominent of the camels while endeavouring not to
swallow them!

Our disagreement, I suspect, centres around a few vital
issues such as the nature of a valid profession of
Christianity and whether or not we are entitled to make
the straight leap, that his argument seems to require, from
the ecclesiology of the New Testament to the current
church scene. Can it seriously be maintained that today:

the believers = the baptized = the church?

The equivalence that such an equation suggests is too
strict. And certainly today, and possibly in the New Testament period, the equation would be better represented by:

the believers < the baptized > the church.

Leaving aside the rightness of infant baptism, even
when administered in the context of a thought-out covenant theology, and with due discipline, it is straining cred-

140

ulity to describe the 'baptized' of today as the 'church' and
to suppose that in so doing you are speaking the same
language as the church of the New Testament era. The
presumptive evidence then was that the person being
baptized was a Christian, that is to say that he or she had
been born again by the operation of the Spirit of God and
had turned to Christ in repentance and faith. The fact of
the matter today is that often baptism has developed into a
social custom that in reality makes no subjective affirmation of the faith of the person involved. One may therefore be forgiven for wondering how appropriate it is to
attribute to the contemporary scene assumptions that
could be made two thousand years ago.

Secondly there is the matter of what Gordon refers to as
'principled comprehensiveness' – his preferred option. To
me, such comprehensiveness seems remarkably unprincipled, in that, in practice, it would appear to tolerate the
widest extremes of heterodoxy, as I shall endeavour to
explain. Now, in several respects, his response to false
teaching is admirable, in that he warns against prejudice,
party spirit, self-righteousness, precipitate action, and the
many other sins to which those who have been zealous for
the truth have sometimes succumbed. Such warnings are
always relevant, particularly in the light of the long-
suffering and patience of our God, and in view of the fact
that often Christians have failed lamentably in these areas.
However, I come away from his protestations wondering
just when, and in what circumstances, he would advocate
and implement the discipline of exclusion from office and
fellowship of church members who were set in their heretical views. The acid test is this: Can he name one
recalcitrant advocate of heresy who has come under the
discipline of his church – the Church of England? It is a
notorious fact that such men exist there. They are highly
intelligent, articulate and conscientious. But they have
held, and in some cases still hold, high office in the
Ecclesia Anglicana. By all means let patience, love,
humility, kindess and all the other necessary virtues be
fully exercised. Let planks be removed from one's own
eye before one starts remonstrating over specks of dust in

the eyes of others. But in the end I remain totally unconvinced that the position Gordon argues would do anything other than result in a process of politely agreeing to
differ. And in this the apostolic precept and practice is
quite other. I find great difficulty in understanding how
members of a church holding mutually contradictory
views of the gospel can nevertheless describe each other
by the same term 'Christian'.

A similar confusion seems to exist regarding the doctrine of the church, and the assumptions that Gordon
makes about the 'separatist' position. (Unfortunately the
vocabulary is loaded with innuendo. Its use, however, can
hardly be avoided in the on-going debate!) No 'separatists'
of my acquaintance affirm categorically that they belong
to a 'pure' church now, or that they have reasonable hope
of doing so in this world. They know their New Testaments too well, and have too realistic an assessment of the
deceitfulness of the human heart to fall into that rather
simplistic error. It is a pity, therefore, that Gordon repeats
the old canard that 'Christians must be wary of appeals to
form another "pure" church ...' Who makes such
appeals? No separatist known to me – certainly that was
not what the late Dr Martyn Lloyd-Jones was calling for.
What some would regard as the high-water mark of Puritan ecclesiology, the Westminster Confession, affirms that
'The purest churches under heaven are subject both to
mixture and error ...'[1] Significantly the statement is
adopted verbatim by the independents[2] and the Baptists[3],
both of whom figure largely as villains in Gordon's potted
version of post-Reformation English church history! The
parallel with the sanctification of the Christian is exact.
We are to aim at that which we know we shall not achieve
here upon earth, namely perfection. It follows, therefore,
that one does look for a *credible* profession of faith from
those who wish to join themselves to the church, and also
that one does seek to exclude those who lack such evidence. The corollary is that those who deny the faith can
scarcely be held to maintain a credible profession of that
faith – that is unless words have ceased to function as
communicators of meaning. In brief, the 'pure church'

syndrome is an Aunt Sally that is not on the so-called separatists' ecclesiastical agenda this side of glory – and, what is more, it never has been.

Evangelical separation

Graham Harrison

What is the gospel? ● What is the church? ● An
evangelical response ● Toleration of error ● One
gospel or many? ● The pluralist church ● When
the crunch comes

When the late Dr Martyn Lloyd-Jones made his celebrated,
or some would say notorious 1966 'call' to evangelicals in
the denominations to come out and come together in a
united evangelical fellowship of churches, he put the
issue of secession firmly on the ecclesiastical agenda.[1] For
a large part of the evangelical constituency it was equally
firmly removed from that agenda by the pronouncements
less than six months later of the Keele Congress.[2] Mis-
understandings soon abounded, motives were queried,
positions were ridiculed and sometimes misrepresented,
with the result that today there is the danger of the reasons
that prompted the call being either ignored as historically
irrelevant a quarter of a century on, or dismissed as biblically misconceived.

'Separatism' – as it tends derisively and inaccurately to
be called – is therefore discounted by a large part of
evangelicalism as both non-viable and theologically
flawed as a solution to any of the problems presently
confronting the churches.

As a position, separatism is easily pilloried. Take, for example, Sir Norman Anderson's passing anecdotal reference:

> I always remember a story I once heard about a church which went by the name of 'The Church of God'. Before very long there was a split in its membership about some matter of doctrine or practice and the splinter group called itself 'The True Church of God'. Once again there was a difference of opinion, and the seceders then chose the title 'The Only True Church of God'. So where can anyone go from there?[3]

To which I suppose one might answer, 'Back to the Church of Rome' – for that would seem to be the inevitable logic behind the telling of the story. And yet such a conclusion would be one at which one presumes the raconteur would rightly demur!

What then can be the reasons that give grounds for asserting that Christian people ought to come together in a fellowship of churches which not only avow the fundamental elements of the Christian faith in an unequivocal and unambiguous way, but which also seek to mark themselves off from those who, albeit conscientiously, cannot make such an avowal?

On the face of it, a certain plausibility attaches to the argument usually advanced against the separatist position, namely that Scripture and history are against it. The Revd John Stott, the chairman of the meeting at which Dr Lloyd-Jones had been invited to declare in public the views that he had already put in private to the Commission of the Evangelical Alliance, declared at the close of the Doctor's address, 'I believe that history is against Dr Lloyd-Jones in that others have tried to do this very thing. I believe that Scripture is against him in that the remnant was within the church and not outside it.'[4]

Let it be clearly stated that it is no light matter thus to separate oneself from those who also lay claim to the title

'Christian' and whose churches likewise make that claim. At the time of the Reformation nobody expressed this more clearly and forcefully than John Calvin:

> For the Lord esteems the communion of his church so highly that he counts as a traitor and apostate from Christianity anyone who arrogantly leaves any Christian society, provided it cherishes the true ministry of Word and sacraments . . . From this it follows that separation from the church is the denial of God and of Christ.[5]

So there need to be substantial reasons if the case for separation is to have any validity. There are. Basically they are presumed in the answer to two preliminary but fundamental questions: What is the gospel to which the church is committed? and, What is the nature of the church as defined by that gospel? These carry the corollary: In what sense, if at all, is it legitimate for a church to exist in denominational fellowship with other churches whose understanding of and commitment to that gospel is radically different from theirs? In other words, can the comprehensivist view of the church be considered in any sense legitimate biblically?

What is the gospel?

All evangelicals would surely agree that the church is founded on the gospel, and has as its duty and privilege the responsibility of proclaiming that gospel to the world. At the heart of the gospel is a complex of historical truths that insist that the Christian faith is rooted in God's intervention in the world that he has made. These truths include the incarnation of the Son of God by means of his virginal conception, his sinless life and substitutionary atoning death for sinners, and the miracles that he performed which were, amongst other things, signs authenticating his claims. The greatest sign of all was his bodily resurrection, and this was neither a ghostly apparition nor a psychological state of mind produced in his shell-shocked disciples by their collective wishful thinking. It was on facts such as these that the gospel was based and then announced to men in order that they might cast themselves in humble repentant trust on the one who had accomplished all this for them. The resulting faith in him constituted the instrumental means by which the benefits of Christ's saving work was to be appropriated by sinners and in the sight of a holy God these same sinners were justified or reckoned righteous. All this and more is, of course, contained in the Holy Scriptures, a God-given and inspired collection of writings under whose authority the church is to place herself, and by whose teaching alone she is to regulate her beliefs.

Convictions such as these were once the inheritance held in common by the major Protestant churches of the land, as even a cursory reference to their formularies and confessions will reveal. They are in fact the very foundation principles of Christianity and thus of the Christian church.

However, the truth is that many of these facts and principles have been increasingly called into question in recent years. The most persistent challenge to Christian orthodoxy has come not from without but from within the ostensible boundaries of the church. It would not be difficult to illustrate how each of these fundamental tenets of Christian belief have been not simply questioned but repudiated. Furthermore, those who have been to the fore in mounting that challenge have not been in obscure positions on the periphery of its councils, but often they have been men with responsibilities of leadership and of teaching within the church. Nor has the malaise been confined to one denomination. It is virtually endemic throughout all the major denominations in Britain. The result has been that those whose beliefs correspond most nearly to the founding principles of these various denominations – the evangelicals – have found themselves to be in a minority, and have had to contend not before the world but within 'the church' for the faith once delivered to the saints. The situation has, with but minor variations, been repeated

147

amongst the Anglicans, Baptists, Congregationalists, Methodists and Presbyterians.

Thus instead of advancing into the world's hostile territory shoulder to shoulder with those who are united both in their diagnosis of that world's need and in their prescription for its remedy, evangelicals have had to pause to fight for the truth with those who in theory are their allies. If that which calls itself the church is thus confused as to the very message that it is to carry to the world, its testimony far from lightening the darkness will but increase the prevailing gloom.

What is the church?

At this point perhaps it is necessary to make some comments regarding the nature of the New Testament church. When Stephen called Israel the *ekklēsia* in the wilderness (Acts 7:38) and Paul described the church as 'the Israel of God' (Gal. 6:16) continuity was clearly established between the Old and New Testament communities of faith. Continuity, however, does not mean the same thing as identity in the sense of one-to-one equivalence. Perhaps no factor illustrates this more clearly than the way in which the church of the New Testament allowed no distinctions of a racial or familial sort to intrude into the fellowship of the people of God. At this point the differentiation of the two communities is most marked. In the very concept of a national Israel such distinctions were inherent, whereas in the transcultural, supra-national church that was to emerge in the period following Pentecost they had ceased to be valid. They were in fact anathema.

Thus the church of the New Testament was regarded as a church of believers, a church of saints, corresponding to the Israel within Israel of which Paul speaks in Romans 9:6. No longer was mere physical membership of the chosen people sufficient grounds for recognition that one belonged to the visible community of the redeemed. What had been present typologically and prophetically in the Old Testament community had become by dint of historical necessity a reality in the New Testament church. Just as in a physical sense Israel had been a separated nation distinct from the pagan nations around it, so now the church was a separated community and such as wished to join it had to 'go forth therefore unto him without the camp, bearing his reproach' (Heb. 13:13, AV).

To that separated community were entrusted the Scriptures. The foundation on which the community was built was Christ and the edifice that he was raising on that foundation was to be structured and ordered by those Scriptures.

Joining such a gathered community could never have been easy. Social advancement was likely to be brought to a speedy halt by membership of this discrete body. Before long, persecution would be the rule rather than the exception for those who joined, whether the convert was racially Jew or Gentile.

In other words, identification with this emerging ecclesiastical body brought no perks, resulted in no social esteem and conveyed the very opposite of material privilege upon those who sought it. Given such a scenario, it might seem surprising that there were any hypocrites at all among these emerging churches of the New Testament period. That there were some, however, is clear from the evidence of the book of Acts and the letters of the New Testament. But they were very much the exceptions rather than the rule, for here was a community that you did not join because your family belonged and had always belonged. Nor was it a body that drew to itself all right thinking people with a concern for moral rectitude and a basic God-awareness. Perhaps more literally than you realized you were taking your life into your hands when you joined such a church.

All this needs to be said by way of preamble, if only to help us understand that when the apostles addressed the people who made up these New Testament churches as 'saints', they were not mouthing pious platitudes that bore resemblance to reality only in a minority of cases, but were giving realistic and accurate spiritual descriptions of the generality of church members. As Robert Haldane put it:

He ... addressed them all as saints, making no exception. It is to such exclusively that the apostolic Epistles are written, whether as churches or individuals – as being all united to Christ, children of God, heirs of God, and joint heirs with Jesus Christ. In the first churches, in which everything was regulated by the Apostles according to the will of God, there may have been hypocrites or self-deceivers; but as far as man could judge, they were all believers; or if any among them appeared not to be such, the churches were told it was to their shame. If any were discovered who had crept in unawares, or were convicted of unbecoming conduct, or who had a form of godliness but denied its power, from such they were commanded to turn away. They were not to be unequally yoked together with unbelievers; wherefore it is said, 'Come out from among them, and be ye separate.' It was in the confidence that they obeyed such commands, that the Apostles addressed them all ... as the children of God ... In these Epistles we find no exhortations to unbelievers. This ought to be particularly observed, as being a key to them, without which they cannot be understood.[6]

It does not follow, therefore, in the present day that whatever calls itself a church of necessity deserves that title and ought in consequence to be regarded as such. In fact, it is at least arguable that many if not most of the institutions that lay claim to the name do so on questionable premises. The phraseology may sound a little quaint to some modern ears but perhaps the Westminster Divines had it right when they said that, 'some have so degenerated as to become no churches of Christ, but synagogues of Satan'.[7] Or as Calvin, writing almost a century earlier, had put it:

For me it is enough that it behooved us to withdraw from them that we might come to

Christ ... If those were churches, then the
church is not the pillar of the truth [1. Tim.
3:15], but the prop of falsehood; not the Taber-
nacle of the living God, but a receptacle of idols
... In the same way if anyone recognizes the
present congregations – contaminated with
idolatry, superstition, and ungodly doctrine – as
churches (in full communion of which a Christian man must stand – even to the point of
agreeing in doctrine), he will gravely err.[8]

In other words, both faithfulness to the gospel and credibility
before an unbelieving world can demand that separation
becomes the painful but necessary duty of churches when
faced with a situation such as that which prevails today.

It would be irresponsible, however, to put it no more
strongly, to advocate such drastic action without first considering various lesser remedies that have been proposed.
There is, after all, a regrettable streak of self-righteousness
and the attendant spirit of Pharisaism in us all. It can be
simpler to make a grand exit accompanied by suitable
rhetoric than to address oneself to the realities of a situation that, while desperate, is yet retrievable.

An evangelical response

The question arises, therefore, given that there is something very deficient about the current situation: What is the
responsible manner in which evangelical churches are to
respond to it? To which the initial answer must surely be –
that one aims at reformation within the limits of the visible
church. The removal of misconceptions, instruction,
debate, persuasion will all play their part in this process. It
is a responsibility fraught with risk, but one that must not
be shirked. It is, moreover, one that many of us who now
strongly advocate the 'separatist' position have engaged in,
imperfectly it might have been, but sincerely, conscientiously and we hope in an attitude of love towards those
whom we were attempting to convince.

When that policy has been pursued and one has been faced with a residuum of conscientiously held differences over certain quite basic issues, what then? It is at this point that church discipline becomes a factor in the situation. In one sense, of course, it has been at the heart of the previous stage in the proceedings. The discipline of the word of God will have been involved as one has sought to bring its teaching to bear upon those whose views have been in contention. But when this apparently has failed to have its desired effect, discipline of a more recognizable form is required.

What we have been attempting to describe has been the *de facto* situation in all the major denominations for many years. Hence the problem, which should be an acute one for anyone seeking to order their church as well as their personal life by the Scriptures. How is it possible to maintain a pretence of fellowship with those whose departures from the faith are not minor and inconsequential but integral to the very nature of the religion one professes?

The matter becomes a crunch issue at the level of those who hold a teaching office in the church – in other words, those who are in the church's recognized ministry and those who are involved in the training and preparation of men for the ministry. Can heterodoxy be tolerated at this level?

The answer of the New Testament to this question would seem to be an unequivocal 'No!' Indeed, such is the forthrightness with which the apostles expressed themselves in this area that some might think there to be almost an element of intemperance in the language employed by them to describe, denounce and disown these teachers of error. For example, Paul is quite explicit as to the attitude to be taken by the church towards such people: 'Now I beseech you, brethren, mark them which cause divisions and offences contrary to the doctrine which ye have learned; and avoid them.' He is not exactly complimentary either about their motives or the results of their activities, 'for', he continues, 'they that are such serve not our Lord Jesus Christ, but their own belly; and by good words and fair speeches deceive the hearts of the simple' (Rom. 16:17–18, AV.) The true apostle recognized that there were 'false apostles, deceitful workers, transforming themselves into the apostles of Christ' (2 Cor. 11:13, AV). Nor was he averse to calling down the malediction of God upon those that troubled the churches and perverted the gospel of Christ (Gal. 1:8–9). Titus 1:9–14 makes it abundantly clear that it is the responsibility of the spiritual leaders of the churches both to hold fast the faithful word and to convince the gainsayers, as well as to stop the mouths of the unruly and vain talkers. John and Jude are equally explicit about the duties incumbent upon the churches to maintain the truth by contending for the faith and refusing to extend fellowship to those whose teaching constitutes a denial of the faith (2 Jn. 7–11; Jude 3–4).

It is quite evident that what is not envisaged as an appropriate response to such men is the toleration of their error as a legitimate option within the church and continuing permission for such men to promulgate their teaching under the auspices of the church. The reasons for this are obvious. Too much is at stake – the destiny and eternal welfare of men and women. What a person believes is of crucial importance and therefore what he or she is taught is not a matter of indifference but has to be regulated by the truth.

Toleration of error

That brings us to the present-day absence of discipline in the case of open and notorious error in doctrines that are at the very heart of the Christian message by those who are intelligent and well read enough to know what they are affirming or denying as the case may be.

Take the instance of the Baptist Union Assembly of 1971 when, in a keynote platform address, the Principal of one of that denomination's theological colleges, Michael Taylor, denied the deity of the Lord Jesus Christ. When protests were made, the then General Secretary, David Russell, affirmed that he had been driven back to his New Testament to see whether these things were so. But calls for the disciplining of the Principal and his removal from the office of preparing men for the ministry fell on deaf ears. Instead, the Council of the Union and later its Assembly reaffirmed positively its acceptance of the Union's Declaration of Principle and refused to do anything about a man who had flagrantly denied it.[9]

Or, to vary the denominational scene, consider the Bishop of Durham, David Jenkins, to whom each recurring festival of the Christian year seems to provoke a media-induced opportunity for denying one or other of the historical facts constitutive of the gospel. The man is no fool. Nor is he in some sort of a mental fog about what he believes. Rather, backed so it seems by his provincial Archbishop, John Habgood, he continues to enunciate his disbelief in the literalness of these fundamental truths as they have been historically perceived and taught in the church from the era of the New Testament down to the present day. And nothing is done about his pronouncements.

It is true that, back in 1978, the Church of England Evangelical Council produced a statement which, among other things, said: 'In the last resort (i) if a central Christian doctrine is at stake, (ii) if the clergyman concerned is not just questioning but denying it, (iii) if he is not just passing through a temporary period of uncertainty but has reached a settled conviction, and (iv) if he refuses to resign, then we believe the bishop ... should seriously consider withdrawing his licence or permission to teach in the church.'[10] The statement hardly smacks of bigotry, nor could it be construed as being likely to produce precipitate action. Indeed, judged by its tone and the advice it offers to the episcopate one might be pardoned for thinking that the writer of Galatians went more than a bit over the top both in what he said and how he said it! *Sed quis custodiet ipsos Custodes?* (Who watches over the custodian?) we might ask.

To highlight two such prominent examples is simply to illustrate and identify what anyone who has been involved in the life and work of the major denominations knows full well runs through each of them. What then is to be done about such defections from the truth? Theological debate, discussion, dialogue – call it what you will – by all means. Let misunderstanding and misrepresentations from whichever side they appear be stripped away. But when all this has been done – and in fairness it should be acknowledged that sincere attempts have been made at it by men not animated by hatred, prejudice and narrow mindedness – and there still remain basic differences concerning the centralities of the faith, what is the next step?

Now at this point it is important to distinguish between some different attitudes that have emerged in answer to that question. Pre-Keele evangelical Anglicanism, along with the evangelical minorities parallel with it in the Free Churches, was generally perceived to reason thus: The church/denomination belongs to us. We are the ones who stand basically where our forefathers stood. The formularies of the church essentially are evangelical. They certainly do not countenance a comprehensivist view that gives all and sundry the right to shelter under the ecclesiastical umbrella. For the time being we evangelicals are in the minority and we have to accommodate ourselves to things that are undesirable, even wrong. But when things improve, and with the blessing of God we are in the majority, with the result that the power structures of the church are under our control, things will be different. When attempts at reclamation fail, responsible discipline will be exercised. Not only will heresy be repudiated, but those who purvey it will have to do so outside the boundaries of the church. In that way the true faith will be identified, confusion avoided and the church will be able to get on with its God-given task of winning a lost world for Christ. No longer will there be public confusion as to what is the faith of the church. Nor will the festivals of Christmas and Easter be the occasion for high-ranking clerics to profess their disbelief in the historical facts on which Christianity itself is based. Indeed such men who prove to be inveterate and incorrigible in their heterodoxy will no longer be allowed to hold pastoral office in the church.

That was a position once widely held among many 'old style' evangelicals of various denominational affiliations. It was a position that had a measure of intellectual coherence about it even if one may have doubted whether it was a practically viable option with any realistic hope of success. Few, it would seem, advocate it today. Following the lead given by the Keele Congress, and reiterated ten years later at Nottingham,[11] a wider working party representative of many Anglicans, Methodists, United Reformed and Baptists, under the chairmanship of the then Secretary of the Evangelical Alliance, expounded essentially the same line.[12]

The older view seems to have been overtaken by one that apparently would allow what those evangelicals of a former generation would never have countenanced: namely, that the church/denomination is *permixtus* in the sense that traditions other than evangelicalism belong in that body alongside our own. Naturally it is assumed that the truest and most biblically authentic variety of denominational belief is that generally circumscribed by the parameters of evangelicalism. But, it is emphasized, one has to be careful not to unchurch other traditions. An illuminating example of this occurred at the time of the proposed Anglican-Methodist merger. Writing in *The Church of England Newspaper*, Dr Hugh Gough, one time Bishop of Barking, and later Archbishop of Sydney, said:

> In their opposition to the proposed Anglican/ Methodist unity scheme some members of both the extreme wings of the Anglican Church seem to be guilty of trying to force upon the whole Church their own particular interpretation of certain Anglican doctrines and practices. The so-called 'ambiguity' of the Service of Reconciliation in actual fact bears the hallmark of that true comprehensiveness of the Anglican Church which is one of its most valuable features ... When I was ordained ... I, as an evangelical, was well aware that there were many kneeling with me who believed that at ordination something 'happened', which I did not believe! But we recognized that the Church of England deliberately allowed, indeed welcomed, holders of both opinions ... It is simply

un-Anglican to condemn such comprehensiveness as wrongful ambiguity.[13]

The occasion might have been peculiar and in some ways
scarcely relevant to the changed ecumenical scene but the
attitude is still with us. Not merely tacit but explicit
acknowledgment seems to be given to the position that
these other groups have a legitimate place within the
church. Those who dare say otherwise are usually cat-
egorized as being theological relics of a bygone era, a
species on the point of extinction now that the lunatic
fringe has departed. So it was that no incongruity was
perceived between having an Anglo-Catholic liberal
Archbishop of Canterbury address the first National Evangelical Anglican Congress, who had poured scorn on
'fundamentalism' just over a decade earlier[14] and more
recently was to toy with the idea of there being atheists in
heaven and who had neither changed nor retracted his
position. Similarly two Congresses later one of his suc-
cessors from a basically similar theological stable was
invited to do the same thing and was given a standing
ovation by the serried ranks of evangelicals for so doing.

One gospel or many?

Now in so far as this is arguing that all wisdom does not
belong to the evangelical consensus alone, well and good.
Simple Christian humility, and an awareness of our own
proneness to wander intellectually, demands that we say
as much. But if in effect we go on to convey the impression, or worse still explicitly affirm it, that evangelicalism
is but one expression of the gospel among several, we
have done something more than acknowledge our own
humility. We have in fact denied the gospel. For just as a
man's inconsistent life may invalidate his verbal profession
of the faith, so too with a church. For all its positive avowal of
the biblical gospel it may, by its actions in embracing in
ostensible fellowship those who do not believe that gospel, deny it. The message being proclaimed loudly and

clearly to the world is that evangelical distinctives are subordinate to denominational harmony.

It is because of what we perceive to be the futility of the first option and the basic, if unrecognized, inconsistency of the second that the path of separation becomes the one that a church, resolutely determined to be faithful to that gospel, must tread when genuine attempts at reformation have failed.

Martyn Lloyd-Jones put both the negative and positive aspects of this case memorably and incisively in his 1966 address:

> The church, surely, is not a paper definition. I am sorry, I cannot accept the view that the church consists of articles or of a confession of faith. A church does not consist of the Thirty-Nine Articles. A church does not consist of the Westminster Confession of Faith. A church does not consist of the Savoy Declaration. A church consists of *living people*. You cannot have a church without living people. You can have a paper constitution with a majority in that church denying that very constitution. That is no longer a church as I see it. The church is not a paper declaration, important as that is. A church must always consist of living people. Sometimes we are told that the church is a place in which a man can 'fish'. Is that a church? Does the church consist of people who are unconverted and who need to be converted? Surely not! A church consists of saints. That is the New Testament view ... So I say we must come back and realize that this is our basic view of the Christian church, and that what we need, above everything else at the present time, is a number of such churches, all in fellowship together, working together for the same ends and objects.[15]

It can hardly be denied that the New Testament church was hugely intolerant of heresy. Where heresy surfaced it had to be dealt with, first by argument, but then, if necessary by excision. What it would emphatically not allow was the possibility that truth and error could be congenial bedfellows, for certain very clear convictions marked these New Testament churches. To begin with, the belief of a church was important. Many philosophical and religious systems competed for people's allegiance. Christianity faced up to these at the level of truth. It argued its case against them. It did so on the basis of a recognizable core of facts that constituted divine intervention in history. On the basis of these facts it drew certain conclusions and derived various inferences that, together with these facts, formed the body of truth that came to be known as 'Christianity'. Confusion as to some of these truths existed periodically in certain churches, but these were speedily, and often exhaustively, dealt with by way of apostolic correspondence or visits or both. What a church believed was recognized as foundational to its existence.

Thus there were no 'evangelical' churches or churches of 'the evangelical tradition' over against those of other more or less equally valid traditions. The faith once delivered to the saints was both the common possession and the common confession of them all and for it they were commanded to fight and that earnestly (Jude 3). When people departed from these convictions and persisted in such departure they were dealt with by way of exclusion from the church – if they had not already done the honourable thing and made themselves separate from it (1 Jn. 2:19).

Doctrinal indifferentism whether born of intellectual conviction or of diplomatic convenience simply did not exist. Had it done so and been recognized as valid, Christianity as such would soon have been snuffed out. As it was, the world was being turned upside down by men of crystal-clear convictions, men who were intolerant of error to the extent that they were willing to die if necessary rather than tone down what they believed for the sake of peace.

It followed that between such churches there existed

bonds of fellowship. Despite the limitations imposed by geography there seems to have been a great deal of coming and going between the churches, if the closing chapters of several of Paul's epistles are anything to go by. Hospitality was both enjoyed and practised. Spiritually gifted men journeyed around the churches edifying and evangelizing as they went. But all was done on the basis and within the limits of a recognizable body of truth held from the heart by all. To compare all this with the religious situation in the western world today is to be driven to the conclusion that there is not so much a difference in degree as in kind between the contemporary church scene and that which the New Testament describes.

True, there were aberrations from the doctrinal as well as from the practical norm among these New Testament churches. In fact that is why we have most of the epistolary contributions to the New Testament. But these aberrations, as we have pointed out, were dealt with. Instruction was given. Spiritual reasoning was applied. But if and when these failed, discipline was instituted, anathemas pronounced, and the errors, and sometimes the persons, of the deviants were disowned.[16]

The pluralist church

The New Testament picture is a far cry from the prevailing situation today. Religious pluralism within the professing church is endemic. An assertive declaration of historic evangelicalism at best is frowned upon as 'divisive' and is likely to be labelled 'fundamentalist' – a collective pejorative term that covers everything from ayatollahs to revisionist Marxist-Leninists, and somehow manages to include historic Christianity en route.

It is sometimes argued that a church can maintain an uncompromising vigorous evangelical testimony while remaining loyal to a denomination that in practice is dominated by views which are quite out of sympathy with that testimony. Not only is it possible, so the argument runs, but it is that church's duty to maintain these ties and testimony until such time as it is ejected by the denomination, or until that denomination explicitly repudiates one of the foundational principles of its credal or confessional basis. On the surface there is much plausibility that attaches to such an argument. 'Quit and run' has surely never been the motto of any church worthy of the name. But even if plausible there is something specious about the argument.

Firstly, it takes no account of the subtle but profound change that has come over the religious no less than over the more general philosophical scene. Relativism is in and, by the same token, absolutism is out. Whereas it used to be assumed that if 'A' were true then 'non-A' was false, that assumption is no longer regarded as valid. Yet this very assumption is the one on which so much of the logic of the New Testament depends. At any rate, so Paul seems to argue in 1 Corinthians 15:12–17. Paul, of course, was not arguing merely as a Christian when he used that logical structure for his argument. He shared a common 'universe of discourse' with his secular contemporaries. But times have changed and with them the universe of discourse, so that relativism now prevails in religious as well as in secular circles. What Francis Schaeffer called 'the methodology of antithesis' no longer obtains.[17] Instead it seems to have been replaced by the philosophy of 'All have won and all shall have the prizes.' It was otherwise at the time of the Reformation and the years following that saw the compilation of the doctrinal formularies that ostensibly still undergird many of the major denominations.

The practical implication of this is simply that one waits in vain to be ejected for one's vigorous evangelicalism. It simply is not done today. But by the same token neither is it done to discipline those whose open and publicly expressed views contradict the doctrinal formularies of the church to which they belong. It surely cannot be gainsaid that each of the major Protestant denominations contains within its ranks a whole spectrum of theological opinion ranging from the simple orthodox to the most extreme heterodox views. The latter are held not by some occasional maverick or eccentric tucked away in pastoral obscurity, but often by those holding high and influential office within the structure of the denomination and by many of those responsible for the training of candidates for the ministry.

The second consideration that exposes the speciousness of the argument often advanced by those who claim to be 'in it to win it' is equally important. Perhaps it can best be approached along the lines of the question: What is involved in a 'vigorous evangelical testimony'?

At the very least there must be certain things on which surely all evangelicals would be agreed. There needs to be clarity with regard to the evangel, the gospel. The holiness, majesty, justice and love of the triune God as demonstrated in the great work of atonement are essential elements, as is the substitutionary and penal nature of that atonement offered by the Son of God for sinners, and justifying faith as being the only means of sinners laying hold of that work.

Not only must these truths be believed, however, they must be preached and asserted fearlessly, for what the church has to offer is not their opinion but God's revelation. As a corollary of this there comes the principle that all that is inconsistent with or contradictory to these truths needs to be repudiated. This must be done in a reasoned, courteous and loving manner. In particular every effort must be made to instruct, with a view to correcting, those who are in error or confusion concerning these issues, or whose views have been expressed in such a way as to leave open the way for misunderstanding. Whether it is the discreet ministry of an Aquila and a Priscilla to an Apollos or the more vigorous exposure of, for example, the Galatian heresy, the New Testament abounds in examples of such 'redemptive reasoning' that more often than not seems to have been successful. This common agreement, however, would appear to terminate when the matter is raised of how one is to deal with those who, having been reasoned with and prayed for, still remain adamant and unrepentant in their error.

When the crunch comes

Klaas Runia years ago asked the question: When and under what circumstances is separation necessary? He went on to cite certain contexts in which the problem becomes acute. There is the situation such as that faced by the Protestant Reformers when the church (in that case, Rome) in its official doctrinal statements opposed the gospel and refused to abandon its errors. Secondly, there is the not unrelated situation in which Christians are compelled under penalty of ecclesiastical censure to accept or do things contrary to the Scriptures. Thirdly, sometimes Christians are no longer permitted by the church to believe or do that which is required by the Scriptures. Runia argues, rightly in my view, that these situations rarely exist in the Protestant church scene today. However, there is a fourth possibility that most certainly is with us. It occurs whenever 'the church in its official capacity (the Bishop or the Assembly or, at the local level, the session) *refuses to deal with notorious heretics*, in spite of protests or charges'.[18]

Silence and inactivity in the face of such a situation is culpable and in fact speaks its own message to the listening world. The truth of the gospel and the integrity of the church alike demand action that will not only identify the falsehood and the false teachers purveying it, but will also result in a withdrawal from them if, through ecclesiastical weakness, the evangelicals are unable to bring discipline to bear upon them. Our responsibility as members of the body of Christ surely demands no less, for the unity of the New Testament church was a unity in the truth.

It is strange how sometimes history seems to repeat itself. For what has been happening in recent years is but a re-run of the so-called Downgrade Controversy that occupied the last years of the life of C. H. Spurgeon. The logic he applied to that controversy still applies today.

As a matter of fact, believers in Christ's atonement are now in declared union with those

who make light of it; believers in Holy Scripture are in confederacy with those who deny plenary inspiration; those who hold evangelical doctrine are in open alliance with those who call the fall a fable, who deny the personality of the Holy Ghost, who call justification by faith immoral, and hold that there is another probation after death ... Yes, we have before us the wretched spectacle of professedly orthodox Christians publicly avowing their union with those who deny the faith ...

It is our solemn conviction that where there can be no real spiritual communion there should be no pretence of fellowship. *Fellowship with known and vital error is participation in sin.*[19]

Iain Murray has well summarized the logic of the case we are presenting when, with reference to Spurgeon's actions, he wrote:

For Christians to be linked in association with ministers who do not preach the gospel of Christ is to incur moral guilt.

A Union which can continue irrespective of whether its member churches belong to a common faith is not fulfilling any scriptural function.

The preservation of a denominational association when it is powerless to discipline heretics cannot be justified on the grounds of the preservation of 'Christian unity'.

It is error which breaks the unity of churches, and to remain in a denominational alignment which condones error is to support schism.[20]

For those of us who have found it necessary to act on the foregoing principles there remains a problem, and it is an acute one. What is to be our attitude towards those who undoubtedly are our brethren in Christ but who refuse even to contemplate taking such drastic action as we have felt compelled to take? We recognize fully that we are not lords of other men's consciences. 'To his own master he stands or falls' (Rom. 14:4). But our judgment is that their position is essentially compromised, confused and confusing. The question which we face is whether we can hold church fellowship with them while they are happy to hold church fellowship on an equivalent basis with others who deny the very gospel that we (and, we believe, they) cherish. Regretfully we have to decline to do so, not because we are sectarian bigots vainly pursuing the will-o'-the-wisp of a perfect church here on earth, but because our very commitment to the gospel demands that we do not deny with our ecclesiastical alliances what we affirm with our evangelical voices.

In summary then, what we believe to have been forfeited is the conviction that a vigorous evangelical testimony must surely recognize that the distinctiveness of the gospel has an ecclesiastical dimension. This in turn carries with it a refusal to co-operate with, or even to accommodate, those who have departed from the faith of the Scriptures. Not to act on this point is to be partaker of their evil deeds. You can issue as many disclaimers as you wish, but the world in its simplistic wisdom will find it hard to believe that the issues that you say are at the heart of the gospel really matter very much when you act in this way. It will draw the conclusion – and who is to say it is wrong in so doing? – that ecclesiastical politics have taken precedence over evangelical conviction yet again.

Response to Graham Harrison

Gordon W. Kuhrt

I shall examine several key issues in the previous essay. I cannot agree that all its assertions are true, and some I find uncharitable. Most significantly its general thesis and conclusion is inconsistent with biblical and evangelical principles.

The early church is seen by Graham through rose-tinted spectacles. The New Testament's evidence is simply not treated fairly. There were the most enormous problems of heresy, immorality, disunity and opposition to apostolic leadership. The story of the early church is an amazing mixture of faith and unbelief, of triumph and tragedy. Certainly the apostles took a strong line on truth, morality and unity, but we have little evidence of how their appeals, anathemas and disciplinary procedures worked out. In fact we do not have a single command about, or example of, the apostles or their followers 'withdrawing' from a church or group of churches. The writer talks of the 'crystal-clear convictions' of early Christians. However, the controversies about the nature of Christ, his resurrection, entry into his community and matters of morality show indisputably that convictions on these matters were far from crystal clear in the early church at large.[1] Careful study of Acts, the epistles and Revelation 2 and 3 will reveal the early church's life 'warts and all'.

Judgments on Christians are made all too easily. The majority of members of the mainstream churches, it is implied, do not really trust in Christ or worship him in spirit and in truth. They are judged to have denied the faith of the crucified one and to be unsuitable for Christian fellowship. It is said that their churches may well be a 'synagogue of Satan'. And what is the evidence for all this judgment? It is that one or other leader is alleged to be heretical. Surely this sort of judgment should be kept for anti-Christian cults where the official teaching is a denial of the Christian faith. In major denominations there may well be leaders and members who err in matters of doctrine and life, people who need better teaching, correction and discipline – but to condemn whole denominations and their entire membership seems to have no biblical warrant whatsoever unless they all obviously subscribe to heresy or immorality.

This judgment is made more specific with respect to theological traditions other than 'evangelical'. Graham admits that 'all wisdom does not belong to the evangelical consensus alone', yet he clearly implies that people who use a different theological label or move in another tradition do not believe the gospel and should therefore be 'unchurched' (pp. 155–157). This sort of argument shows either great confusion or great ignorance about many people who are in theological traditions that may be called 'catholic', 'liberal', 'neo-orthodox', 'charismatic' or whatever. I certainly believe strongly that the evangelical tradition is on the whole the theology most faithful to the Scriptures. However, many friendships and dialogue with others, compel me to believe that most other Christians I meet are 'evangelical' in the sense of loving and believing the gospel and the Lord Jesus, even when they would not describe themselves as evangelicals. Confused they might often be, and indeed wrong at certain points – but that they are unbelievers outside of Christ and his church, I dare not assert without evidence that is overwhelmingly clear and explicit.[2]

It is alleged that discipline in the Church of England

scarcely exists. Graham seems unaware of the enormous amount of evangelical and biblical preaching, teaching, writing, argument and correction that goes on daily. Most observers of the English scene will agree without cavil that overall the outstanding evangelical contributions to biblical study and theology, liturgy and ethics in the last generation have been from the Church of England. When there are issues requiring theological correction evangelicals are deeply involved in writing, scholarship and synodical debate. Frequently observers from other situations do not fully understand the issues and their complexities. Where there are moral problems among clergy and church leaders, the bishops generally deal with them with pastoral gentleness but also firmness. However, this is done privately and quietly where possible. I am certainly well aware of the similar problems that can and do occur in all church traditions, and that all of us live in 'glass houses'.

Separation, in the sense of withdrawal from other Christians, is never encouraged in the New Testament. I have explained in my essay that the only separation I see commanded is excommunication of an inveterate and impenitent offender. However, in the previous chapter, Graham justifies not only separation from non-evangelical Christians, but also separation from evangelicals who do not agree with them on this issue (p. 165). This is supported by C. H. Spurgeon's dictum 'fellowship with known error is sin'. But this needs much more attention. There were tremendous problems of erroneous belief, immorality and disunity in the church of Corinth, but the apostle Paul still addressed his readers as 'the church of God, sanctified in Christ Jesus' (1 Cor. 1:2).

Church separations occur for a variety of reasons – many of them not really theological, but to do with patterns of church order, leadership, psychology and personality. More honesty is needed here. For instance, independent churches in the evangelical tradition are quite numerous in England, yet they differ from one another on many issues. It is instructive that those that place a particular stress on orthodoxy (right belief) do not always exhibit the same zeal for orthopraxy (right behaviour). Church life is frequently marred by division, spiritual elitism, legalism and other problems.

Heavy-handed authoritarian discipline has been a major problem in many Brethren assemblies, independent evangelical churches and new restorationist house churches. Where this has been admitted, and legalism avoided, many independent evangelical churches have warm and close fellowship at many levels with churches in other traditions.

Part 4

The issue of charismatic experience

Michael Cole and David Matthew

- Are charismatic experiences to be expressed by the renewal of traditional denominations, or by establishing new fellowships in which God's gifts are being restored?
- Is it the gospel alone which constitutes the ground of unity within and among local churches, or do different experiences of spirituality and the exercise of gifts of oversight call for new structures of church order today?

A renewed tradition

Michael Cole

Issues that divide us • Testimony • The unity of the church • Local church membership • The ministry and leadership of the church • The tradition and structures of the church • Pastoral care • Discipline in the church • Worship and liturgy in the traditional church • The kingdom of God and restoration • Is there a way forward?

Two books rested side by side. One was *Hope for the Church of England?* edited by the Revd Gavin Reid; the other, by John Noble, was *House Churches – will they survive?* Perhaps that expressed how Christians on either side of the divide feel about each other.

Issues that divide us

There are a number of important issues about which Christians in the two traditions understand and apply the Scriptures in different ways. These issues include the basis of the unity of the church, membership and leadership, the place of tradition, church structure, and worship in the church. What does the New Testament teach about the renewal of the church and the restoration of the kingdom? Does the divide between the restorationist churches and the renewal movement in the traditional churches have to continue on separate lines, or is there a better and greater purpose that God might have for his church? These are some of the issues that I shall try to explore in this chapter.

My hope is to explain to my brothers in the house church movement – among whom I have friends – why I can hold to the teaching of the Bible and yet remain, hopefully, a faithful and committed evangelical Anglican with some charismatic experience. I hope to explain the truth in such a way that those younger Christians who move away from their home denominational churches and encounter house church fellowships among the churches to which students and other young people go will not need to reject their spiritual heritage and feel that others have got it wrong.

Some readers may well feel that I face an impossible task. As Canon Tom Walker has written:

> Some feel that the structures are so firmly established and the pattern of liturgical worship so rigid, that the sort of freedom [which he had earlier described] can never be truly experienced in such a traditional setting. As well as rigidity in the local church, there seems to be so much bureaucracy and such a top-heavy hierarchy in the wider church at its central and diocesan levels, that some give up hope of God breathing into such dry bones and freeing such formality. It is partly because there is such little hope for changing the heavy structures of the Church of England that so many turn to the House Churches for warmth of fellowship and freedom to express spiritual gifts within the Renewal Movement.[1]

It is my belief that 'these bones can live' (Ezk. 37:1–14). The Lord is able to turn 'rock into a pool, the hard rock into springs of water' (Ps. 114:8).

Testimony

There are nine reasons why I belong to and value the Church of England and its partnership in the Anglican Communion.

1. It is biblical in its authority. Article Six of the Thirty-Nine Articles of Religion in the Prayer Book states:

> Holy Scripture containeth all things necessary to salvation, so that whatsoever is not read therein, nor may be proved thereby, is not to be required of any man, that it should be believed as an article of faith or be thought requisite or necessary to salvation.

In the time of James I, it was said that the English became the people of the book, and that book was the Bible.

2. It is credal in its affirmations. The Nicene, Apostles' and Athanasian creeds sum up in historic formularies, the biblical and unchanging faith of the church. It may be attacked and even denied by some, but it will not be altered.

3. It is liturgical in its worship. I believe that in the Anglican churches we can have the best of all worlds, with the experience of the past, and the enthusiasm of the present, but hold form and flexibility together.

4. The Church of England is parochial in its organization. That provides unique evangelistic and missionary opportunity. Whether we always use this opportunity to the full is another question, but the facts remain that in England every person belongs to some Anglican church's parish.

5. The church is episcopal in its oversight. The origin of the bishop may be traced back to the *episkopos* of the New Testament, and linked it with the function, but not the name of apostle. Thus we have the best of both worlds – the local control and the wider overview and oversight.

6. With the two sacraments of baptism and Holy Communion, the church is sacramental in its life.

7. With regard to the nation it is an established church.

Many will question this. There are voices both within and without the church calling for the disestablishment of the Church of England. Such a relationship, however, gives it, potentially, a powerful link and witness into every walk of life.

8. The church, linked with the Anglican Communion, is universal in its scope. One of the great joys is to be able to go as far as New Zealand, Singapore, or South America – as I have done – and share familiar forms of worship made alive by the presence and inspiration of the Holy Spirit. At the same time, you discover in those parts of the world a growth, courage, faith and vision which are vitally needed. Just as each member of a local church belongs to and encourages another member, so one member church can fulfil a similar function in fellowship with other churches in the world-wide communion. This surely is a powerful instrument for the gospel that the restoration churches do not have with their youth and lack of history.

9. I am also glad to belong to a church which is willing constantly to refer its life back to the yardstick of the Scriptures. Bishop Stephen Neill writes:

> Firmly based on the Scriptures as containing all things necessary to salvation, it still throws out the challenge, 'Show us that there is anything clearly set forth in the Holy Scriptures that we do not teach, and we will teach it. Show us that anything in our teaching or practice is clearly contrary to Holy Scripture and we will abandon it.'[2]

I thank God for the grounding that I received in the Scriptures. I resolved that I would embrace no teaching that did not accord with God's word. Slowly, as I worked my way through the Scriptures in 1977 I became convinced theologically that the renewal movement was scriptural, and I then entered experientially into more of the work of the Holy Spirit.

When I arrived at All Saints', Woodford Wells in Essex in 1975, the church was known as an Anglican evangelical church. God was drawing an increasing number of individuals into the experience of renewal. The period of sabbatical leave between January and April 1984 led me to clarify the principles upon which I believe a ministry should be founded.

We faced a challenge – should we limit the renewing work of the Holy Spirit to individual believers, or should it be allowed to affect the church in its corporate life? We had no choice, and the leadership began to follow the guidelines I believe had become clear – namely:
– The headship of Jesus over his church.
– The first task of the church is to worship the head in ways that are appropriate.
– The need for the body to learn to listen to the head for its direction and work.
– The centrality of the cross in our lives.
– The unanimity of the leadership in its decisions.
– The ministry of the local church as the body of Christ.
– The gifting, anointing and empowering of the Holy Spirit for service.
– The need to move forward by faith in the living God.[3]
It is out of this local church background of renewal that I write. There is also testimony from two wider contexts.

The first concerns the extent of the charismatic movement in the world-wide traditional churches. Writing in the *Church Times* in November 1989 Canon Michael Harper, the International Director of SOMA (Sharing of Ministries Abroad), described the growth of the renewal movement in the world-wide Anglican Communion – even in the United Kingdom:

> Lambeth '88 gave the thumbs up to many of the insights the renewal movement has pioneered. The official Lambeth Report – 'The Truth shall make you free' – includes positive references to free, spontaneous and flexible worship, powerful evangelism, every-member ministry, deliverance or exorcism, healing, inner healing, charismatic renewal and speaking in tongues.

The renewal movement is well established in some countries like the United States and Australia, and growing rapidly in Third World countries. Michael Harper continues, 'The world-wide Pentecostal/ Charismatic Movement has grown from 16 million in 1945 to 247 million in 1985. Today it numbers around 350 million and is still growing fast.' Detailed figures are available from Dr David Barrett for individual countries and denominations for those who would wish for more specific information. What is also clear, in view of the amazing political developments in the Eastern European and former communist countries is that a vast majority of the Christian churches in those countries have not only faithfully survived, but also grown and are charismatic churches.

The second concerns the scene in Britain. Anglican Renewal Ministries claim that out of 3,000 people on their mailing list, 1,300 are clergy. The Group for Evangelism and Renewal in the United Reformed Church suggest that out of 1,200 active ministers, some 350 are likely to be involved in some experience of renewal. The figures for other Protestant churches are similar. Some of us also perceive a powerful movement of the Holy Spirit within the Roman Catholic, Orthodox and Lutheran churches. Another mark of the work of the Spirit is seen in the emergence of the church planting movement, and the fact that at least one new church is planted every week in Britain by the traditional churches.

We cannot dismiss the renewing work of God's Spirit within the traditional denominational churches as a passing phase or a dying ember. God is at work in a most powerful and unmistakable way by his Spirit, reviving and renewing his church throughout the world.

I now turn to eight issues of belief and practice where this renewal movement differs from the restorationist churches.

The unity of the church

The heart of Christian unity is being 'in Christ'. 'Therefore, if anyone is in Christ, he is a new creation; the old has gone, the new has come' (2 Cor. 5:17). One essential meaning of baptism, according to Jesus, is incorporation into him (Mt. 28:19). He commands his disciples to baptize 'in [or into] the name of the Father and of the Son and of the Holy Spirit'. Paul elaborates on this, when he writes:

> Make every effort to keep the unity of the Spirit through the bond of peace. There is one body and one Spirit – just as you were called to one hope when you were called – one Lord, one faith, one baptism; one God and Father of all, who is over all and through all and in all (Eph. 4:3–6).

Later, in the same chapter, Paul exhorts the church to be so built up that they reach unity in the faith and in the knowledge of the Son of God and become mature (Eph. 4:13). Thus there is a unity of the Spirit, through being in Christ, which is fundamental to our position. There is a unity of the faith to which we strive.

Local church membership

The distinction that Christians today make between the universal church, the local church, and various denominational expressions of the church, was unknown in New Testament times. The Christians at Corinth, for example, did not debate whether they should worship at St Cephas', or the Apollos True Church of Christ. They all belonged to the church in Corinth – even though they had their factions and different emphases. There was one local church, and that was part of the world-wide church.

The New Testament provides us with various pictures

of the church. It is likened to a family, a body or a building. Entry into, or membership of, that church is expressed in simple ways. As I am born again into the family of God, and made his child by adoption and grace so I become a member of the family (Jn. 1:12; Rom. 8:15–16). As I am baptized by one Spirit into the one body, so I become a part of that body (1 Cor. 12:13), and as I am 'in Christ' so I become an essential part of the building of the church in which God dwells by his Spirit (Eph. 2:21–22). As with the early church, the Lord is still adding to the church those who are being saved (Acts 2:47).

My becoming a member of the church of God is partly the work of God – Father, Son and Holy Spirit – and partly my response to that work through repentance and faith. The ideal entry into the church of God is set out for us in David Pawson's book, *The Normal Christian Birth*.[4] His thesis is that many Christians have been badly 'delivered'. So often, he claims, later spiritual disease can be traced back to an inadequate initiation into the kingdom of God. From an examination of many New Testament texts David Pawson expounds the 'four spiritual doors' of Repentance, Belief in Jesus, Baptism in water and Reception of the Spirit – to use his short hand, *RuBBeR!*

Today Christians face two dangers regarding membership of the church. Firstly, we in the major denominations take church membership too lightly, and often ministers and clergy have not explained as carefully as they should what God requires of us if we are to be truly members of the church of Jesus Christ. We may have stressed faith, but not repentance. We may have urged baptism in water – whether for the children of believing parents, or for adults on profession of their faith – but said little or nothing about the gift of and baptism of the Holy Spirit. Those of us who have fallen into this error are rightly rebuked by our brothers and sisters in other parts of the church.

Secondly, there is, in the restorationist movement, the opposite error of demanding a whole list of qualifications before admitting a brother or sister to membership – such as sharing the vision of the church, tithing our total income, accepting the authority and leadership of local elders, and so the list would continue. I do not find the New Testament teaching these things as a *condition* of becoming a member of the local church. It seems to me that sometimes more is asked of a man or woman in order for them to be a member of the local church, than is asked about the vital issue of being a member of the body of Christ. Is it possible to be a truly committed believer and yet not to be welcomed into a local house church fellowship as a member?

These two errors come about because there is a confusion between *becoming* a member of the church, and *being* a member of the church. Of course, the New Testament sets out clearly the obligations and the privileges of membership of the local church. Hebrews 13, for example, stresses quite clearly the mutual obligations of the leaders for the members and the members for the leaders.

Just as Acts 2:38–39 helpfully sums up what it means to become a Christian and a member of the church, so Acts 2:42–46 expresses the essential life and activity of the effective local church. It is clear that the early Christians met frequently in their homes for social and spiritual fellowship, prayer, teaching and worship. They observed the more formal times of worship in the Temple, as well as the unstructured times for worship in their homes.

The ministry and leadership of the church

It is on the nature of the ministry, more than any other, that the traditional charismatic will differ from those in the restoration and house church movement.

I personally rejoice in the three-fold ministry of the Anglican Church. I believe that the biblical justification for the ministry of bishop, priest and deacon set forth fully and clearly by Bishop Lightfoot in his commentary on the letter to Philippians is still sound.[5] The New Testament teaches the area-wide and supervisory role of the bishop (episkopos); the leadership of the local church by the elder or presbyter (but not the priest in the Old Testament sense), and the role of the deacon as a servant in the local church.

It would be foolish to pretend that these three ministries have not departed from the biblical model in some ways. However, there is debate in the church today over the rediscovery of the ministry of the deacon along New Testament lines. There is a growing understanding and appreciation of Paul's teaching in Ephesians 4:11–12. More and more clergy and ministers are discovering that their role is to enable other Christians to fulfil their ministry in order that the body of Christ might be built up.

Linked with this is the demise, in many 'renewed churches', of the one-man-band style of ministry, and the creation of teams of ministers – whether officially or unofficially. More and more people are appreciating the distinction between the office, ministry and gifting of the leaders. For example, in our own church, alongside the full-time leadership appointed to their office, and the elected leadership of wardens and parochial church council, is the gifted leadership – in the areas of administration, counselling, music, and the like.

Where traditional and restoration leaders would differ is over divergent views of 'ordination'. The Church of England has more than one view about the meaning of ordination. This confusion lies at the heart of the problem over issues of ministry. It affects, for example, who may officiate at the celebration of the Holy Communion or Lord's Supper. Many would press for lay presidency at the Eucharist. It is an urgent matter on the mission fields of the world. The house churches on the other hand believe that any Christian is able to celebrate the sacrament.

I see my ordination as a recognition, and authorization by the Anglican Church of a ministry, role and responsibility that has been entrusted to me, and to which I have been commissioned, and for which I have to give an account both to the church, as well as to the Lord who will call me to account (Heb. 13:17). I value the role and the ministry of the bishop with his trans-local responsibility, his experience, his unifying role, and his ability to share a wider vision of the work. This is, for me, the *episkopos* of the New Testament.

It is at this point that we part company with the house church movement. John Noble writes:

> Should ultimate authority in the local church lie with the leadership of the congregation? Should it be in the hands of apostles and elders, or in the saints'? ... In Matthew 18:15–20, Jesus, speaking to his apostles, made it plain that unresolved disputes were to be judged in the church, not by the apostles and elders alone.[6]

Is a continued use of the ministry of the *apostle* supported by the New Testament? It is clear that the apostles in the New Testament were both foundational and functional. Their ministry related to the message of the gospel, the mission of the church, and the maturity of the church (Acts 8:1, 14; 11:1; Eph. 4:11). Part of this ministry cannot be repeated and maintained. Yet in so far as the church must continue to grow and mature until Jesus returns, then the apostolic ministry referred to in Ephesians 4:11 will be required. As I have written elsewhere, 'Our fellow-Christians in the house church movement believe they are right in recognising some of their leaders as apostles.'[7] These people are not elected or called; rather they are appointed in recognition of the trans-local church ministry they have been given by the Lord. In other parts of the Christian church a similar ministry is needed, and should, I believe, be recognized even if such leaders are not termed apostles. Local superintendents, district moderators and Anglican bishops all have the ministry of linking the churches together, understanding pioneer situations where initiatives can be taken, and acting as kindly older brothers, whose objective view of a local church will enable it to assess itself and correct any imbalance or error in its life. They will seek always to bring that church into fellowship with others, to the maturity of faith and life that the Lord intends for it.[8]

Dr George Carey, when Bishop of Bath and Wells, expressed the episcopal view of this apostolic ministry when he wrote about the exciting movement of church planting in the Church of England:

> We are not a collection of independent churches, but rather a body held together by episcopal leadership, Anglican liturgy and church order. The vision must be shared with those who have authority and I hope I can say for other bishops that any visionary enterprise will be greeted with joy if we are consulted right from the very beginning. Don't treat bishops as rubber stamps for your ideas . . .[9]

Let me return to Ephesians 4:11–12 for a moment. 'It was he [Christ] who gave some to be apostles, some to be prophets, some to be evangelists, and some to be pastors and teachers, to prepare God's people for works of service, so that the body of Christ may be built up.' These verses make clear, firstly, that leadership in the church should be corporate, and never the prerogative of one person. The reasons for this are clear – i.e. no one person will possess all the gifts that the leadership and the church require. It is spiritually unhealthy for one person to lead alone. Vision may die, faith will fade, and the work of the body of Christ decline. The nature of plural leadership, however, is not so clearly spelt out. Is it the leadership where every member of the leadership team is involved in every decision (popularly known as 'y' decisions)? Or is it leadership where a *primus inter pares* (a 'first among equals') is called upon to take some decisions (in this instance regarded as 'x' decisions)? Many of us rejoice that a re-discovery of the truth of

Ephesians 4:11–12 has led us to corporate leadership.

Secondly, these verses teach the purpose of leadership. It is to equip the members of the body so that they are able to fulfil *their* ministries. It has often been said that sheep and not shepherds give birth to lambs! But the shepherds must make sure that the sheep are able to do that, and also to care for their lambs.

Thirdly, Ephesians 4:11–12 speaks of the five-fold gifts of ministry – apostolic, prophetic, evangelistic, pastoral and didactic. Each aspect is vitally needed today. The traditional churches are steadily recovering the vision of the role of evangelists. They are vitally required as the church moves through the Decade of Evangelism. I have already explained why I am personally happy to accept the apostolic role and ministry of those who have the title of superintendent or bishop, but not to give them the unique title of apostle.

Likewise, some in the church are cautiously considering the nature of the prophetic ministry. We need to affirm that the Bible is God's word given to all people for all times and places and needs. It is always God's word. It was given as holy men of God spoke from God, and as God spoke out through the Holy Spirit. Prophecy, on the other hand, is the specific word of God to a specific occasion and need, for specific people. We must never add to the words of Scripture through prophecy today, but we may still claim that God can and often does speak to his church and people through the word of prophecy.

Prophecy today, however, can never become Scripture, and a part of God's unchanging revelation, in the way that Old Testament prophecy did. A distinction is often made between *biblical* or *apostolic* prophecy [Eph. 2:20) and Christian prophecy. I find that helpful. The New Testament refers to Anna (Lk. 2:36), Agabus (Acts 11:28 and 21:10), and others mentioned in Acts (13:1–3; 15:32) as prophets. There were also some other unnamed believers who prophesied but who are not termed prophets (Acts 19:6; 20:23; 21:4–9).

Fourthly, I believe that the New Testament teaches that leadership can be both appointed and elected. We find, for example, that the leaders of the church prayed and fasted before sending out Paul and Barnabas on their first missionary journey (Acts 13:1–3). When, however, the Grecian Jews of the church at Jerusalem chose the seven deacons from among their own numbers, they were taught to select seven men who were known to be full of the Holy Spirit and wisdom (Acts 6:3). After their appointment the responsibility of caring for the neglected widows was handed over to them.

Clearly, those within the renewal and restorationist movements have different views of ministry – apostles and prophets, bishops and clergy, their appointment, election and ordination – even though we go back to the same Scriptures.

The tradition and structures of the church

Sadly, many Christians – in all churches – are growing up ignorant of the great movements, lessons and heroes of church history. We have not learned the lessons of the Dark Ages. We seem to be unable to appreciate the vast sweep of history from the medieval age to the Reformation and on to the Renaissance; from the Age of Enlightenment on to the period of humanism, and secular thought up to the present day, with the emergence of the thought and teaching of the New Age.

Such an historic perspective gives a church leader great strength and understanding. History, tradition and structure are great bulwarks for the faith. We can trace the heroes of faith who have lived and died since the list in Hebrews 11 ended. We can recount the events about the faith once entrusted to the saints (Jude 3). We can see the sovereign and protecting hand of God in his world and over his church.

Unfortunately, so Dr Andrew Walker suggests, some of the brethren in the restoration movement want to re-write or re-interpret the history of the church. He writes:

> It might seem as if the writers are unaware of
> the Greek fathers and have certainly not read

their Kelly. Perhaps they do not know that Calvin and Charles Wesley were saturated in the theology and spirituality of the Chalcedonian thinkers? Perhaps, too, the writers do not really know their catholic history? Whether they do or not, it is a mistake to understand the interpretation of Church history by Restorationists as an intellectualist exercise. They are concerned with discerning the survival and gradual restoration of the true church – amidst the apostasy of denominational history.[10]

John Noble falls into a similar trap. He quotes Bishop John Robinson, 'Is the church not an archaic and well protected institution for the preservation of something irrelevant and incredible?', and then comments:

> I guess there are some folk who have already assumed that I'm writing off all the denominations and every historic tradition in one fell swoop. Well, I'm not. God is the one who decides what is relevant and what is not, but if the cap fits . . .[11]

The attack from the restorationists upon denominations comes in two ways, suggests Andrew Walker:

> Firstly, it is insisted, denominations have perverted the teaching of the New Testament. Secondly, many churches are made up of people who are not Christian at all. Infant baptism is seen as pernicious, not only because it is seen to be unbiblical, but because it allows people to be in denominations and participate in Communion without having to be regenerate.[12]

The restoration churches, by contrast, see themselves as the 'foci of God's final chapter in the history of His people – and thus the whole world. This is made clear by surveying the list of recovered truths of the twentieth century as spelt out in the Restoration magazine'. This consists of: baptism in the Holy Spirit; the return of the gifts of the Spirit for both corporate and individual life; a belief in a world-wide end-time revival; the restoration of apostolic and prophetic ministries as a major means of bringing about the unity of the church; the establishment of apostolic teams to supplement and complement the work of apostles; the growth of discipling practices, under godly leaders, in the local churches; a recognition that denominations are not in God's plan, and are ultimately unrenewable; and a new freedom in worship and praise.[13]

I have to confess I find this to be a rather proud and arrogant attitude, strong on truth and purity, but lacking in love, and a willingness to acknowledge that other Christians might also be equally loyal and committed to their Lord, but seeing the Scriptures in a different light. For example, both the Old and New Testament histories record times of spiritual decline among God's people, yet his love is unchanging towards them. Similarly, the risen Lord has to warn – simply because he loves – that if his church continues in that way he will spit them out of his mouth (Rev. 3:16). Christ is the Lord and judge of the church. We need to heed that warning. But is it the role of other Christians – and especially Christian leaders – to teach that God has cast sections of his church away from him?

There is also, in restoration teaching, one specific view of church history and of the end times. There is a particular eschatological view about the coming of the kingdom, and the return of Christ the King. Such a view seems to take little notice that down the years Christians have differed in their view of the coming of the kingdom and the millennium.

There is also a wrong understanding of Jesus' teaching about the new wine and new wine skins. The synoptic gospels all refer to this teaching (Mt. 9:16–17; Mk. 2:21–22; Lk. 5:36–39). Jesus is teaching about the contrast between the life of Israel under the law before the coming of the Messiah, and the life of the new Israel through grace now that the Messiah has come. There is a fundamental incompatibility of the old Israel with the new Israel. 'The old garment could not contain the new cloth. The new wine of messianic forgiveness could not be preserved in the parched wine-skins of Jewish legalism.'[14] There is no reference here to creating different churches, fellowships and structures because of the work of the Spirit. Rather, Jesus is teaching about the new structures needed for the coming of the gospel. Traditional renewed churches are just as much the new wine skins that God can use in this day as the house churches of the restoration movement.

Again, there is a wrong attitude to tradition. 'How should we view traditions?', asks Arthur Wallis.[15] He quotes, without comment, but helpfully for myself, John Stott's view that there are three important principles implicit in the Lord's teaching: 'First, that Scripture is divine, while tradition is human. Secondly, that Scripture is obligatory, while tradition is optional. Thirdly, that Scripture is supreme, while tradition is subordinate.'[16]

Towards the end of his chapter on Christ and tradition, Wallis writes, 'Let us turn from the stuffy atmosphere of traditional Christianity to where the fresh air from heaven is plainly blowing'[17] and then goes on to describe in first-century terms the sort of church life and practice that would be typical of twentieth-century restoration meetings. He appears to have completely rejected Christ's teaching about tradition, namely, that while there are very real dangers in giving tradition a wrong place (it must never be exalted to a status equal to Scripture) yet, there is a valuable tradition and custom – such as going up to the feast, and attending the synagogue – that was part of the spiritual life and discipline of Jesus' own life.

Those who reject tradition fail also to acknowledge the need for worship and church life to be expressed in the cultural milieu appropriate to the believers. What is culturally acceptable for one group of people would be unhelpful to another group. Paul expounds this in 1 Corinthians 14:40 when he is writing about the worship of the church. Everything must be done 'in a fitting and orderly way' for 'God is not a God of disorder but of peace' (1 Cor. 14:33). Paul is stating an unchanging principle concerning Christian worship. The principle is one of order. We are right to combine freedom and form in worship. Disorderly or irreverent worship is usually unedifying and is not the atmosphere in which the gifts of the Spirit will flourish. Paul uses the word 'fitting'. It is a relative term that will vary from culture to culture. The low-key, unemotional way that is right for many English people would be unfamiliar and restrictive for those who worship with a greater degree of noise and activity. My warning is against exalting tradition alongside Scripture, but equally against dismissing tradition and confusing it with culture, only to replace that tradition which we have inherited, with another tradition that we are creating!

Instead of abandoning the past, and leaving a sinking denominational ship (as some have done, and others were forced to do against their will) is it not better to work for, and believe that God is able to breathe new life, the life of his renewing spirit, into dead and dry bones?

Charles Hummel, previously of the American IVCF staff, once entitled a book *The Fire in the Fireplace*. Some traditional fireplaces are unattractive, dull and cold. Some fires burn, but without an adequate fireplace. The traditional churches have their fireplaces and the fire of the Holy Spirit is burning brightly in some of them. The warmth and light of the fire is increasingly attracting those who are cold and hungry in today's world.

Pastoral care

David Watson put many in his debt when he wrote his book *Discipleship*. He expressed for many churches and Christians around the world the recognition that Jesus calls us to go into all the world and make *disciples*.

While both traditional and restoration leaders would agree with this aim, they would depart from each other on some of the methods. Andrew Walker expresses the tension when he writes:

> In the typical Evangelical churches, believers
> are expected to 'give their hearts to Jesus', and

> there is an expectation that some demands
> will be made on free time. Restorationists,
> however, are prepared to give their all to the
> kingdom, whether it be time, money, personal
> possessions or skills. Being an Anglican or a
> Baptist can be a part-time pursuit (almost a
> leisure activity). To become a Restorationist is
> to adopt a total way of life.[18]

These comments may be true for some members of the
traditional churches. I know, however, a good number of
my own church members who are utterly committed and
give of their time, skills and possessions because that is
the response they wish to make to the love and grace of
the Lord. What I am unhappy about is the demand from
the leaders of house churches that members are expected
to accept an intrusive amount of pastoral care in making
such a commitment. John Noble explains:

> Pastoral authority concerns the welfare and
> direction of the body and its individual mem-
> bers: where they live, what work they do in
> the church, how they bring up their children,
> how much money they give and a thousand
> and one other things.[19]

That seems to me to go beyond the limits of pastoral care
outlined in the Bible. One of the best summaries of biblical
pastoral care is found in Ezekiel 34, where the prophet
rebuked the shepherds for not fulfilling their duty, and
then expounded what it was. We are justified in taking this
as a pattern of pastoral care for the leaders of today's church
on this ground. Although Ezekiel levelled his accusations
against the kings of Israel for exploiting the people under
their care, the proper pattern of pastoral care is provided by
God himself, described by Ezekiel as a good shepherd. It is
a pattern similar to that fulfilled in the life and ministry of
Jesus, as the good shepherd (Jn. 10:11).

Thus, pastors are called to take care of and to feed the
sheep. They will lead the sheep to good teaching and

ministry and seek to satisfy the spiritual hunger of those in their care. They will strengthen the weak and encourage, value and affirm people. Rather than burdening the congregation they will seek to build them up. They will heal the sick and seek to minister to every part of their being, body, soul, spirit and mind. They are called upon to bind up the wounded (and all of us know how Christians can become hurt, and bruised in the spiritual battle). Finally, they are called upon to bring back those who have strayed (and for all sorts of reasons individual Christians stray away from the local fellowship). The pastoral ministry is a ministry of encouragement and watchfulness, not of duty and demand. There are many within the traditional church who perceive the pastoring and shepherding ministry of some in the restoration movement to be 'heavier' than the biblical emphasis would suggest.

Discipline in the church

It is a short step from the question of pastoral care in the local church to discipline of the individual members. It is impossible to have one without the other.

We do not find it easy to exercise discipline when members sin. What about the handling of sexual sin, and the breakdown of marriage, the issue of remarriage, and the mis-management of business and financial affairs? I believe we have things to learn from others. For example, a guideline of discipline which I have found most helpful has been outlined by Floyd McClung – 'A good rule to follow is, if it is a secret sin, confess it to God; if it is a private sin, ask forgiveness of the one you have sinned against; and if it is a public sin, ask the group's forgiveness.'[20]

In my own local church, we are becoming increasingly firm about the administration of baptism, and especially infant baptism. More and more churches are rightly teaching parents that the privilege of baptism for children relates only to the children of Christian parents – on the grounds of covenant theology. What many of us find hard to cope with are the occasions when our teaching and emerging discipline have been undermined by others in the renewal movement who believe only in being 'properly baptized', or as I would regard it, being re-baptized. Most ministers in traditional churches have faced this dilemma. We understand the pastoral considerations, and the pressure of the Spirit on the individual, but theologically we hold to the position that a Christian is baptized only once, and we do not intend to undermine the power and the validity of the sacrament of baptism.[21]

Is it not possible for Christians to respect each other's church discipline without undermining the pastoral care and teaching of their members?

Worship and liturgy in the traditional church

I have touched on this already, but I want to explore it at greater length. Traditional churches in general, and the Anglican Church and Communion in particular, will never be short of their critics. Their leadership and structures will be one target. Another will certainly be their worship and liturgy. My task is not to defend this, but rather to express my appreciation, as an evangelical charismatic Anglican, for them, and to illustrate how form and freedom can be, and must be, held together.

It is true that the liturgy and worship in many a parish church is dull, boring, lifeless and antiquated. It is equally true that the liturgy and worship can become inspiring, thrilling, full of awe and of the presence and reality of the living Lord. Our worship can be majestic and glorious with thousands gathered in our cathedrals and churches. It can also be personal and intimate in our local churches and home groups. It is not the form of the worship that is the key, but the life-giving breath and power of the Holy Spirit at work in the leader of the worship, all who are taking a role such as organist, choir member, reader and pray-er, and also the members of the congregation. I believe that this can be true for our traditional Prayer Book services as well as for our freer and more modern forms of worship using, for example, John Wimber's *Songs of the Vineyard*, whether accompanied by organ, guitar, or music groups, whether clergy or lay-led.

I do not believe we have to go as far as our restorationist brothers who believe that they have to 'dance before the Lord'. As Andrew Walker writes:

> What is known as 'body worship' or free expression in worship, is seen as a sign of the kingdom. David, that great Restorationist archetype, 'danced before the Lord'. It is expected that the Holy Spirit will affect the body and emotions, too, not only the mind and will.[22]

The key in this whole issue of worship and liturgy is not found in changing the furniture of the church, or the forms of the worship, or in giving freedom to individuals to worship 'as they wish to', but in allowing the fullness of the Spirit to possess our hearts so that we all 'worship in spirit and in truth' (Jn. 4:24).

The kingdom of God and restoration

We need to ask, 'How does the Bible describe the kingdom, and what does it teach about restoration?'

The word 'restoration' basically means to 'set in order again'. It refers usually to the restoration of the covenant relationship with God (Mt. 17:11; Mk. 9:12); to the bringing of an individual believer back into a life of obedience to the Lord or of enjoying personal fellowship once more (Gal. 6:1; Heb. 13:19); and to the restoration of the kingdom.

The question that the disciples asked the risen Lord, 'Are you at this time going to restore the kingdom to Israel?', was greeted with, 'It is not for you to know the times or dates the Father has set by his own authority. But you will receive power when the Holy Spirit comes on you; and you will be my witnesses . . .' (Acts 1:6–8). The restoration of the kingdom is something in the future. That is underlined by Acts 3:21 (the key verse of the restorationists): 'He [Jesus] must remain in heaven until the time comes for God to restore everything, as he promised long ago through his holy prophets.' The job of the church, renewed in the power of the Spirit, is to proclaim the gospel and to preach the kingdom (Mt. 10:7). It is God's right to restore the kingdom in his sovereign time.

The kingdom of God has come, and is still to come. The kingdom is both now and not yet. We live between the victory of the resurrection and the ascension, and the glory and dominion of the return of Christ. Jesus, in his parables, taught that the kingdom has come, and is to come. He taught that the kingdom was growing, and yet was imperfect. (See, e.g. Mt. 13:11, 24–30, 41, 47).

The kingdom of God and the church of God are not one and the same instrument. The kingdom of God means the rule and reign of God. The church of God is constantly to be renewed in the power of the Spirit, and reformed according to the plumb-line of God's word. Our business is to proclaim and manifest the kingdom of God in words, works and wonders. We are engaged in a power encounter and conflict against the forces of darkness, against the kingdom of Satan and evil. All this I would defend from my study of Scripture. I do not, however, believe that God calls me to reject the testimony of past generations of faithful men and women of God and to see God working only through the new house churches for the restoration of the kingdom.

Is there a way forward?

It would be foolish to pretend that tensions did not exist between those of us in the major churches who wish to speak about the renewal of the church, and leaders in the house churches who wish to work for the restoration of the kingdom. Such leaders have usually come out from the institutional church, and believe that a radical restoration of the corporate life of the church is called for. They long to see the kingdom of God established in the world, and believe this will come about through the work and witness of the growing restoration churches, and not through the major denominational churches.

My belief, however, is that there is a united way forward together. I submit that it has been suggested by the Old Testament, prayed for by the Lord Jesus, outlined in books, and is being discovered in practice.

1 Suggested in the Old Testament

Ezekiel 37 records the vision of the valley of dry bones. It is a picture of the whole house of Israel. The dry bones become a vast army standing ready for battle (v. 10) through the work of the servant of God (Ezekiel), through the preaching of the word of God, and through the coming of the Spirit of God upon and into the people of God. A powerful picture of the renewal of the church!

The story, however, does not end there. Ezekiel goes on to describe how he was told to take one stick of wood and write on it 'Belonging to Judah'. He was told to take another stick and write on it 'Ephraim's stick'. God then commanded him, 'Join them together into one stick so that they will become one in your hand' (Ezk. 37:17). I do not believe that we can make a direct link between the uniting of Israel and Judah in the Old Testament, and the uniting of different streams of Christendom at the present time – Scripture does not go that far. Nevertheless, I believe that we have, spelt out in Ezekiel 37, principles of the way in which God works which are true for all times. Thus we have to ask the question: Is God, in some sovereign way, wanting to bring together the two sticks of the renewed traditional churches and the restoration fellowships, that they may become one in his hand? It is an exciting prospect.

2 The prayer of Jesus

Jesus prayed to the Father that his church would be one 'So that the world may believe that you have sent me' (Jn. 17:21). We must not only be glad that God is renewing and restoring his church, we must also be willing for the Lord to reunite his divided church, in order that the world may believe, and glory be brought to the one to whom we all bow the knee, Jesus Christ the Lord.

3 The teaching of others

Writing in *One Lord, One Spirit, One Body*, the Roman Catholic priest, Peter Hocken, suggests a way ahead. His major burden is to avoid the extremes of 'denominationalism' on the one hand and 'non-denominationalism' on the other. He sees both as detrimental to the unity of believers. Rather, he points to a third way.

> The non-denominational rejects the traditions, and seeks to build afresh from the New Testament, as though the intervening history had never happened. The denominational seeks to bring renewal to the church, but keeps one's own church at the centre. The non-denominational makes an absolute of the present work of the Spirit, the denominational makes an absolute of the past. Each position seems very logical and reasonable to its supporters. But both fail to grapple successfully with the ecumenical grace at the heart of renewal ... The ecumenism of the third way goes beyond occasional inter-church collaboration and occasional inter-church fellowship because God has gone beyond these limited steps ... This third way is itself a new thing, unexplained and uncharted, precisely because the renewal is new. The churches do not know how to receive a fully ecumenical work of the Spirit. But the Spirit will teach those who humbly seek to know.[23]

Peter Hocken is raising issues, true to Scripture, which perhaps few have yet had the courage to face. But the work of the Spirit, and the prayer of Christ for the unity of his church, surely demand that we do face these issues.

4 Appreciating and meeting each other

The traditional churches have much to learn from the restoration churches. I wish to pay tribute to this stream of God's work, and I am grateful for the growing willingness of most house church leaders in the charismatic movement to be involved with their 'traditionalist' counterparts. There are, sadly, a few who still seem intent on 'empire building' rather than 'kingdom-building'. We are called to be interdependent and not independent like the leaders of the Exclusive Brethren of a former generation.

I also appreciate the sharing of common issues. For example, the experience of the house church leaders responding to the issue of the ministry of women has some things to say to those in the Anglican Church battling with the issue of the ordination of women to the priesthood![24] I appreciate the opening of their leaders to the work of the Holy Spirit, their vision of planting churches, and the example of many member's practical and loving support of their pastors. The house churches can teach many of us in the traditional churches about sacrificial giving. The house churches also seem to have an ability to communicate the gospel to 'the person in the street' in a way that is not always true of the local parish church.

Whatever our differences now, they must be seen in the light of the fundamental oneness that lies at the heart of God, the Scriptures and the gospel. There is an essential unity that is found within the Trinity, which is one in character and purpose. We are called to reflect that unity, just as the Father is in Jesus, and Jesus is in the Father (Jn. 17:20–21). There is a oneness created through the saving work of Christ upon the cross. There he brought together Jew and Gentile and created in himself one new person out of the two, thus making peace (Eph. 2:15). There will be a oneness at the end of time when all things are seen to

be subjected to the lordship and dominion of Jesus Christ
(1 Cor. 15:27–28).

Is it not therefore clear from the teaching of the Scriptures, from an understanding of the heart of the Father, the
outworking of the death and resurrection of Jesus, and
what is expressed in the work of the Spirit, that renewed
denominations and restoration fellowships should seek
more and more to be 'one in Christ Jesus'?

Response to Michael Cole

David Matthew

There is much Michael Cole and I agree on: church history is important; prophecy today must be tested against the Scriptures, not vice versa; renewal in the 'traditional churches' is alive and well; the unity of the faith is less accessible than the unity of the Spirit; David Pawson's *The Normal Christian Birth* presents a scriptural ideal.

Even in these areas, however, questions arise. Church history, for example, has to be *interpreted*. I have stated my own perspective at length elsewhere,[1] but have yet to find a clearly-stated alternative view, except that of the Roman Catholics, who see all post-Reformation developments as a tragedy and would like to draw us all back within their fold. As with history, so with Scripture. We are taken to task for failing to acknowledge that Christians in other streams 'see the Scriptures in a different light'. What that light is remains a mystery.

Michael leans too heavily, I suspect, on Andrew Walker's book. It was out of date even before it was first published in 1985. And its title is odd – *Restoring the Kingdom* is an expression I have never heard in my circles. Restoring the *church*, yes, as a starting point for pressing on to the biblical ideal of the restoration of *all things* (Acts 3:21) – including righteousness and justice in society. Judgment begins at the house of God.

We in the restorationist movement do not teach 'that God has cast sections of his church away from him'. No-one can pluck the redeemed out of his hand. We do, however, question the slack use of the term 'church', and reserve the right to accept *people* as the Lord's while rejecting the amorphous *systems* to which many of them belong.

Nor do we accept Andrew Walker's gross statement, quoted by Michael, that the restoration churches are seen as the 'foci of God's final chapter in the history of His people' (p. 187). At the same time, we do enjoy liberty to move and change at the command of the Spirit, without the baggage of tradition, which perhaps enables us to be a healthy provocation to our brothers and sisters in other groups.

Ministry is a major area of disagreement. I am not familiar with Lightfoot's arguments for the three-fold Anglican ministry but, from the references I noted in my essay, it seems to me beyond argument that *episkopos* (overseer) and *presbuteros* (elder) are one and the same. And it will not do to water down the trans-local ministry of the post-resurrection apostle and squeeze it into the category of *episkopos* under such labels as district moderator!

The only case of *elected* church leadership is in Acts 6. These 'deacons' (only the related verb 'serve' is used, not the noun 'deacon') were to be handling the people's hard-earned cash, and thus needed their vote of confidence.

Michael takes us to task for misusing our Lord's 'wineskins' metaphor. Yet he himself several times quotes the 'dry bones' passage (Ezekiel 37) in relation to the traditional churches, claiming it offers 'principles of the way in which God works, which are true for all times'. I take the wineskins passage in the same way, no more, no less.

The pastoral ministry is indeed 'a ministry of encouragement and watchfulness'. We repudiate the extremes of so-called 'heavy shepherding'[2] but dare not overlook the fact that watchfulness may at times require commanding and rebuking (e.g. Tit. 1:13; 2:15; 3:10).

The support for what Michael calls 'Christ's teaching about tradition' is weak: his going up to the feast and attending the synagogue. But isn't that pre-Pentecost 'old wineskin' practice (Rom. 9:4)? And while it is true that the early believers in Jerusalem attended the temple, as well as meeting in homes, AD 70 put an end to that, in what I see as God's final judgment on building-specific religious ritualism.

Christianity has no holy places, only holy people. Believers are themselves the house of God, especially in their corporateness.[3]

Michael condescendingly refers to our churches' 'youth and lack of history'. Nonsense! We trace our roots – as *all* God's people must surely do – back to Noah, Abraham, Moses, the Old Testament, Jesus, the Twelve and the New Testament church. More recent loyalties are of necessity lesser loyalties – and the very ones that keep us apart.

Worship, because of its centrality, cannot be made dependent on 'cultural milieu'. Many British people are reserved and might opt for a front-facing pew, a polite handshake and a set service. Filled with the Spirit, however, they can become like Italians! We do not *have* to 'dance before the Lord', but it is good to be freed up enough to do so when appropriate.

Infant baptism, in my view, is made no more acceptable by appeals to covenant theology and a declared trend towards offering it only to the children of believers. Lack of space forbids further discussion, but I would endorse David Pawson's appendix on the subject.[4]

Clarity is often misconstrued as exclusivity. We are not exclusive. I myself preach and teach in a variety of denominational churches, and count leaders of many pedigrees (including Peter Hocken) as my friends. But we *are clear* – in our biblical basis of action, in our vision and in our determination to press on towards the mark.

Can't we travel that road together?

A perspective from the restoration fellowships

David Matthew

I Unity within the local church ● The full-orbed gospel ● Repentance and faith ● Baptism in water ● Receiving the Holy Spirit ● Summary: the essential gospel ● II Unity between local churches ● Practical problems ● III Gifts of oversight ● Local leaders ● Trans-local leaders ● Trans-local leaders and unity ● Unity and truth

True unity between Christians is organic, not organizational. Existing, as it does, only between those who share the same spiritual life, it is the 'unity of the Spirit' (Eph. 4:3). From the start, then, we touch on the charismatic dimension, which is the peculiar dimension of the Holy Spirit, for he is 'the Spirit of grace' (Greek *charis* – Heb. 10:29).

Immediately we are faced with the fact that some people are born again by that Spirit while others are not, and that between the two groups is a total distinction – 'What does a believer have in common with an unbeliever?' (2 Cor. 6:15). Let Paul answer his own question: 'The man without the Spirit does not accept the things that come from the Spirit of God, for they are foolishness to him, and he cannot understand them, because they are spiritually discerned' (1 Cor. 2:14). Unity without a common spiritual life is impossible.

Scripture describes this ultimate distinction in a variety of ways. Each individual is either dead in sin or alive to God, 'in Adam' or 'in Christ', a goat or a sheep, lost or saved, darkness or light. Either he or she is still in the dominion of darkness or has been transferred into the kingdom of God's beloved Son. Either his or her name is in the book of life or it isn't.

Any meaningful discussion of unity, therefore, must be based on this premise. Attempts to join the unjoinable will be doomed to failure before they start, as unproductive as nailing planks of wood together at angles in the hope of making a tree. No, the sap of spiritual life is the *sine qua non* of true unity, whether it be between individuals or churches.

Recognizing who lies at which side of the distinction is no problem to an omniscient God: 'The Lord knows those who are his' (2 Tim. 2:19). But what about us? Can *we* know? Not infallibly, perhaps, but surely enough to ensure that we do not try to establish unity outwardly and organizationally when none exists inwardly and spiritually. I have elsewhere identified as follows some of the distinguishing marks by which we may recognize God's children:

> To begin with, 'deep calls unto deep' at a spiritual level and any elder worth the name will have a level of *discernment* by which he will be able to recognise true spiritual life in others (1 Corinthians 12:10). Then, on a more concrete level, we can look for a *clear confession of faith* in Christ (Acts 8:37; Romans 10:9–10; 1 John 4:15) and a bold *testimony to the Holy Spirit's inner witness*. Also, *the way a person prays* can often be an indicator of the

reality of his profession, a heartfelt 'Abba, Father!' testifying to his spiritual sonship (Galatians 4:6; 1 John 3:24).

Then we can look for *character change* (not all necessarily instant) as the fruit of the Spirit begins to appear (Galatians 5:22–23; 2 Corinthians 3:18). We can observe *godly sorrow for lapses into sin* (1 John 1:9; 2 Corinthians 7:10; James 5:16) and an obvious heartfelt *love for the Lord* (1 Corinthians 16:22; Ephesians 6:24; 1 Peter 1:8). Such love will spring from *a heart that is obedient*, for a real Christian is one whose watchword is 'Jesus is Lord', that is, governor or ruler, and 'we know that we have come to know him if we obey his commands' (1 John 2:3).

Brotherly love will also be evident towards fellow-believers (1 John 2:9–10; Romans 12: 4–10; Philippians 1:9; 1 Thessalonians 4:9). And because hunger is always a sign of healthy life we can look for that *hungering and thirsting after practical holiness* which, along with charismatic manifestations, will always attend a genuine baptism in the *Holy* Spirit (1 Thessalonians 4:3–4; 2 Corinthians 7:1; Ephesians 1:4, 13–14; 1 Peter 1:14–16).[1]

Acceptance, then, of the vital distinction between the saved and the lost, and of the impossibility of oneness across the divide, is crucial to any biblical understanding of Christian unity. It forms the background to the present study, in which we will consider – with particular reference to 'charismatic experiences' – first, unity within the local church and, second, unity between local churches.

I Unity within the local church

The full-orbed gospel

Local church elders, like the Good Shepherd whom they represent (1 Pet. 5:1–4), are the gate of the sheep. Whom, then, do they admit to membership?

The answer must be: *those who have made an active faith-response to the Christian gospel*. Others may attend the church's meetings from time to time (1 Cor. 14:24), but they do not figure in any discussion on unity because they do not partake of the common spiritual life which is its basis. They are not part of the church by New Testament definition.

In specifying 'an active faith-response to the Christian gospel', however, we need to define what we mean by 'gospel', because the word has become debased. So let us ask, 'What is the gospel we preach?' Few Bible passages offer a more succinct gospel summary than Peter's statement in Acts 2:38: '*Repent and be baptised, every one of you, in the name of Jesus Christ for the forgiveness of your sins. And you will receive the gift of the Holy Spirit.*'

Repentance and faith

The first element, repentance (and the accompanying faith in Christ which it implies – Acts 20:21), is not in dispute among evangelicals generally, and it is not my intention to develop the doctrine here.

Baptism in water

Baptism in water certainly is in dispute – as to its subjects, its mode and its significance. It is a restoration issue, a neglected and distorted truth needing restoring to its proper foundational place in the church. Many would omit discussion of it here, however, on the grounds that it does not qualify as a charismatic experience. But that very attitude is part of the unity problem, for, in my view, it surely does qualify!

Let us, then, briefly summarize the biblical position on water baptism in general.

A dangerous wedge

The two elements of repentance/faith and baptism belong together. While water itself does not cleanse from sin, of course (1 Pet. 3:21), Scripture associates baptism so closely with repentance and the washing away of sin that we drive a wedge between them at our peril (Mk. 16:16; Acts 2:38; 22:16).

In spite of the fact that the one is meant to follow hard on the heels of the other, many churches persist in separating them in some way. Some leaders, taking the line, 'When you feel led to be baptized, let us know and we will arrange it', find that many members never seem to 'feel led' at all.

Other leaders require those repenting and believing to attend a series of baptismal classes, so that they know what it is all about in the finest detail. Paul, however, seems to suggest action first and understanding later. 'Don't you know,' he asks the Roman believers, 'that all of us who were baptised into Christ Jesus were baptised into his death?' (Rom. 6:3). Their apparent failure to grasp this important baptismal principle had not prevented their being baptized in the first place – and properly so.

Some drive in the wedge even further by requiring a probationary period before baptism, in which new converts can prove the genuineness of their faith by consistent godly living. But, ironically, prompt baptism could well be a decisive factor in making that godly living possible, precisely because it is a means of grace, a truly charismatic act which becomes a springboard for faith, with positive practical results, as we shall see.

A far more gutsy approach is needed by church leaders, following the example of Peter who 'ordered that they be baptised' (Acts 10:48). Indeed, baptism, far from being an optional extra for the seriously committed, is an essential part of the gospel and should figure in our evangelism. Judging by the Ethiopian eunuch's comments, it was certainly part of Philip's gospel (Acts 8:35–36), and was put into effect without delay as soon as the eunuch expressed faith in Christ.

This should come as no surprise, because Jesus prepared the way for such a gospel: 'Go and make disciples of all nations, baptising them ...' he instructed the Eleven, adding, 'teaching them to obey everything I have commanded you' (Mt. 28:19–20). Is not baptism in fact the very first item of that 'everything' which Jesus commanded?

If it is true that a Christian is, by definition, someone who says 'Jesus is Lord' (Rom. 10:9; 1 Cor. 12:3), how can a claim to submit to Christ's lordship be taken seriously if the one making it baulks at this very first command? A willingness to submit to baptism at the earliest opportunity is, I suggest, a more biblical indicator of response to the gospel than raising the hand, coming forward for counsel, kneeling at the 'mercy seat', repeating the 'sinner's prayer' or signing a 'decision' card.

While the *act* of baptism is non-negotiable, we could not take quite as firm a line as to its *mode*. Only immersion, however, adequately fits the imagery of death and burial in Romans 6, quite apart from the fact that the essential meaning of *baptizō* is 'immerse' (see also Jn. 3:23; Acts 8:38–39).[2] Everything points to total immersion as the desirable norm.

As for the candidates, in spite of learned books written to the contrary, baptism is not for infants since they are incapable of the active repentance and faith with which the Acts 2:38 package begins. And faith by proxy is a nonsense – accountability to God is a personal affair (Rom. 14:12).

We argue not for adult baptism as opposed to infant baptism but for *believers'* baptism (Acts 2:41; 8:13, *etc.*). Under the old covenant, the covenant sign of circumcision was performed on natural babies, those who had not long been born. Under the new covenant, the covenant sign of baptism is performed on spiritual babies, those just born *again*.

While many of these will be men and women of mature years, some may be quite young children. My own children were all baptized, on the basis of a clear confession of faith, between the ages of six and ten, and have gone on to prove by their continuing walk with the Lord the validity of their early baptism. This, I believe, is how we should view the New Testament's references to the baptism of households (Acts 11:14; 16:15, 32–33; 18:8; 1 Cor. 1:16).

A charismatic act

Whether the candidates are young or old, the essential nature of water baptism is charismatic, that is, grace flows in it by the Spirit. It is meant to be more than just getting wet all over – more even than a mere act of obedience. It is an act in which we are to expect as positive a cutting off of the 'flesh' in the spiritual sense (the power of the old nature) as, under the old covenant, there was a cutting off of physical flesh in circumcision (Col. 2:11–12).

The Holy Spirit is active in baptism. I have often seen new believers cut off from evil habits as they released their faith during the act, some of them leaving behind under the baptismal waters the paraphernalia of those habits – cigarettes, syringes, occult objects or pornographic magazines.

We must remember, too, that the majority of believers are not tidy-minded students of doctrine. They will never read a book like this one, for instance. For them (and indeed for all of us), baptism serves as a piece of personal theatre, a Spirit-directed drama of death and resurrection far more powerful and persuasive than any number of teaching sessions. We can easily forget what was taught in the classes. We can lose our notes. But there can be no forgetting being plunged beneath the water and rising again, spluttering and elated (and in many cases simultaneously baptized in the Spirit and speaking in tongues), to begin the rest of our life in union with Jesus.

Baptism thus becomes a personal milestone to which

the candidate can look back and from which he can draw confidence, especially in times of pressure. 'No,' he can assure himself when temptation presses, 'I took the plunge. I died with Christ that day, and there can be no going back.'

Baptism in water, then, is part of the gospel we preach. True, it has no validity apart from the repentance and faith which it both presupposes and expresses. But with that proviso understood, it is essential to Christian initiation and, as such, is a requirement for local church membership. As such, also, it is pivotal to any concept of church unity – there is 'one baptism' (Eph. 4:5), and each member of the church must have experienced it.

That goes also for those baptized in infancy. Paedobaptists often claim that to immerse those who were baptized as infants, and who later make a personal commitment to Christ, is to re-baptize them. We reject that claim in the conviction that infant baptism is no baptism at all.

Receiving the Holy Spirit

Receiving the Spirit is the final element of the Acts 2:38 package, and the one which, in popular thinking, is the thorny charismatic issue.

The terminology used of receiving the Spirit in Acts is varied and interchangeable – baptism (1:5; 11:16), the Father's promise (1:4), coming upon (1:8; 11:15), filling (2:4), receiving (10:47), God's gift (11:17). Of all these terms, 'baptism' in particular implies not only complete immersion in the Spirit but also initiality. This may be applied at two levels: to the initial outpouring of the Spirit at Pentecost (Mk. 1:8; Acts 1:5), and to the initial experiencing of the Spirit by individual believers since then in a personal Pentecost (1 Cor. 12:13). The statement, 'One baptism, many fillings' makes good biblical sense.

With respect to 1 Corinthians 12:13 – 'we were all baptised by one Spirit into one body' – I concur with John Baker's interpretation which sees Paul as saying, 'We were all baptised in (rather than "by") one Spirit in relation *to* one body.' If his argument for this interpretation, and particularly for translating the Greek *eis* here as 'in relation to' or 'with a view to', is correct, we have in this verse a powerful statement for the indispensability of baptism in the Holy Spirit for Christian unity.[3]

In line with western individualism, the baptism in the Spirit has become over-personalized. It is not meant to be an end in itself, but a means to an end: the unity and maturing of the church. The manifestations to which it is the gateway are 'for the common good' (1 Cor. 12:7; see also 14:4–5, 12, 17, 26, 31).

A conscious experience

Baptism in the Holy Spirit is experiential – a conscious experience. No-one in the New Testament was ever baptized in the Spirit and didn't know it.[4]

How, then, can some maintain that it happens automatically, and in many (perhaps most) cases without conscious awareness, upon repentance and faith? John Stott is typical of those who argue for this approach: 'The gift of the Holy Spirit is a *universal* Christian experience because it is an initial Christian experience,' he states. 'All Christians receive the Spirit at the very beginning of their Christian life.'[5]

Such a view, which makes receiving the Spirit a synonym for becoming a Christian, must be rejected on biblical grounds – if the implication is that it happens unwittingly. If, on the other hand, the implication is that, in our preaching of the gospel, we should, like Peter, lead our hearers to expect to 'receive the gift of the Holy Spirit' as a conscious, powerful experience as part of the package deal of salvation, we would wholeheartedly agree.

When Paul makes his categorical statement that, 'if anyone does not have the Spirit of Christ, he does not belong to Christ' (Rom. 8:9), he is reflecting normal New Testament experience, in which people repented, believed, were immersed and 'charismatically' received the Spirit more or less together as part of becoming a Christian. To take his statement and turn it on its head, making it an argument for automatic, often unconscious reception of the Spirit, is to do Paul an injustice.

The New Testament, after all, argues not *towards* the baptism in the Spirit as something which 'must have taken place, I suppose, because I gave my life to Jesus', but *from* the baptism in the Spirit as an identifiable experience in its own right. We should expect this, in normal circumstances, to be part of Christian initiation.[6]

Misunderstandings about receiving the Spirit

The fact that some in the New Testament who believed in Jesus had to wait before they received the Spirit (Acts 1:4–5) does not require us also to wait.

The Spirit could not be given until Jesus was first glorified (Jn. 7:39; Acts 2:33). But now that he is glorified, he is permanently ready and willing to release the Spirit, without delay, to all who will reach out in faith (Lk. 11:13), and our preaching should reflect this. Failure to grasp the fact of the Spirit's immediacy probably accounts for the popularity in some circles of that misleading expression, 'the second blessing'.[7]

Many Christians today, the victims of a deficient doctrinal background, are entering into their inheritance piecemeal and, for many of them, the receiving of the Holy Spirit as a powerful conscious experience has indeed been a second blessing. Better late than never. But in our reaching out to the unchurched and the doctrinally ignorant – who now make up the great majority of the western population – we must preach the full-orbed gospel and expect to see an appropriate response. Why should they wait, just because some of us had to?

Seeing people being born again, immersed and baptized in the Spirit all in a matter of days, or even hours, is happily becoming more normal.

Another false notion must be laid to rest: that baptism in the Spirit is a kind of spiritual 'A'-level, a reward for stickability and maturity. Far from it! Immature children may receive it (Acts 2:39), and the Corinthians, for all their blatant immaturity of character, did not lack any of the charismatic gifts to which baptism in the Spirit opens the door (1 Cor. 1:7). The Spirit's fruit takes time to grow; his charismatic anointing is instant (1 Jn. 2:20, 27; *cf.* Lk. 3:21–23; Acts 10:38).

Nor is that anointing something to be passive about: 'If the Lord wants to do it for me, he will.' In most cases he won't! His blessings must be received by faith, and faith is always active. Just as the land of Canaan, though promised, had to be appropriated, so it is with the Holy Spirit and with his gifts, which are to be earnestly coveted.

In Paul's statement, '. . . that by faith we might *receive* the promise of the Spirit' (Gal. 3:14), the Greek *lambanō*, normally translated 'receive', is capable of an active interpretation: 'to take, take hold of, grasp, seize' (Liddell and Scott). The inner working of the Spirit in conviction of sin and regeneration may well be quiet and mysterious (Jn. 3:7–8), but never the baptism.

In today's spiritual climate, those who are still catching up on the fundamentals of Christian experience after many years of faith in Christ must understand that not to have experienced the baptism in the Spirit does not mean that they are devoid of the Spirit. Sadly, Christians from pentecostal and charismatic circles have sometimes given that impression. Can we reasonably expect a person who, after a clear personal commitment to Christ, has walked with him according to his or her understanding for thirty years or more, to agree that he or she has wasted all that time? Dare we denounce such a person as a total stranger to the Spirit?

Never! Christian love forbids it. And in any case, it is not true: the person was awakened by the Spirit, convicted by the Spirit, born again by the Spirit, and he or she is indwelt by the Spirit. But we can encourage the person with the fact that Jesus himself, though conceived by the Spirit and Spirit-directed throughout his life, was nevertheless additionally anointed for his public ministry (Acts 10:38).

And what about the disciples? Before Pentecost they knew something of the Holy Spirit's revelation (e.g. Mt.

16:17) and his power in healing and the casting out of demons (Lk. 10:17), but they nevertheless needed an additional enduement of 'power from on high' before the fullness of their ministry could begin (Acts 1:4, 8).

It is never too late, and 'piecemeal' believers can come confidently to the Lord for a dynamic experience of the Holy Spirit today. The Spirit may be imparted by the Lord sovereignly to spiritually hungry people (as in Acts 10:44), or through the laying on of hands (as in Acts 8:17).

Speaking in tongues

Examples of all the manifestations of the Spirit listed in 1 Corinthians 12:7–10 can be found in the Old Testament and in the ministry of Jesus and his apostles before Pentecost – *except speaking in tongues.*

Isaiah prophesied this phenomenon (Is. 28:11, quoted in 1 Cor. 14:21), and so did Jesus (Mk. 16:17). In fulfilment of those prophecies, speaking in tongues appeared at Pentecost and remains the distinctive hallmark of the post-Pentecost work of the Spirit (Acts 2:4; 10:46; 19:6).[8] It is the only manifestation with a personal as well as a church-oriented value, and the only one that can be used at will. As David Edwards (a non-tongues-speaker) concedes, it was 'an experience common in the early church, so common that it did not need to be explained'.[9]

The tongue, James assures us, is the hardest human member to tame (Jas. 3:8). In yielding it to the Holy Spirit as he comes upon us, we are implicitly yielding the whole of our being to him.

The benefits of speaking in tongues are enormous. It provides an ever-ready means of personal edification (1 Cor. 14:4) as well as opening up a two-way channel of communication with God which operates at a deeper level than normal propositional language (Rom. 8:26–27; 1 Cor. 14:2, 21). It becomes a powerful vehicle of praise to the Lord, both spoken and sung (1 Cor. 14:15). Used publicly, along with the gift of interpretation, it edifies gatherings of the church (1 Cor. 14:5). And, when first received, it assures the joyful recipient that the Lord has opened up to him or her the whole spectrum of spiritual gifts, which are essential to the proper function of a New Testament church.

Summary: the essential gospel

Peter preached the receiving of the Holy Spirit as part of his gospel, and so should we. Repentance towards God and faith in Jesus Christ, baptism in water and the receiving of the gift of the Holy Spirit – this is the essential gospel message, for too long emasculated in most evangelical evangelism.

We dare not suggest that the elements of baptism in water and the Holy Spirit are optional extras and that the 'gospel proper' is repentance and faith. To opt for unity around a gospel lacking in these vital elements is to deny the biblical gospel completely.

In preaching the full Acts 2:38 gospel, we should expect an appropriate response, for experience shows that, by and large, *what we preach is what we get*. If we urge people only to give their lives to Jesus, they will. If, in addition, we urge baptism upon them as an outward expression of repentance and faith, they will respond accordingly. And if we preach the empowering of the Spirit, with speaking in tongues, as part of Christian initiation, we will (and do) find people entering into that, too.

Faith comes by hearing the message of the word of Christ (Rom. 10:17), who spoke clearly about the baptism in the Spirit. If the message, as we proclaim it, contains no reference to the Spirit, faith has nothing to latch on to with regard to the Spirit and our hearers will miss out on the experience.

But the day is coming when the average Christian, not the exceptional one, will look back at the great turning-point in his or her life and say, 'What a time that was! It dawned upon me that I was a lost sinner. I cast myself in desperation on Jesus. I said a definitive goodbye to the old life in the waters of baptism. Then – oh what joy! – the Spirit of God came upon me and I found myself glorifying

God in an unknown language. What a day!'

In restoring this ideal, the local church benefits by having all its members living in the good of the whole package *as a starting point* for growth. That is New Testament normality.

The need for forbearance

In the meantime, some slowness to enter into the baptism in the Spirit may well have to be tolerated. Several factors may combine to inhibit this aspect of Christian experience: previous anti-charismatic teaching; an over-emphasis on the mind and rationality (making it hard to submit the mind to the Spirit); cultural reserve which stifles emotion; and wild tales about losing control, especially over speaking in tongues.

The latter is an ironic misunderstanding, for the fruit of the Spirit includes self-control (Gal. 5:22–23). The NEB renderings, 'tongues of ecstasy' and 'ecstatic utterance', are not only a bad and misleading translation but a testimony to the translators' lack of experience of glossolalia.

Loving, patient explanation and acceptance by caring church leaders of believers with such difficulties over receiving the Spirit or speaking in tongues can usually solve the problems.

With these provisos understood, the Acts 2:38 package should be seen as *the irreducible minimum* for local church membership. It is the biblical pattern to which the issue of in-church unity must be related. Why should we settle for less?

More than meetings

Experience shows that local churches established on this basis are robust in Christian living and aggressive in evangelism. They contrast sharply with churches where there is a major element of mere church-going or loose attachment.

A high degree of church commitment is essential, if only because the corporate goals of the church, being higher than those of the individual (Eph. 3:10, 18), require the sinking of the latter into the former. Indeed, it is only in full fellowship with our fellow-believers that even our personal spiritual goals can be fulfilled.

The phrase 'when you come together' figures frequently in Paul's first letter to the Corinthians (11:18, 20, 33, 34), but being part of the local church is more than attending meetings. Beginning with submission to Christ's lordship in personal life (Mt. 28:20; 1 Cor. 9:21; 12:3; 1 Jn. 5:2–3), it extends to submission to local church leaders as delegated authorities under Christ (Acts 20:28; Heb. 13:17), and submission to one's fellow-disciples (Eph. 5:21; Col. 3:16). It involves willingness to contribute actively to the church's corporate life: in practical love and care,[10] in spiritual contribution (1 Cor. 12:27; 14:26, 31; 1 Pet. 4:10), and in finance (Acts 4:34–35; 1 Cor. 16:2; 2 Cor. 9:7).

When people are evangelized in the way we have outlined, they receive a touch of the Holy Spirit which makes then instinctively want to be joined to the local church at this deep level. Interestingly enough, the church growth movement takes the view that 'a person is not regarded as evangelised unless and until he or she becomes a disciple of Jesus Christ *and a responsible member of a local church*'.[11] It is often in Christian communities committed to the restoration of the church that this strength of loyalty and internal unity is seen at its best.

II Unity between local churches

Unity between local churches would be easy if they all operated to the standards we have outlined, or at least aimed in that direction. But many do not. How then do we relate?

Obviously it is right that brotherly love in Christ be extended, first of all, to individuals from other local churches who claim new birth, even though not baptized in water or the Holy Spirit. A work of grace is clearly evident in many such people.

What is more, some of them may have had a real experience of the Holy Spirit but for one reason or another choose to play it down publicly. They may, for instance, want to avoid rocking the denominational boat if charismatic experiences are frowned upon, or they may have temperamental reservations about 'letting go' in manifestations of the Spirit.

In some cases, their experience of the Spirit, though radical, may not have issued in speaking in tongues. This may be because of the interpretation which insists (by a distortion of 1 Cor. 13:8–10) that the gifts of the Spirit died out with the formation of the New Testament canon. Or maybe the negative answer presupposed by Paul's question, 'Do all speak in tongues?' (1 Cor. 12:30) has convinced them that this gift is not for all. If so, they have failed to distinguish the public use of tongues, which is not every Christian's ministry, from its personal devotional use, which is evidently available to all (1 Cor. 14:5, 18–19). They should be welcomed as brothers in the Lord (and encouraged towards active co-operation with the Holy Spirit for a release into speaking in tongues).

In practice, however, some Christians recoil from the hand offered in fellowship. Coming from militantly anti-charismatic churches, they see a claimed charismatic experience as both a threat to their more cerebral Christianity and a compromise with error. Unity, even at the individual level, is the last thing they want.

Practical problems

When it comes to expressions of unity between whole churches, the problems are often even greater. To begin with, some 'churches' are not churches at all by New Testament definition, even though some individuals within them may be truly the Lord's. I would recognize as valid those local churches where there is some evident desire on the part of the leaders for purity of membership – that is, the admission of genuine believers only – even where baptism in the Holy Spirit is not actively taught or practised.

Experience has shown that there is a great danger, however, that contact between a charismatic church and a non-charismatic evangelical church can lead to a desire in some members of the latter to transfer to the former, attracted by the life and flexibility in the Spirit which they witness. Accusations of 'sheep-stealing' quickly follow and the leaders tend to steer away from further contact.

Joint evangelism – such as in city-wide missions organized by evangelical fraternals – can be difficult because of differences over 'What is the basic gospel we preach?' How many evangelists preach the full package?

When, in the interests of unity, support is given to such ventures, it is painful to see enquirers being directed to paedo-baptist churches or to ones where the charismatic dimension is either played down or even opposed as a matter of policy. It is equally painful to see them directed to churches where traditional trappings get in the way of spiritual liberty, where membership is an unashamed mix of saved and unsaved, or where there is no encouragement to exercise the charismatic gifts which are essential for maximum individual and corporate growth.

But some of the major hindrances to inter-church co-operation lie in the realm of leadership structures and differing views about the nature of the ministry. This topic therefore requires a section in its own right.

III Gifts of oversight

Unity between local churches begins, as often as not, with contact between their leaders.

The 'Holy Spirit dimension' is of particular relevance to leaders, in two respects. Firstly, the Holy Spirit has given a broad pattern for church leadership in the New Testament writings which he inspired. Secondly, he sovereignly anoints individuals for specific leadership roles (Acts 20:28; 1 Cor. 12:28; Eph. 4:11), roles to which he has called them and for which he equips them.

Why should we not defer to the Spirit in both respects? The alternative is the appointment of leaders by some system based on tradition or expediency. Inevitably this makes practical unity more difficult, for how can a Spirit-called and Spirit-anointed man of God find common ground with, say, a minister installed by a remote official as a result of three years at a liberal theological college? On the other hand, unity cannot fail to grow between leaders who, regardless of their denominational pedigree, are men of the Spirit committed to God's own way.

Let me hasten to acknowledge that there are many fine, godly leaders in the church today who have come into leadership by unbiblical routes, and whose fellowship and contribution I value highly. But, let it be said, their spiritual success is doubtless due more to the grace of God than to the system that produced them.

What, then, is the broad pattern of local church leadership recorded by the Holy Spirit in the New Testament?

Local leaders

A local church is led by *elders*. The terms *presbuteros* ('elder', emphasizing character) and *episkopos* ('overseer', emphasizing function) are interchangeable.[12] They also have a shepherding function (1 Pet. 5:1–4; 2:25; *cf.* Jn. 21:16; see also above references in note 12), though not all of them may be shepherds – just as all may prophesy but not all are prophets, all may serve (*diakoneō*) but not all are deacons (*diakonoi*) and all may evangelize but not all are evangelists. I would identify a leader who not only shepherds but *is* a shepherd with the pastor-teacher of Ephesians 4:11 (see below).

Local church eldership in the New Testament is always plural, though plurality (as in the Godhead) does not imply *functional* equality. In any multiple leadership there will always be the 'James', blessed with a greater measure of rule, who concludes discussions with 'It is my judgment, therefore, that ...' (Acts 15:19). But a leading elder must not place himself above criticism; he must stay open to confrontation by his fellow-leaders (Acts 15:36–41; Gal. 2:11–21) and, for that matter, by the people he leads (1 Tim. 5:19–20).

Ideally, elders emerge from within the local church. When Paul sent Titus to Crete to appoint elders there (Tit. 1:5) he was clearly expecting him to appoint those local members showing signs of both leadership ability and the Spirit's anointing. Incidentally, this verse shows that a church can exist in the early stages without officially appointed elders. Grace will keep the believers directly until apostolic men come to establish a local leadership (see Acts 11:20–26).

Eldership training is in the school of life-experience and church fellowship, along with study of the Scriptures and in-service training by trans-local leaders. This is how Paul brought the Ephesian elders through (Acts 20:18–20, 25–27, 34–35). Bible college or seminary training is not thus ruled out. Its effectiveness is enhanced enormously, however, when the college is run in co-operation with the local church and when its teachers are not professional lecturers but, like Paul, men and women in active ministry themselves.[13]

The appointment of elders is not to be democratic, though they must enjoy the confidence of the people. It is not to be automatic after college training or obtaining a degree in religious studies. Nor is it to be a cold 'headquarters decision' divorced from living spiritual relationship – the church is the *body* of Christ, not a skeleton.

Appointment is based on several factors: calling and equipping by the Holy Spirit (Acts 20:28); godly and mature character (1 Tim. 3:2–7; Tit. 1:6–9; 1 Pet. 5:2–3); management ability (1 Tim. 3:5); aspiration to the task under the Holy Spirit's influence (1 Tim. 3:1); and the proven ability to teach (1 Tim. 3:2). The latter, I must add, implies far more than the traditional evangelical 'preaching with a view'.

It is *apostles* or *their delegates* who, recognizing these qualifications, appoint elders in the churches (Acts 14:23; Tit. 1:5), with the laying on of hands (Acts 13:2–3; 1 Tim. 4:14; 2 Tim. 1:6). (We will return later to the question of apostolic ministry today.) And the appointment is not primarily to an office or position but to an often hard and unglamorous task (1 Tim. 3:1).

Deacons (Acts 6:1–6; Phil. 1:1; 1 Tim. 3:8–13) are agents of the eldership, sharing some of their burden in specified areas of responsibility. They are selected on the grounds of their godly character and outstanding serving ability. They are not hirers and firers of pastors!

Trans-local leaders

James Beall has pointed out that, traditionally, there have been three forms of church government: episcopal (a bishop over many priests), presbyterian (multiple eldership) and congregational (membership consensus).[14]

On biblical grounds, we must go for presbyterian-style government, with a large degree of autonomy accorded to the local eldership. But to be truly biblical we must draw in certain elements of the other forms. We reject spiritual democracy, but recognize that elders cannot function without the approval and support of the people. We also reject episcopacy, with its geographical and hierarchical basis, but assert the need for the trans-local ministries of apostles and prophets.

Apostles and prophets are not, like bishops and superintendents, posts to be kept filled. They are men with supernatural, charismatic enablings whom local church leaders recognize and to whom they voluntarily relate and defer.[15] Together, they are foundational to the local churches (Eph. 2:20) – and one does not pull out the foundation once a building has gone up.

The emergence of apostles and prophets in our generation is a phenomenon of the utmost importance. It is as much an act of the Spirit as was the charismatic renewal. 'It is my opinion,' wrote Arthur Wallis in 1981, 'that recognising apostles and prophets, and letting them function,

will yet prove the most important restoration breakthrough of our time.'[16]

Contrary to the fears of many, apostles in particular do
not claim to be on a par with the Twelve, or to rewrite or
add to Scripture. Nor do they plan to carve up the country
(let alone the world) into papal territories where each can
establish his authority. Far from occupying thrones, they
end up in practice 'on display at the end of the proces-
sion', 'the scum of the earth, the refuse of the world'
(1 Cor. 4:9, 13).

Apostles and prophets are gifts of the ascended Christ to
his church (Eph. 4:10–11). Having ascended, he poured
out the Spirit, whom we may receive directly, but who
also blesses us, if we will allow it, through human
channels in the form of these ministries.

Inevitably there will be false apostles and false prophets, just as there were in New Testament times, and their
claims must be tested by their fruits. But the recognition
of those who are genuine and a releasing of them to their
God-given ministry is a major key to the reshaping of
today's church in its progress towards unity.

Equally significant today is the emergence of apostolic
companies, or teams. Paul's team operation, as described
in Acts and in his epistles, provides a sound pattern for
today. Apostolic companies are flexible, their composi-
tion changing in order to meet constantly-changing
needs.[17] Their members are there to do a job, not to claim
some kind of 'team status' which puts them a notch above
local church leaders. Already such companies, learning as
they go, are having a powerful effect on the church in
many lands.

Apostles and prophets are not, of course, the only
ministries listed in Ephesians 4:11–13. Regarding the
others – evangelists, pastors and teachers – little New
Testament data is available, but they appear to be leaders
of exceptional stature. Not only do they have gifts, they
are gifts, and while the Greek word Paul uses of them is
domata (Eph. 4:8) rather than *charismata*, all the evidence
is that they are charismatic gifts – gifts of God's grace – to
the church, raised up by the Holy Spirit and directed by

him in their trans-local work. Certainly that was Paul's view of his own ministry (1 Cor. 3:10; 15:9–10; Eph. 3:7–8).

The New Testament envisages only one, united church in a city (1 Cor. 1:2; Phil. 1:1; 1 Thes. 1:1) – in many congregations, perhaps, but united by a common eldership. The *pastor-teacher* (one ministry rather than two?) is probably to be seen, then, as a leader of city-level stature, with an active role towards all the congregations. There could well be several such pastor-teachers in a city, with one deferred to as the first among equals. He is a man not intimidated by other teachers.

The only New Testament model for the *evangelist* is Philip, who was based in the church at Caesarea (Acts 21:8). Though an evangelist will have a roving commission in reaching the lost, he is described as a gift not primarily to the world but to the church, 'to prepare God's people for works of service' in evangelism (Eph. 4:12). Not only does he do the job himself, he inspires and trains others to do it too.

Trans-local leaders and unity

The role of all the Ephesians 4 ministries is inseparable from the question of inter-church unity. In one of the clearest statements in the New Testament about God's plan for the unity and maturity of the church, Paul states that these ministries are given 'so that the body of Christ may be built up until we all reach unity in the faith and in the knowledge of the Son of God and become mature' (Eph. 4:12–13).

Why is it, then, that some Christians today oppose these ministries, especially that of apostles and prophets? The uniting factor in the New Testament church was not a common 'faith and order' programme nor denominational affiliation. It was first and foremost the ministry of anointed trans-local leaders, especially of apostles like Paul and Peter. I suspect that, before the 'unity of the *Spirit*' (Eph. 4:3) can blossom into 'unity in the *faith*' (Eph. 4:13), God's people will have to remove the barriers they have raised to the ministry of such men.

Let me again acknowledge the fact that much blessing has often attended individuals, local churches and leaders who have resisted both the broad leadership pattern set forth by the Holy Spirit in Scripture and his charismatic enablings. That blessing, however, is a token, not of their rightness but of the amazing grace of God. He blesses because that is the kind of God he is.

But if we are ever to reach the 'unity in the faith' which we desire and which is God's declared intention for us, we must stop presuming upon his grace and begin to fall into line with his will as declared in Scripture and his sovereign appointments by his Spirit.

Unity and truth

Prior to the sixteenth-century Reformation, the western church could claim unity – but only at the expense of truth. At the Reformation, when Christians began to implement some of the long-neglected truths of God's word, they soon found that they could do so only at the expense of unity. Each move of the Spirit since then has forced Christians to the same conclusion: unity at the expense of truth is unacceptable.

Today, yet another shaft of light has broken forth from God's word: we live with the twentieth-century phenomenon of the baptism and gifts of the Holy Spirit. Though it has had its precursors in previous generations, today it is here to stay on a massive world-wide scale.

It appeared first in the pentecostal movement almost ninety years ago and, more recently, in the charismatic renewal and associated movements. Those of us who view this as part of God's sovereign restoration of an element vital to personal and (more importantly) corporate Christianity cannot let it go. It accords with Scripture and is a truth which we cannot sacrifice on the altar of unity. On the contrary, we are convinced that no real unity is possible without it.

The time must come, however, when Christians will no longer have to choose between truth and unity, a time when a lasting marriage will take place between the two. Isn't this the 'unity of the *faith*' which Paul sets as our goal?

It will come about when all God's people do all God's will. And whatever else that means, it must mean jettisoning everything which prevents our being lifted by the Holy Spirit – by means of his direct operations, his leadership anointings and the Scriptures which he inspired – into the full purposes of God.

Response to David Matthew

Michael Cole

I appreciated David Matthew's clear, biblical and straight-forward presentation but I am left with two reactions. Has he said too little on some aspects and has he claimed too much for others? For example, he has written virtually nothing about the basic restoration position and its view of the kingdom of God; about the tradition and history of the church; and about the nature of worship. As I have attempted to show in my contribution the Bible has very important statements to make on all these matters, and it would have been good to have heard David's side.

There are two main areas where I am left with the feeling that David has claimed too much from the Scriptures. Those concern Christian initiation and Christian leadership.

Christian initiation

The first area of Christian initiation relates to baptism in water. While we both turned to Acts 2:38–40, we have interpreted it in different ways. David does not refer to the promise of the section: 'The promise is for you and your children, and for all who are far off – for all whom the Lord our God will call.' He has dismissed in almost a line the whole infant baptism position. I believe that there are two groups of people who have the right and privilege to be baptized – namely, believers on their profession of faith, and the children of at least one believing parent on the grounds of the covenant promises in the Old Testament to Abraham. There are parallels between the sacraments of the old covenant, namely circumcision and the Passover (both of which involved the shedding of blood), and the two sacraments instituted by the Lord – baptism and the Lord's Supper (neither of which involved the shedding of blood, since Christ had shed his blood, once for all upon the cross).

While I agree that the mode of baptism is strongly suggested by the teaching of death and resurrection in Romans 6, yet there has been disagreement down the ages as to the precise meaning of the word – 'baptize'. 'Sprinkling' and 'dipping' are also accepted means of baptism. I have already made my comments, and expressed my concern, over the matter of 're-baptism', to which David refers.

The second area of Christian initiation relates to baptism in the Spirit. I support David's statement, 'One baptism and many fillings', and I agree with much of his interpretation of the Scriptures, but I want to question two issues.

Firstly, is this the only possible interpretation of the New Testament teaching about the baptism of the Spirit? In his recent book, *Baptism with the Spirit*,[1] Michael Eaton surveys the teaching and preaching ministry of Dr Martyn Lloyd-Jones on this theme. It is the most comprehensive examination of this central scriptural teaching in modern times. Martyn Lloyd-Jones taught that in historical theology there have been at least nine different understandings of this doctrine. These range from the non-experiential at the moment of conversion to the experiential reality that might occur at any time after conversion. While we should be persuaded of our own position, we should also be aware of other Christian leaders who hold equally firmly from the Scriptures a different understanding. I would prefer to be less dogmatic in my presentation.

Secondly, I believe that David Matthews claims too much for biblical teaching on 'speaking in tongues'. He sets forth the classic pentecostal position which is not tenable from 1 Corinthians 12 – 14. Tongues are not the sign of baptism of the Spirit. Rather, Paul teaches that all can speak in tongues, some do, but none *must*. I agree that there is a real blessing received through the gift of tongues, and my personal wish is that all spoke in tongues. It is so often the key to the release of other charismatic gifts. But it is not commanded for all.

Christian leadership

I have written at length about the appointment, authority and nature of Christian leadership. I am, therefore, concerned about some of the emphases that David has, and also the implications he makes. For example, is the authority of the local elder the same as the authority of the Chief Shepherd himself? Surely not! Yet David seems to imply that when he writes 'Local church elders, like the Good Shepherd whom they represent (1 Pet. 5:1–4), are the gate of the sheep. Whom, then, do they admit to membership?' (p. 206). Again, membership of the local church 'extends to submission to local church leaders as delegated authorities under Christ' (p. 217).

David has already raised the matter of the spiritual discernment required by the local elder to recognize true spiritual life in a potential member and to admit to membership. Surely, the Lord adds to his church. Shouldn't David be referring to the maturity that the New Testament requires of believers?

I don't understand how David can hold the position he does about membership and also about admission to baptism. He writes, 'Paul seems to suggest action first and understanding later.' Doesn't baptism imply membership?

I wish to take issue, not only over the authority of local leaders, but also over their appointment. David suggests that our positions differ radically, but is that really so? Does he not hold that there must be the inward call of the Spirit in the life of the future leader, together with the recognition of that call by the local church, and the appointment by the church of that person to ministry? If that is his position, then that is basically similar to what the traditional churches hold. The means may be different, but the biblical principles are the same.

I am glad that David sets out fully his position about apostles and prophets. I can only repeat that I do not believe the Scriptures need to be interpreted in that precise way.

The final impression and reaction I have is very simple. If every church and fellowship would understand the Scriptures in the way that David and the restoration fellowship do then all would be well, because 'we are right'. I have sought to show that there are other ways of looking at the same issues by brothers who hold the Scriptures equally firmly. I should have loved to have seen more recognition that others can hold an equally tenable position, and that we can learn from one another. Where there is the 'unity of the Spirit' are we not able to reach the unity of the faith (Eph. 4:3, 13)?

Where does this leave us?

Alan F. Gibson

At least one conclusion is glaringly obvious to us. We can now see why all the endeavours of twentieth-century ecumenism have not demolished our denominational walls. Even by reducing the problem to differences between those sharing evangelical convictions we are still left with yawning gaps between our contributors.

Although they are all concerned to work towards the kind of unity they see in Scripture, they represent a wide spectrum of views about who comprises the church itself. David Holloway, for instance, in defending his position on the national church is perceived by Derek Prime and David Matthew as if he were including people they cannot accept as Christians at all. David Matthew, in particular, on the other hand, would exclude from his concept of unity those whom David Holloway would regard as genuine believers seeking to obey Scripture. All of which shows how important it was for us to look at the issue of membership in the first place.

The exercise, however, has not been without profit. We have identified some of the points at which those reasoning from the same Bible start to diverge towards their different conclusions.

Some crucial watersheds

1 Realism or idealism?

Given the history of the church in our own nation (whichever nation hardly matters at this point in the discussion)
how do we view its present form? Realism demands that
we recognize the heritage we have received from the past.
We are not drawing a new ecclesiastical map on a clean
sheet of paper. We must start from where we are. That is
why David Holloway begins with the paradox of the
church as it is and the church as it is meant to be. He is
arguing from within the national church as a sociological
reality, already established by, and having a responsibility
to, the state. He is less concerned about the existence of
nominal believers in the church than Derek Prime is.
From that standpoint he then looks back to the New Testament and finds support for his acceptance of the mixed
character of the professing church in the 'serious faults of
the apostolic church'.

Using such a perspective, what is sometimes called the
'folk religion' of baptism, weddings and funerals provides
an opportunity to meet real people who may not be 'born
again' but who have not deliberately rejected the label
'Christian'. Even the religious dimension of state
occasions is thus seen positively as a way to witness
before kings and rulers.

It is perhaps surprising that only Michael Cole among
three contributors from the Church of England begins to
give us a systematic statement of the Anglican view of the
church. This may be because of the way the initial questions were framed. The parish system, its hierarchical
structure, synodical government, the evangelical societies
and the (decreasingly?) common liturgy, are all a far cry
from the connectionalism defended by Harry Uprichard.
And yet this is the immediate context of church unity
experienced by many Christians. What they may perceive
as the Church of England's strength, however, others see
as its weakness. Its genius for middle-of-the-road policies,
and its 'establishment' image, has made the Anglican

Church vulnerable to domination by a liberal leadership. That is why we find evangelicals in the Church of England who feel closer to some of their Free Church neighbours than to some of their Anglican partners.

In reality all denominations are capable of degenerating into an institutionalized bureaucracy too inflexible to allow spiritual initiatives to flourish. In this respect Harry Uprichard's example of church planting in rural Ulster may not be typical. What about the vast challenge of the inner cities? Does the parish system in fact stifle church planting initiatives?

Some forms of idealism, on the other hand, are not without their own dangers. David Matthew, for example, sees the uniting factor in the New Testament church as 'first and foremost the ministry of anointed trans-local leaders'. As a result he calls upon all evangelicals to 'fall into line with his [God's] will as declared in Scripture and his sovereign appointments by his Spirit' (p. 225). By David's own admission, however, this presents a practical problem. He is ready to 'recognize as valid those local churches where there is some evident desire on the part of the leaders for purity of membership . . . even where baptism of the Holy Spirit is not actively taught or practised' (p. 218). The enormous problem here is how these churches can be expected to accept the ministry of trans-local leaders whose charismatic theology they do not conscientiously share. It is idealistic to look for the unique circumstances of the immediate post-Pentecost church to be mirrored in the ecclesiastical pluralism of our own day. This needs an injection of more than a little realism if it is to forward church unity. Understandably, there are evangelicals who conclude, with Eryl Davies, that too much connectionalism, of whatever kind, only frustrates the headship of Christ over the local congregation.

We can see that so much depends on where we start from. There is such a reality as 'the professing church' in our nation or, more to the point, a number of professing churches. To do justice to biblical teaching about the church and its unity we must avoid the extremes on the one hand of a too uncritical acceptance of the status quo and on the other hand the wishful thinking of unrealistic idealism. In this respect the scene in, say, the United Kingdom is not essentially different from that in any other country where denominations have proliferated and diversity is a fact of life.

2 Remaining or changing?

By and large only a minority of Christians actually change their denominational allegiance. Even in an age when many young people leave home to study and when mobility of employment is commonplace, most people stay in the denomination they joined after they were first converted. This is understandable. If God has met you and blessed you in one particular kind of church then it can't be all that bad, can it? What is it then, which provokes a Christian to make such an important change? Derek Prime's own snippet of personal testimony is interesting. He does not use the word 'conscience' but he does speak of 'my conviction that I must obey the New Testament' (p. 44). He was clearly acting on principle, not merely going along with what his parents, and later his Anglican friends, expected of him.

I am well aware that we can all think of others who have made the same move in reverse. Although he does not say so in his essay, one of our Anglican contributors did exactly that. He was brought up in a Christian home and his parents were Baptists. Today he is contending against the views he once held. Now it would be easy to get cynical and to conclude that the whole topic is so subjective that there is little point in further discussion. In reality, the opposite is the case. Both those I have quoted made their eventual choice of church association by prayerful consideration of Bible teaching and then acted according to their conscience.

What we are seeing nowadays is more flexibility about church loyalty. When a Christian moves to another area he or she will look first for a church committed to the gospel and it may then be ease of transport, a suitable Sunday School, or the warmth of welcome they receive which determines where they settle. But we must distinguish between an enforced transfer of church allegiance and merely drifting around. There are instances in which it is not principle but pragmatism or personality which tips the scales. In many towns we have the luxury of a choice of churches, and worshippers may believe they are showing a worthy ecumenical spirit by alternating between two (or more!) of the churches accessible to them. Such an attitude, however, belongs more to the age of consumer choice than to that of dedicated discipleship.

The New Testament calls us to embrace a doctrinal Christianity which sees our regular fellowship in the body of Christ as a serious commitment. When choices have to be made our perception of the biblical issues should be the basis of our decision. When the hard choice of moving from one church to another has to be made, it is the conscience captive to the word of God which should be the final arbiter.

3 Biblical Christians or New Testament Christians?

Some of the more intransigent difficulties of biblical interpretation have their origin in the debate about the relationship between the old and the new covenants. David Holloway, for example, finds the first example of the national church (p. 25) and the background to infant baptism (p. 35) in the Old Testament. Harry Uprichard finds connectionalism evident in the Old Testament (p. 105). The Old Testament is also the source for those holding the covenant view of infant baptism so central to this whole debate, as is argued in Gordon Kuhrt's *Believing in Baptism*.[1]

Now every evangelical believes that all of the Bible is the word of God. We are not seriously suggesting that only the New Testament should be used as data to discern our doctrine of the church. Some differences are apparent, however, when we begin to ask whether all Old Testament teaching is valid unless contradicted in the New Testament or whether the New Testament is normative in our understanding of the Old Testament. At a very superficial level, the continuing use of the term 'priest' in some churches today may be defended by saying that it is a corruption of the New Testament term, 'presbyter'. In reality, however, its sacrificial overtones lend credence to the sacramental theology at the back of much of the 'women priests' controversy.

David Matthew has over 200 Bible references in his chapter. Not one is from the Old Testament. We may legitimately infer that he is concerned that the church of today be a 'New Testament' church. Some denominations nowadays even have that in their title. But are we to be 'Bible' Christians or 'New Testament' Christians? The canons of hermeneutics lie behind most differences which divide evangelical Christians and among those principles of interpretation perhaps none is more fundamental than the relationship of the Old to the New Testament. All there is space to do here is to suggest that we watch out for it in our discussions with fellow Christians on the issues of the church.

4 Integration or co-operation?

Our contributors were not asked to provide a blueprint for practical policy but some have indicated the direction of their own thinking. Even here wide differences emerge. The logic of David Holloway's position is that we should all be ready to join an existing national church and provide a stronger evangelical wing. Eryl Davies urges independent churches to work for greater interdependence with occasional 'synodical' consultation. The model of the Evangelical Alliance is commended by Gordon Kuhrt but, as he points out, it has not proved possible for all evangelical churches to remain within this body with a clear conscience. Michael Cole hopes that leaders from restoration fellowships and renewed denominational churches will begin, at least, 'appreciating and meeting each other' without necessarily expecting any formal union scheme.

There is no agreed picture of how evangelical churches should work together, whether on a national scale or even within one locality. What is represented, however, is a growing conviction that churches should be seeking fellowship and mutual encouragement in the tasks all Christians face in an increasingly secular age. It cannot be enough for us to remain so committed to our own sub-cultures that we do no more than raise a reluctant wave to our fellow evangelicals making the same journey in another vehicle.

Some practical suggestions

Having listened to our contributors, let me suggest some steps which evangelical churches might realistically pursue.

1 We must take seriously the ultimate goal

We are all convinced that one day our Lord's petition to his Father will be granted so that his people will 'be brought to complete unity to let the world know that you sent me' (Jn. 17:23). This eschatological hope is what can provide the stimulus for us to work for its realization in this life and for some greater measure of its fulfilment in our own generation. Although not all evangelical churches, by any means, have been enthusiastic about the international impetus of the ecumenical movement, its emergence in this century has had one beneficial effect. It has provoked Bible-believing Christians to think about the doctrine of the church and to work out a credible ecclesiology. Few are now content that our lights should shine, 'You in your small corner and I in mine.' The existence of this book is one indication of that.

To take this seriously, however, must involve a humble recognition of the fact that some of those professed Christians we mix with, and some of the churches we are formally linked with, may not be part of the genuine body of Christ at all. 'The Lord knows those that are his', but not even all who have done miracles in his name will be acknowledged as his on the last day. Sadly, the mixture of genuine and spurious makes it a complex task to bring together in one church structure as many as we can of those who will be together in heaven. The endeavour is made all the more difficult because of disagreements about what such a structure would be like and because some evangelicals do not believe such a constitutional re-alignment is called for. Does this mean, therefore, that nothing at all can be done to move, however slightly and slowly, closer to Christ's goal?

2 We must seek to make our fellowship constructive

There are numerous examples of trans-denominational activity in para-church societies committed to specific roles in evangelism, social concern, Bible-teaching and so on. Several private conferences and study groups exist to facilitate mutual study and fellowship with the particular aim of crossing existing denominational boundaries. Evangelical churches from a wide spectrum, some with no tradition of inter-church links, have identified with the Evangelical Alliance. Many churches which have separated from comprehensive denominations on conscience grounds, have joined the British Evangelical Council. Recent years have seen growing opportunities for genuine co-operation between the EA and the BEC in areas where their different perspectives on churchmanship are not an issue. Joint submissions were made to government bodies about religious broadcasting legislation and more than one coalition now exists where representatives from the widest evangelical constituency meet regularly to discuss mutual concern over matters such as sexuality in society.

3 We must grasp the local opportunities

There is a sense in which the local application of evangelical unity is both more difficult and more important than what is attempted at national level. It is more difficult because neighbouring congregations can appear to compete for the loyalty of local Christians. It is more important because, unless we are careful, the new ecumenical bodies in Britain will promote more co-operation at the grass roots level between churches indifferent to gospel essentials than committed evangelicals can achieve among themselves.

What opportunities there are will differ from place to place. Some evangelical churches are too small to have a viable youth work in each congregation. With so many young people now owning cars a combined youth meeting after church on Sunday is a workable proposition. One such group meets on a county-wide basis in the north-east of Scotland. An annual camp is jointly arranged by a number of small churches in Yorkshire. Recent years have seen growing opportunities for Schools' Workers to encourage Christian Unions and to assist Religious Education teachers. To fund a worker of this kind is expensive and it has been good to see how many are now being sponsored by local groups of evangelical churches.

Of course there are limits to these initiatives. A March of Witness may have such broad support that some evangelicals will conclude that appearing in public alongside a Roman Catholic priest merely confuses their neighbours about the nature of the gospel. Other marches may incorporate features of deliverance ministry which not all evangelicals can support with a good conscience. In such circumstances it is good to distinguish between our standing aside from what our brothers and sisters are doing and our standing against them. It is vital to our integrity that we all remain true to our own principles but it is equally important for us to remember that one of those principles is our common membership of the body of Christ.

This is well illustrated by the true story of a Scottish minister pledged to uphold in his own church their historic practice of singing only the Psalms and that without instrumental accompaniment. When invited to the funeral of a godly Baptist in his home village he not only sang the hymns but he made sure the widow saw that he did so. He later explained that his debt of love to his grieving sister derived from his sharing with her and her departed husband an eternal fellowship in the body of Christ. This bond he perceived to stand higher in the hierarchy of Christian duties than those he had accepted by ordination to the ministry of a particular church.

4 We must recognize that unity is not an end in itself

One of the mistakes of the ecumenical enthusiasts is to assume that church unity can be separated from other features of the church's maturity and sought for its own sake. Sometimes it is projected as the one key which will unlock other treasures for the churches, such as impressing the ungodly and reducing our running costs.

At whatever level, whether in one local church or between churches, a sense of unity is the result of something else. It is one facet of the holiness of the body of Christ to which God, in his mighty grace, will one day bring his church. Numerous scriptures bear witness to this fact. Our Lord's oft-quoted prayer for the unity of his people in John 17:20–26 follows his earlier petition for them to be 'truly sanctified'. Aware of the dangers they face from the evil one, he has already prayed, 'Holy Father, protect them by the power of your name . . . so that they may be one as we are one' (Jn. 17:11). The apostle Paul's urging of his Philippian friends to 'make my joy complete by being like-minded, having the same love, being one in spirit and purpose' (Phil. 2:2) is set in the most challenging context of those already united to Christ and in fellowship with his Spirit then imitating his unique demonstration of unselfish humility (Phil. 2:5–11). The Bible's emphasis, both in the Old Testament (Ps. 133) and in the New Testament (Rom. 15:5–6), is on the spirit of unity which only God can grant.

Seeing unity as a feature of holiness is illuminating. It puts so many other things into perspective. Think, for example, of the 'already, but not yet' language of the Bible. At a personal level Christians are called 'saints' but they are not yet sinless. If we gave up striving to be more holy we would be disobeying clear Bible commands. The same is true of the holiness and the unity of the church. There is only one body of Christ and we are already united to each other in him (Eph. 2:19–20). Yet this given unity we are to

guard and work at (Eph. 4:3) until the progressive sanctification of the church brings this work to completion (Eph.
4:13). That this has not yet come about is evident. But to
give up the battle because our unity is not yet perfect is to
ignore our biblical duty.

What we must be doing is moving in the direction of
God's ultimate goal, no more dependent on carnal methods
for the holiness of the church than in attaining personal
godliness. So dependent must we be upon the Spirit of God
that when some advance is made which makes more visible the unity of Christ's church then the world must see
that the only explanation is not ingenious organization but
divine grace. We have already seen how great the obstacles
are. When they are overcome, God must have the credit for
it.

Now the essence of sanctification is in the heart, neither
in an outward show of piety nor in a legalistic avoidance of
'wordliness'. So it is with the church. To belong to a
'united' church structure and to care nothing for the needy
members of a neighbouring church is sheer hypocrisy. That
is why improving attitudes and the nurturing of genuine
Christian love is of far more significance to church unity
than a thousand committees making well-meaning plans
for joint ventures which no-one is motivated to pursue.

This brings us right back to the matter of priorities. If
biblical unity is essentially spiritual and only secondarily
institutional then the questions about spiritual life and
concern for the truth must be high on our agenda. It was in
the context of unity that our Lord prayed, 'Sanctify them by
the truth; your word is truth' (Jn. 17:17). A spirit of unity is
not a warm glow engendered by a shared worship experience. Nor is it merely the friendship we discover in working alongside former strangers. It is the result of God's word
exposing our sins of pride, selfishness and self-sufficiency
until we repent and seek his grace to become more like
Jesus Christ. It is hammered out in the real-life conflicts of a
church comprising such different personalities and tem-
peraments that when love is displayed there it can only be
explained as a supernatural work of the Spirit of God.

5 We must remember that we are in a spiritual battle

Nothing spiritual is accomplished without overcoming the enemy of God and of godliness. The devil delights to divide and rule. He is the father of lies and the master of intellectual disguises. He can masquerade as an angel of light whilst promoting rank heresy. So we must be watchful. All that passes for the genuine Christian is not necessarily so. Neither is all that goes under the title of a 'church'.

In John Bunyan's classic, *The Holy War*, he acutely observes that the devil's most effective agents are those elements of the old nature remaining in the life of the Christian. These he employs so cleverly that we are often unaware of his strategy. Take, for example, the effects of our own personality on our Christian relationships. Some by nature are authoritarian and see every issue in black and white. Others are very sensitive and will too readily take the easier path to avoid criticism. Some church leaders find it difficult to manage change and can only keep going by sticking to paths familiar to them. Others over-compensate for their own feelings of insecurity by adopting a strident tone in debate. We cannot alter our own personality but we can learn to recognize our own propensities and the way the devil is likely to exploit them. If there are factors affecting our capacity to relate to other Christians which are non-theological they are not to be seen as non-spiritual. They are recognized as potentially significant by the devil and he is ready to abuse them. They should be recognized also by us and we should be ready, with the help of God, to handle them.

In a battle we must learn to get on with our fellow soldiers, even if our different regiments, or nationalities, mean that we do have very different traditions. The devil will do all he can to keep us locked up in our own worlds, minding our own business, doing our own thing and perpetuating as many divisions among God's own people as he can. He will go further. He will split churches and denominations, persuading us all the time that this is a 'necessary' evil. If we are engaged in controversy, as sometimes we must be, he will stoke up our zeal for the truth until it passes into an unholy rancour and we end up fighting not our enemies but our brothers and sisters.

It is really a matter of priorities. Richard Baxter is said to have advised, 'When a small controversy endangers the unity of the church, raise a larger controversy.' The devil will make mountains out of molehills. Much division is the result of a loss of spiritual perspective which makes doubtful questions into reasons for schism. Alternatively, to make a bogus unity out of agreement on superficial issues is to cheapen truth and holiness. It is the larger controversy for the great gospel principles which separates the true church from the thinking of our secular world. The challenge is for evangelicals to recognize that and to work out policies centred on the gospel itself.

Thank God then, that ours is a gospel of hope. The devil will not have the last word about church unity. Nothing can ultimately frustrate our Saviour's purpose that one day there will be one flock, forever safe under the care of the one shepherd. Until then, however, we still have some work to do. The expression in Ephesians 4:3 is 'Make every effort'!

About the contributors

Alan F. Gibson, the editor of this volume, is General Secretary of the British Evangelical Council, based in St Albans, England. In this capacity, he is concerned about the unity of evangelical churches on both a national and international scale.

Canon Michael Cole has been in the ministry for more than thirty years. About half that time was spent in the north of England in Leeds, Sheffield and Manchester. At one time he was a Chairman of the Evangelical Alliance and therefore closely concerned with unity among Christians. He has written a number of books and is a regular contributor to *Renewal* magazine. As well as writing he is widely known as a speaker. He also fulfils a busy ministry within the parish of All Saints', Woodford Wells, in Greater London.

Eryl Davies is Tutor and Principal at the Evangelical Theological College of Wales, and editor of *Foundations*, the theological journal of the British Evangelical Council. Dr Davies has pastored churches in Wales and is the author of several books.

Graham Harrison is minister of Emmanuel Chapel, Newport, in Wales, and lecturer in Christian Doctrine at the London Theological Seminary. He is also Principal of the

Theological Training Course run by the Evangelical Movement of Wales.

David Holloway is Vicar of Jesmond Parish Church, Newcastle upon Tyne, in the north of England. Formerly he was tutor and lecturer in Doctrine and Ethics, Wycliffe Hall, Oxford. He has written several books, including *Ready Steady Grow: Principles for the Growth of the Church in Britain* (MARC, 1989) and *The Church of England: Where is it Going?* (Kingsway, 1985).

Gordon W. Kuhrt is Archdeacon of Lewisham and a member of the General Synod of the Church of England. He is author of *Believing in Baptism* (Mowbrays, 1987).

David Matthew has been linked, since 1975, with the Covenant Ministries team led by Bryn Jones. For many years he was editor of *Restoration* magazine, and is now deeply involved in the Modular Training Programme of Covenant College, Coventry, England. He is Editor-in-Chief of Harvestime Publishing Ltd, and author of many books.

Derek Prime was, until 1987, minister of Charlotte Chapel, Edinburgh, in Scotland, and now carries on an itinerant ministry, as well as writing. He is affiliated to the Fellowship of Independent Evangelical Churches, and is based in Edinburgh.

Harry Uprichard is a minister of the Presbyterian Church in Ireland. He is presently minister of Trinity Presbyterian Church in Ahoghill, near Ballymena, Northern Ireland. Dr Uprichard has written a number of booklets, including one on baptism. He is a frequent contributor to various periodicals and theological journals, and serves as one of the editors of *Evangel*.

Oliver Barclay, the series editor, was formerly General Secretary of the Universities and Colleges Christian Fellowship.

Notes

The national church David Holloway (pp. 21–38)
1 William Temple, *Citizen and Churchmen* (Eyre and Spottiswood, 1941), p. 48.
2 Quoted by William Temple, *Citizen and Churchmen*, p. 48.
3 Report of the Archbishops' Commission, *Church and State* (Church Information Office, 1970), p. 1.
4 Ralph D. Winter, *The Two Structures of God's Redemptive Mission* (William Carey Library, 1974), p. 128.
5 Ernst Troeltsch, *The Social Teaching of the Christian Churches* (University of Chicago Press, 1981), vol. 1, p. 331.
6 Troeltsch, *Social Teaching*, p. 331.
7 Troeltsch, *Social Teaching*, p. 334.
8 Troeltsch, *Social Teaching*, p. 334.
9 Troeltsch, *Social Teaching*, p. 339.
10 Troeltsch, *Social Teaching*, p. 333.
11 Timothy Hoare, 'Established to Serve the Nation', *Hope for the Church of England?*, ed. Gavin Reid (Kingsway, 1986), p. 67.
12 John Calvin, *Institutes of the Christian Religion*, IV. 20. 2.
13 Alec Vidler, *The Orb and the Cross* (SPCK, 1945), p. 133.
14 Quoted in John Henry Newman, *On Consulting the Faithful in Matters of Doctrine* (Collins, 1986), p. 72.
15 *Kant's Political Writings*, ed. Hans Reiss (Cambridge University Press, 1970), p. 54.

Independency Eryl Davis (pp. 69–90)
1 See also, 1 Tim. 3:1; 4:14; 5:17, 19; Tit. 1:5, 7; 1 Pet. 5:1–2.
2 *Manual of Congregational Principles*, published by the Congregational Union of England and Wales, 1884. Books I and II of the *Manual* were published separately in 1885 by the same publisher under the title *Congregational Church Polity*.

Notes

3   John Murray, *Collected Writings* (2 vols., The Banner of Truth Trust, 1976, 1977), vol. 1, p. 260.

4   Murray, *Collected Writings*, vol. 2, p. 348.

5   Louis Berkhof, *Systematic Theology* (The Banner of Truth Trust, 1958), p. 590.

6   Murray, *Collected Writings*, vol. 2, p. 349.

7   See Acts 8:1; 11:26; 14:27; 15:3–4, 22; 20:17, 28; Rom. 16:1; 1 Cor. 1:2; Col. 4:16; 1 Thes. 1:1; *cf*. Rev. 2:1, 8, 12, 18; 3:1, 7, 14.

8   Jn. 15:1–11; 1 Cor. 12:12–27; Eph. 1:23; 2:16; 4:21.

9   John Calvin, *Christian Institutes* (James Clark), vol. 2, p. 281.

10 See Murray, *Collected Writings*, vol. 1, pp. 231–236, for a good discussion of the subject.

11 R. B. Kuyper, *The Body of Christ* (The Banner of Truth Trust, 1967), p. 91.

12 R. W. Dale, *Systematic Theology* (Pickering and Inglis, 1956), p. 903.

13 James Bannerman, *The Church of Christ* (The Banner of Truth Trust, 1869), vol. 1, pp. 241–242.

14 Murray, *Collected Writings*, vol. 1, p. 262.

15 *The Church: God's Agent for Change*, ed. Bruce J. Nicholls (Paternoster Press, 1986), p. 199.

16 From 1851 to 1857 the Congregationalists in England built 365 churches while the Primitive Methodists averaged 100 new churches per year.

17 It is estimated there are over 10,000 para-church groups in N. America alone and they are mushrooming in Third World countries.

18 See, e.g. Nigel Lacey, *God's Plan for the Local Church* (Grace Publications, 1985), p. 18; Bannerman, *The Church of Christ*, vol. 1, pp. 6–8; A. H. Strong, *Systematic Theology* (Pickering and Inglis, 1907), pp. 887–889; *We Believe*, The Strict Baptist Affirmation of Faith, 1966.

19 *The Works of John Owen* (The Banner of Truth Trust, 1964), vol. 13, p. 125.

20 Bannerman, *The Church of Christ*, vol. 1, p. 12.

21 Murray, *Collected Writings*, vol. 1, p. 233.

22 Murray, *Collected Writings*, vol. 2, p. 340.

23 Murray, *Collected Writings*, vol. 1, p. 341.

24 Eph. 6:21–22; Phil. 2:19; Col. 4:7–9; 2 Tim. 4:10–12; Tit. 1:5; 3:12, *etc*.

25 Murray, *Collected Writings*, vol. 2, p. 343.

26 *The Works of John Owen*, vol. 16, p. 183.

27 Murray, Collected Writings, vol. 1, p. 344.
28 Gresham Machen, New Testament Introduction (The Banner of Truth Trust, 1971), p. 101.
29 This is confirmed by D. G. Tinder in the Evangelical Dictionary of Theology (Marshall Pickering, 1985), p. 310.
30 See, e.g. Terry Virgo, Restoration in the Church (Kingsway, 1985), pp. 142–148; Gerald Coates, What on Earth is This Kingdom? (Kingsway, 1983), pp. 135–152, and Divided We Stand (Kingsway, 1987).
31 Biblical Interpretation and the Church: Text and Context, ed. D. A. Carson (Paternoster Press, 1984), p. 105.
32 Murray, Collected Writings, vol. 1, p. 269.
33 Murray, Collected Writings, vol. 1, p. 270.
34 P. Hocken, One Lord, One Spirit, One Body (Paternoster Press, 1987), p. 87.

Connectionalism Harry Uprichard (pp. 95–120)

Grateful acknowledgment is made to the Library of the Reformed Presbyterian Church in Ireland and to Claremont Graduate School, California, and University Centre and University Microfilms Inc., Ann Arbor, Michigan, for reference to D. R. Ehalt's Ph.D. thesis as undernoted.

 1 See the discussion in W. Cunningham, Historical Theology (The Banner of Truth Trust, 1960), vol. 1, pp. 73–78; and J. Bannerman, The Church of Christ (The Banner of Truth Trust, 1869), vol. 2, pp. 201–213.
 2 See e.g. C. K. Barrett, Church, Ministry and Sacraments in the New Testament (Paternoster Press, 1985). Cf. L. Morris, Ministers of God, Great Doctrines of the Bible (IVF, 1968); and A. Stibbs, God's Church, Great Doctrines of the Bible (IVF, 1968).
 3 This is the view underlying such publications as: Growing into Union, Proposals for forming a united Church in England (SPCK, 1970); Baptism Eucharist Ministry (WCC, 1982); God's Reign and Our Unity, Report of Anglican-Reformed International Commission 1981–84 (SPCK, 1984); and Ministry in a Uniting Church (Gomer Press, 1986).
 4 For the general thesis of development in the New Testament see F. F. Bruce, 'The Epistles of Paul', Peake's Commentary on the Bible, ed. M. Black and H. H. Rowley (Nelson, 1964), pp. 927–939. Cf. Barrett, Church, Ministry and Sacraments, pp. 77–101. Some tentative approach to this subject is made in my unpublished Ph.D. thesis, 'An examination of the early date

hypothesis for the writing of 1 Thessalonians, with particular reference to development in Paul's theology', Queen's University, Belfast, 1976.

5 Quite a number of publications past and more recent discuss the issue. From the connectionalist or more specifically presbyterian viewpoint the following might be mentioned: T. Witherow, *The Apostolic Church* (Free Presbyterian Publications, 1983), pp. 62–66; Bannerman, *The Church of Christ*, vol. 2, pp. 545–556; J. M. Porteous, *The Government of the Kingdom of Christ* (Johnstone Hunter and Co., Edinburgh, 1873); C. Hodge, *The Church and Its Polity* (T. Nelson and Sons, 1879); J. Murray, *Collected Writings* (2 vols., The Banner of Truth Trust, 1976, 1977), vol. 1, pp. 231–287, vol. 2, pp. 321–365; L. G. Whitlock Jr, 'Presbyterian Polity and Practice', *Presbuterion*, vol. 1, no. 2 (1975), pp. 117–130; G. W. Knight III, 'The Church in the New Testament', *Presbuterion*, vol. 3, no. 1 (1977); *Pressing Toward the Mark*, ed. C. Dennison and R. Gamble (Orthodox Presbyterian Church, 1986), pp. 53–62, 63–81, 99–110.

Those emphasizing independency or congregationalism include the following: J. Owen, *The True Nature of a Gospel Church and its Government* (Originally published 1689. J. Clarke & Co, 1947); R. W. Dale, *Manual of Congregational Principles* (Congregational Union of England and Wales, 1884) and, *Congregationalism Through the Centuries* (Independent Press, 1937); N. Micklem, *Congregationalism and the Catholic Church* (Independent Press, 1943); D. R. Ehalt, 'The Development of Early Congregational Theory of the Church, with Special Reference to the Five "Dissenting Brethren" at the Westminster Assembly', unpublished Ph.D. thesis, 1969. (An excellent historical and theological dissertation of congregationalism. See credit above.)

6 These and other relevant documents can be found in *The Reformation of the Church* (The Banner of Truth Trust, 1965) – a collection of Reformed and Puritan documents on church issues with introductory notes by Iain Murray.

7 Savoy Platform, *The Reformation of the Church*, p. 276.

8 Cambridge Platform, *The Reformation of the Church*, pp. 244–245.

9 For full discussion see under *Kaleō* in *Theological Dictionary of the New Testament*, ed. G. Kittel (Eerdmans, 1979), vol. 3, pp. 501ff.

10 'The Form of Presbyterial Church Government 1645', in *The Reformation of the Church*, pp. 218–222.

11 For a summary of debates see Ehalt, 'Early Congregational Theory', pp. 90–112, 184–238.

12 *The Reformation of the Church*, p. 207.

13 H. R. Jones, 'Are there Apostles Today?', *Foundation*, 13 (Autumn 1984), p. 25.

14 R. Clements, 'Word and Spirit', *Hear the Word* (IVP, 1990).

15 Murray, *Collected Writings*, vol. 2, pp. 342–343.

16 Ehalt, 'Early Congregational Theory', pp. 218–219.

17 Micklem, *Congregationalism*, pp. 25–26.

18 Ehalt, 'Early Congregational Theory', pp. 192–193.

19 Cambridge Platform, *The Reformation of the Church*, p. 249.

20 Dale, *Congregational Principles*, pp. 1–89.

21 *Cf.* R. V. G. Tasker, *Matthew*, Tyndale New Testament Commentaries (IVP, 1976), p. 173; W. Hendriksen, *Matthew* (The Banner of Truth Trust, 1974), pp. 699–700; R. T. France, *Matthew*, Tyndale New Testament Commentaries (IVP, 1985), pp. 255, 274–275; F. Filson, *The Gospel According to St Matthew* (Black, 1987), p. 202; L. Morris, *1 Corinthians*, Tyndale New Testament Commentaries (IVP, 1964), pp. 87–88, 92–93.

22 *Cf.* Morris, *1 Corinthians*, pp. 87–88, 92–93; D. Prior, *The Message of 1 Corinthians*, The Bible Speaks Today (IVP, 1985), p. 73; C. Hodge, *A Commentary on the First Epistle to the Corinthians*, Geneva Series (The Banner of Truth Trust, 1968), p. 83, esp. reference to church 'in the organized capacity'.

23 See 'government' in 1 Cor. 12:28; *cf.* 1 Thes. 5:12, 13; Heb. 13:17; Rom. 12:8.

24 See the congregationalist view of Acts 15 as in Dale, *Congregational Principles*, pp. 84–85; and Ehalt, 'Early Congregational Theory', pp. 222–223. *Cf.* F. J. Foakes Jackson, *The Acts of the Apostles* (Hodder and Stoughton, 1951), pp. 136–137.

25 Gal. 2:8, 10; Acts 15; Rom. 15:24, 28; Tit. 1:5; 1 Thes. 1:4–10.

26 *Cf.* F. F. Bruce, *The Acts of the Apostles* (Marshall Morgan Scott, 1965), p. 314; C. S. C. Williams, *The Acts of the Apostles* (A. & C. Black, 1975), p. 185; E. Haenchen, *The Acts of the Apostles* (Blackwell, 1985), p. 444; p. 451, n. 4.

27 Knight, 'The Church of the New Testament', p. 34.

28 Westminster Confession, I. 6.

29 Cambridge Platform, *The Reformation of The Church*, pp. 265–269.

30 Savoy Platform, *The Reformation of The Church*, pp. 279–280.

31 *The Times*, 19 July, 1988.

Principled comprehensiveness Gordon Kuhrt (pp. 127–139)

1 Andrew Walker, *Restoring the Kingdom* (Hodder and Stoughton, 1985).

2 Gordon Kuhrt, *Believing in Baptism* (Mowbrays, 1987).

3 John Stott, *Christ the Controversialist* (IVP, 1970).

4 E.g. 1 Cor. 15:2; 2 Thes. 2:15; 1 Tim. 6:20; 2 Tim. 1:14; Heb. 13:9.

5 See e.g. Mt. 18:15–17; 1 Cor. 5; Gal. 1; 2 Jn. 2:10.

6 E.g. Dr Martyn Lloyd-Jones in 1966. See *Knowing the Times* (The Banner of Truth Trust, 1989), ch. 13.

7 See Michael Saward, *Evangelicals on the Move* (Mowbrays, 1987); Adrian Hastings, *A History of English Christianity 1920–1985* (Collins, 1986); Randle Manwaring, *From Controversy to Co-existence – Evangelicals in the Church of England 1914–1980* (Cambridge University Press, 1985); *Hope for the Church of England?*, ed. Gavin Reid (Kingsway, 1986).

8 See *Truth, Error and Discipline in the Church* (Vine Books, 1978), re. *The Myth of God Incarnate; A statement about Jesus* (CEEC, 1984), re. David Jenkin's views on Jesus' birth and resurrection; *Bishops, Belief and the Bible* (CEEC, 1986), re. *The Nature of Christian Belief* by the House of Bishops; John Stott, *Evangelical Anglicans and the ARCIC Final Report: An assessment and critique* (Grove Books, 1982); *ARCIC – An open letter to the Anglican Episcopate* (Grove Books, 1988); David Edwards and John Stott, *Essentials* (Hodder and Stoughton, 1988). This list could have been extended to many pages merely with significant contributions in the last ten years.

Response to Gordon Kuhrt Graham Harrison (pp. 140–143)

1 The Westminster Confession, XXV. 5.

2 The Savoy Declaration of Faith and Order, 1658, XXVI. 3.

3 The Baptist Confession of Faith, 1689, XXVI. 3.

Evangelical separation Graham Harrison (pp. 144–165)

1 D. M. Lloyd-Jones, 'Evangelical Unity: An Appeal', *Knowing the Times* (The Banner of Truth Trust, 1989), pp. 246–257.

2 *Keele '67*, ed. Philip Crowe (CPAS, 1967).

3 Norman Anderson, *An Adopted Son* (IVP, 1985), p. 217.

4 *The Christian*, 21 October, 1966.

5 John Calvin, *Institutes of the Christian Religion*, trans. Ford Lewis Battles (SCM, 1961), IV. 1. 10.

6 Robert Haldane, *Exposition of the Epistle to the Romans* (The Banner of Truth Trust, 1958), pp. 37–38.

7 *Westminster Confession*, XXV. 5.

8 *Institutes*, IV. 2. 6, 10.

9 *Baptist Times*, 18 November, 1971.

10 *Truth, Error and Discipline in the Church* (Vine Books, 1978).

11 *The Nottingham Statement* (CPAS, 1977), pp. 40–41.

12 *Include Us In* (Ark Publishing, 1980).

13 *Church of England Newspaper*, 10 January, 1969.

14 *The Times*, 20 August, 1955.

15 D. M. Lloyd-Jones, *Knowing the Times* (The Banner of Truth Trust, 1989), pp. 252f.

16 Compare Acts 20:28–31; 1 Cor. 15; Gal. 1:6–9; 1 Tim. 1:19f.; 4:1f.; 6:3–5; 2 Tim. 3:1–5; Tit. 1:10–13; 3:10; 2 Pet. 2; 1 Jn. 2:18f., 22; 4:1–5; 3 Jn. 9f.

17 *Francis A. Schaeffer Trilogy* (IVP, 1990), pp. 46–47.

18 Klaas Runia, *Reformation Today* (The Banner of Truth Trust, 1968), pp. 121–122.

19 *The Sword and the Trowel*, November, 1887, pp. 558f.

20 Iain Murray, *The Forgotten Spurgeon*, 2nd edn. (The Banner of Truth Trust, 1973), pp. 158–159.

Response to Graham Harrison Gordon Kuhrt (pp. 165–169)

1 Graham confuses historical event and theological interpretation (p. 146). This in itself is a major problem of theology. It means he is unable to recognize the complexity of the position of some modern theologians, e.g. the Bishop of Durham, David Jenkins, who certainly affirms the *theology* of the resurrection whilst doubting aspects of its *historicity*.

2 Graham confuses the relationship of the Old and New Testaments (pp. 148–149) and implies an inadequate view of the status of Old Testament saints. For a further study see Gordon Kuhrt, *Believing in Baptism* (Mowbrays, 1987), pp. 44–49.

A renewed tradition Michael Cole (pp. 173–199)

1 Tom Walker, *Hope for the Church of England?*, ed. Gavin Reid (Kingsway, 1986), p. 119.

2 Stephen Neill, *Anglicanism*, 3rd edn. (Penguin, 1965), p. 417.

3 For more detail see Michael Cole, *He is Lord* (Hodder and Stoughton, 1987).

4 D. Pawson, *The Normal Christian Birth* (Hodder and Stoughton, 1989).

5 J. Lightfoot, *Epistle to the Philippians* (Macmillan, 1885), pp. 181–269.

6 John Noble, *House Churches – will they survive?* (Kingsway, 1988), p. 71.

7 Michael Cole, *Make Way for the Spirit* (Highland Books, 1988), p. 70.

8 Noble, *House Churches*, pp. 18–19.

9 *Church of England Newspaper*, 20 October, 1989.

10 Andrew Walker, *Restoring the Kingdom* (Hodder and Stoughton, 1985), p. 139.

11 Noble, *House Churches*, pp. 18–19.

12 Walker, *Restoring the Kingdom*, p. 142.

13 Walker, *Restoring the Kingdom*, p. 143.

14 R. V. G. Tasker, *Matthew*, Tyndale New Testament Commentaries (IVP, 1976), p. 98.

15 Arthur Wallis, *The Radical Christian* (Kingsway, 1981), p. 105.

16 John Stott, *Christ the Controversialist* (IVP, 1970), p. 70.

17 Wallis, *The Radical Christian*, p. 113.

18 Walker, *Restoring the Kingdom*, p. 127.

19 Noble, *House Churches*, p. 73.

20 Floyd McClung, *The Father Heart of God* (Kingsway, 1985).

21 Cole, *Make Way*, pp. 58–60.

22 Walker, *Restoring the Kingdom*, p. 163.

23 Peter Hocken, *One Lord, One Spirit, One Body* (Paternoster Press, 1987), pp. 69–70.

24 Noble, *House Churches*, p. 95.

Response to Michael Cole David Matthew (pp. 200–202)

1 David Matthew, *Church Adrift* (Marshall Pickering, 1985).

2 See David Matthew, 'Shepherding: A Job for Heavyweights?' *Restoration*, March/April 1990.

3 1 Cor. 3:16–17; 2 Cor. 6:16; Eph. 2:19–22; Heb. 3:6; 10:21; 1 Pet. 2:4–5.

4 D. Pawson, *The Normal Christian Birth* (Hodder and Stoughton, 1989).

A perspective from the restoration fellowships David Matthew
(pp. 203–226)

1 David Matthew, Church Adrift (Marshall Pickering, 1985),
p. 194.

2 Arguments for a looser meaning remain weak, and certainly
not strong enough to warrant the widespread practice of a
different mode. See T. J. Conant, The Meaning and Use of
baptizein (Kregel Publications, 1977).

3 See John P. Baker, Baptized in One Spirit (The Fountain
Trust, 1967). W. F. P. Burton took a similar view. He compared
the verse with Mt. 10:10: 'Take no bag for (eis, to equip you for)
the journey.' On that basis, Paul is saying that baptism in the
Spirit equips us for functioning in the one body.

4 See Acts 2:1–13; 8:14–19; 9:17–19; 10:44–48 and the references later in this section to Scripture's arguments from rather
than to the baptism in the Spirit as an identifiable experience.

5 John Stott, Baptism and Fullness (IVP, 1966), p. 14.

6 Acts 11:15–18; 15:8; 19:1–6; Gal. 3:2; 1 Jn. 3:24; 4:13.
When Philip preached the gospel in Samaria, he baptized
those who 'accepted the word of God'. But they did not
receive the Spirit until Peter and John came down and laid
hands on them (Acts 8:14–17). If, prior to their receiving the
Spirit, they could not legitimately be called believers, Philip
was guilty of baptizing unbelievers.

7 The expression is attributed to John Wesley. The delay in the
receiving of the Spirit by the believing Samaritans (Acts
8:14–17) was in all likelihood because of the need for apostolic representatives to be present to see it happen. This was,
after all, a major breakthrough – the advance of the gospel
beyond Jewish boundaries ('You will be my witnesses in . . .
Samaria'). Peter and John needed to see for themselves the
Spirit's authentication of the Samaritans' claim to believe.
When it came to the next breakthrough – to Gentiles at the
house of Cornelius ('. . . and to the ends of the earth') – Peter
was present from the start, and the Spirit fell upon them
without delay as they responded to the message (Acts 10:34–
48).

8 The listed references make an unquestionable connection
between baptism in the Spirit and speaking in tongues. The
two remaining accounts of baptism in the Spirit concern
Paul (Acts 9:17–18), who informs us in 1 Cor. 14:18 that he
was a profuse speaker in tongues; and the Samaritans (Acts

8:14–19), whose experience was characterized by some observable phenomenon, witnessed by Simon Magus. That this was tongues cannot be proved, but the evidence of the other incidents points strongly in that direction.

9 David L. Edwards and John Stott, *Essentials* (Hodder and Stoughton, 1988), p. 27.

10 1 Cor. 12:24–27; Phil. 2:4; 1 Thes. 5:11; Heb. 10:24–25.

11 C. Peter Wagner, *Strategies for Church Growth* (MARC, 1987), p. 122.

12 Acts 20:17, *cf.* 28; 1 Tim. 3:2, *cf.* Tit. 1:6; Tit. 1:5.

13 It seems probable that students attending the two-year course taught by Paul at the lecture hall of Tyrannus in Ephesus (Acts 19:9–10) played a part in the evangelizing of proconsular Asia, including the establishing of the seven churches of Rev. 2 and 3. See *e.g.* W. M. Ramsay, *St Paul the Traveller and the Roman Citizen* (Hodder and Stoughton, 1908), p. 274; F. F. Bruce, *Acts*, New International Commentary on the New Testament (Eerdmans, 1980), p. 389.

14 James Lee Beall, *Your Pastor, Your Shepherd* (Logos International, 1977), p. 130.

15 For an examination of the apostolic ministry in general, see *Apostles Today*, ed. David Matthew (Harvestime, 1988).

16 Arthur Wallis, *The Radical Christian* (Kingsway, 1981), p. 184.

17 Acts 13:2, 5; 12:25; 15:39–40; 16:1–3, 10–13; 18–5, 18; 20:4–6.

Response to David Matthew Michael Cole (pp. 227–230)

1 Michael Eaton, *Baptism with the Spirit* (IVP, 1989).

Conclusion: Where does this leave us? Alan F. Gibson (pp. 231–243)

1 Gordon Kuhrt, *Believing in Baptism* (Mowbrays, 1987). See also, David Kingdon, *Children of Abraham* (Henry Walter/Carey Press, 1973).